ZONES OF CONFLICT
An Atlas of Future Wars

ZONES OF CONFLICT
An Atlas of Future Wars

by

John Keegan and Andrew Wheatcroft

Simon and Schuster
New York

Published by Simon and Schuster
A Division of Simon & Schuster, Inc.
Simon & Schuster Building
Rockefeller Center
1230 Avenue of the Americas
New York, New York 10020
Published in Great Britain by Jonathan Cape Ltd.
SIMON AND SCHUSTER and colophon are registered trademarks of Simon & Schuster, Inc.

1   3   5   7   9   10   8   6   4   2

1   3   5   7   9   10   8   6   4   2   pbk.

Library of Congress Cataloging in Publication Data

Keegan, John, *date*
Zones of conflict.

1. Strategy – Maps.   2. Strategy.   3. War.
I. Wheatcroft, Andrew   II. Title.
III: Title: Atlas of future wars.
GL046,R3K4   1986   912'.135543   85-675704
ISBN 0-671-60115-6
ISBN 0-671-62411-3 (pbk.)

Photoset by Rowland Phototypesetting Ltd
Bury St Edmunds, Suffolk
Printed in Great Britain by
Clark Constable (1982) Ltd, Edinburgh

For Susanne and Janet

CONTENTS

THE LIGAMENTS OF STRATEGY

MAPS

PREFACE

All the place-names given in this book are in accordance with those given in *The Times Atlas of the World* (1980 Comprehensive Edition). Where a place-name has changed we do on occasion use its former name as well when it relates to an earlier period (e.g. Stanleyville/Kisangani).

Graticule lines are given on the maps to provide accurate points of reference. Road and rail data corresponds to the best available source. We have decided to be anomalous in the way in which we refer to distance and height. In the text these are given in imperial measures only; on the maps in both metric and imperial. Conversion tables are provided on page xvi. We decided to have neither an index nor a bibliography. Neither seemed to be of great significance in the particular case of this book.

Finally, we would like to thank the staff of the following institutions for their work in connection with this book: the Royal Military Academy, Sandhurst; the Map Room, Cambridge University Library; the National Library of Scotland. All the cartography of this book has been carried out by Malcolm Porter to whom we both owe considerable gratitude. We should also like to thank our editor at Cape, Tony Colwell, and in particular Mandy Greenfield, who has imposed consistency on us with a firm but friendly hand.

June 1985   J.K and A.W.

INTRODUCTION

It is said that the 'trick' played by the chess master when he plays simultaneously against forty or fifty amateurs and beats them all lies in a visual ability he possesses and they do not; that of mentally composing each board and the pieces it bears into a two-dimensional map, the barriers, choke points and highways of which he perceives and they do not. It is this gift rather than that of seeing 'a move ahead' which distinguishes the chess champion from the pedestrian player.

Chess was, originally, a 'war game' and the board a simplification of the battlefield on which the ancient armies of cavalry and footmen met each other. Is it possible, in this apparently all-threatening world of military power in which we live, to apply a similar technique of simplification to its military geography?

We believe it is. For all that there are now 140 armies in the world, a dozen major navies and air forces, five strategic nuclear forces and the beginnings of a military apparatus in space, the places in which military power can actually be applied are comparatively few. Geographical or climatic factors prevent military action over wide areas of the world. In many others, where military movement is possible, the absence of targets worth capturing or destroying, or mere distance itself, makes strategic action unlikely. Many states, moreover, pursue good-neighbour policies or, even when they do not, are too weak to put bad intentions into effect. The result is to reduce to a mere handful the spots on the globe where the strategic chess-player will focus his attention. 'When' and 'how' trouble will happen he cannot predict. But 'where' is something he can identify with considerable accuracy.

England shows with absolute clarity how little the basic strategic problems alter over the centuries. England – as long as she controls Scotland and Ireland and maintains a reasonable level of naval force – is a very difficult country to invade. All neighbouring coasts offer disadvantages as points of departure, either of geographical or of long-standing political character, or both. The Norwegian coast is distant, the population in any case too small to mount a threat, and the coastal plain too narrow for an interloper to assemble there the necessary superiority of men and supplies. Denmark is better – the Anglo-Saxons and King Alfred's Danish enemies both set out from it – but it is again distant, lacks good harbours and the country, since the decline of Viking power, has not had the means or will to tackle England. Even Hitler, when in occupation of Denmark, did not include it among the base areas for his projected Operation Sealion. The German North Sea coast itself is an unsuitable invasion base; the ports are deep inland and their exits constricted by shallows and islands. The river outlets from the Low Countries are more promising. But the area's interposition between the German- and French-speaking lands has made it more often fought over than occupied by any one great power, thus neutralising it as a threat to England. The multiplicity of internal waterways which allowed the Dutch to fight successfully for their independence also ensured that, when they achieved it, they could never sufficiently extend their territory to rival England, except in commercial wars at sea.

France is, therefore, left as the main source of threat. But, despite its nearness, it is less than satisfactory from an invader's point of view. The harbours along the north-eastern coast are small and exposed; those in the Bay of the Seine, in Normandy and Brittany, though larger, are comparatively far from the English coast. The very high tides of the Channel make landing on the open beach perilous, and open beaches are fewer than high cliff zones, while the excellent English ports, at Plymouth and behind the Isle of Wight, are both easily defensible and superb bases for attack against surface invading fleets. It is therefore not surprising that the English kingdom has only been invaded successfully once, by William the Conqueror; the coming of air power has, naturally, reduced the extent of England's security, since it threatens to overcome her naval defences,

and so open the way to the chinks in her geographical armour. But the only attempt made at a combined air–sea offensive against her shores – by Hitler in 1940 – failed. Modern missiles would presumably succeed where the Luftwaffe did not; but, had things come to that pass, we would be worrying not about England's but the world's future.

This brief survey of the reasons which make England comparatively impregnable is designed to show that successful conventional warfare – indeed even unsuccessful conventional warfare – can only be carried on within very constricted regions of the world; a fact which remains as true in the twentieth century as in any other. The use of the terms 'desert warfare', 'jungle warfare', 'mountain warfare' and 'arctic warfare' suggests that there is no sort of terrain which armies cannot use. But that is absolutely not the case. Mountains and the polar regions can only be fought over by specialised troops, and then at exorbitant cost in transport and supplies. True jungle warfare is almost impossible, as photographs of the vegetation make instantly clear; what is meant by the term is warfare for the rivers and roads which traverse the jungle. Desert warfare is almost equally difficult. The middle of the Arabian 'Empty Quarter' and the central Sahara have never seen armies which, in the well-known 'desert' campaigns of 1940–3 and of the Arab–Israeli wars, in fact clung to its semi-populated edges.

If we subtract desert, jungle, mountain and polar regions from the land mass, the remaining area potentially suitable for military operations is very much reduced. Almost all the land north of 60°N. can be excluded (northern Canada and Russia north of the line Leningrad–Vladivostok). Desert covers almost the whole of Africa and Arabia between 30° and 15°N., and much of inner Asia north of the Himalayas and their associated mountain massifs.

Those mountains and the nearby highlands and ranges of Iran and the Caucasus effectively divide inner Asia from the Middle East and south Asia; the Mongolian chain separates Russia and China. It is only the ends of the ranges therefore, and certain difficult passes through them, which are of military significance.

In Africa and South America it is vegetation which provides the obstacle to free movement. In South America a belt of rain forest nearly 2,000 miles wide, in central Africa nearly 1,000 miles wide, divides each land mass at the level of the equator. There are also major rain forest belts across the bottom of China which, together with east–west mountain chains, bar easy passage into south-east Asia.

All of this is easily deducible to anyone who applies common sense to a climatological, physical and vegetation map of the world. The analysis will be highlighted by the superimposition of a population and communication map, since people, and the roads and railways which serve them, are found most thickly concentrated where geography and climate make life easiest. And it is people who fight wars and – even in the air age – chiefly roads and railways which allow them to get at each other.

Yet we are still far from a refined analysis of likely areas of conflict. To get closer we must apply the factor of political stability. Wars must, almost always, begin at borders. Certain countries are so large – e.g. the USA and USSR – that their interiors must be regarded, save in the most exceptional circumstances, as non-

military regions. Some borders – notably the American–Canadian – separate states so harmoniously related that war between them is unthinkable. Others mark divisions between states so strong and others so weak – e.g. those between India and Nepal and Bhutan – that they are more akin to internal boundaries than international frontiers. Others again, within alliance systems such as NATO and the Warsaw Pact, are effectively demilitarised. And certain lucky states, of which Switzerland is the most obvious, proclaim a neutrality which seems unlikely to be disturbed.

Two other factors suggest themselves in assessing where conflict may arise. The first is military capability. Although there are now almost as many armies as there are sovereign states, the majority are too weak and ill-equipped to operate beyond their own borders and are best seen as internal security forces. The second is objective discontent, fuelled by ideology, religion, race or language ('irredentism'), envy of material resources or historical reflex. In addition there are a number of 'imperial' states, such as Ethiopia, which are resisting the secession of discontented minorities, and others, such as Libya, which have developed local 'imperial' ambitions.

This constellation of factors – physical, climatic, logistic, economic, military and political – will now allow us to identify where current or latent international disputes may find their geographical focus, how they may develop, and how great their magnitude and how wide their ramifications are likely to be.

CONVERSION TABLES

miles to km		km to miles		ft to metres		metres to ft
1.609	1	0.621	0.304	1	3.2808
16.093	10	6.214	3.048	10	32.81
160.934	100	62.137	30.48	100	328.08
321.869	200	124.274	60.96	200	656.16
482.803	300	186.411	91.44	300	984.25
643.738	400	248.548	121.92	400	1312.34
804.672	500	310.685	152.40	500	1640.42
1609.344	1000	621.371	304.80	1000	3280.84

GENERAL KEY TO MAPS

—·— National boundary

+++++ Railway with strategic significance

Mountain area

//////// Strategic corridor

🌳 Forest

〰️ Navigable river

━━━ Main highway, motorway or equivalent

– – – Secondary road

······· Minor road

🛢️ Oil field

🚢 Oil terminal

—— — Oil pipeline

✕ Former battle site

🏰 Fortified position or strongpoint

Radar location

Army base

Armoured strike force

Naval base

Submarine base

Air base

■ Capital city

● City or large town

• Small town

IRAN Country name

MAINE Region, county or state

R. Rhein River, lake or dam

For other symbols, see the detailed key to each map

ZONES OF CONFLICT

EUROPE

1 Europe: The Central Front

The Central Front, NATO's designation of its military frontier in Central Europe which follows the line of the East German and Czech borders and that of the Federal Republic of Germany, harbours the densest concentration of armed force in the world today. On NATO's side of the Inner German Border, some twenty-six armoured and mechanised divisions, equipped with tactical nuclear weapons and supported by 3,500 tactical aircraft, confront thirty Soviet divisions, also equipped with tactical nuclear weapons and supported by 7,500 tactical aircraft; to the Soviet's strength must be added some twenty-nine non-Soviet divisions which are maintained at operational levels of efficiency. The strategic criticality of the Central Front derives, moreover, not merely from the density of conventional force concentrated there, but also from its potential as a trigger to the outbreak of nuclear war between the Superpowers.

The Central Front is the creation of accident and history rather than geography, since it exactly follows the line demarcating the Western and Eastern Zones of Occupation agreed between the Anglo-American and Soviet leaderships at the Yalta Conference in February 1945. Pre-war Germany was a country with natural frontiers only in the west, where they followed the course of the Rhine and the flanks of the Alps. In the east, except along the high ground of the Bohemian mountains, Germany rested on no natural obstacle, merely following the border of conquest and annexation secured by Germans in 1,000 years of eastward expansion. Russia's advance across Germany in the spring of 1945 therefore carried the border of conquest back from one zone of open territory to another.

As long as the Inner German Border constituted a zonal division between co-operating allies, its divergence from strong terrain features was unimportant. The failure of East and West to agree on the future political settlement of Germany, however, and the growth of a wider antagonism between them which accompanied that failure invested the military weakness of the IGB with increased significance. The foundation of NATO in 1949 and of the Warsaw Pact in 1955 completed its transformation into a line of military

No potential war has ever been more exhaustively planned than the Great Battle on the Central Front. Both sides have analysed every aspect of the ground, although NATO has the advantage of defending its own terrain. Much depends on the capacity of the defence to slow a rapid advance. German villages would become strongpoints in a Real War. But German cities are vulnerable close to the Inner German Border, and beyond a conventional defence lies the threat option of nuclear weapons, which introduces an incalculable wild card into the game.

KEY

—·— National boundary
+++++ Main railways with strategic significance
——— Autobahns
Land over 500 metres (1640 feet)
NATO armoured units
NATO tactical air bases
Other NATO military units
Warsaw Pact armoured units
Warsaw Pact tactical air bases
Other Warsaw Pact military units
//////// Strategic corridors
● Cities
· Towns

miles
0   20   40   60
0 20 40 60 80
kilometres

Europe: The Central Front (north)

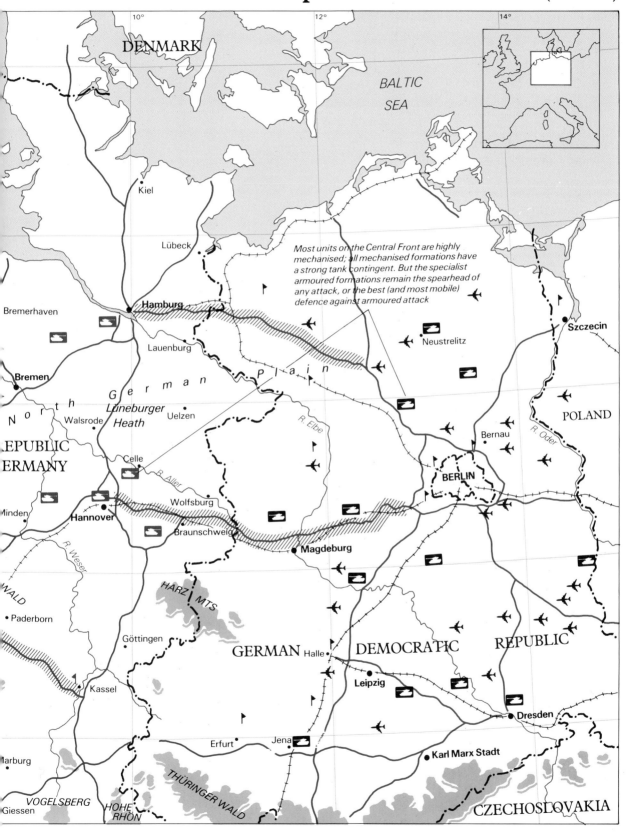

DENMARK

BALTIC

SEA

Kiel

Lübeck

Bremerhaven

Hamburg

Lauenburg

Bremen

German

Lüneburger Heath

North

Plain

Neustrelitz

Szczecin

POLAND

Walsrode

Uelzen

R. Elbe

Bernau

R. Oder

REPUBLIC

ERMANY

Celle

R. Aller

BERLIN

Minden

Wolfsburg

Hannover

Braunschweig

Magdeburg

HARZ MTS

Paderborn

Göttingen

GERMAN

Halle

DEMOCRATIC

REPUBLIC

WALD

Kassel

Leipzig

Dresden

Erfurt

Jena

Karl Marx Stadt

arburg

THÜRINGER WALD

VOGELSBERG

Giessen

HOHE RHÖN

CZECHOSLOVAKIA

R. Weser

Most units on the Central Front are highly mechanised; all mechanised formations have a strong tank contingent. But the specialist armoured formations remain the spearhead of any attack, or the best (and most mobile) defence against armoured attack

Much of the northern part of the Central Front is open 'tankable' country, obstructed only by low hills and the odd patch of high ground. In the south the outcrops and the great Alpine mass begin to dominate the terrain. Mobility is restricted to the valleys, especially in winter; it is also limited by the borders of the neutral states, Austria and Switzerland. East-west access has recently been improved by the creation of fast motor routes, but entry to Italy and the south is entirely controlled by the tunnels running under the encircling mountains.

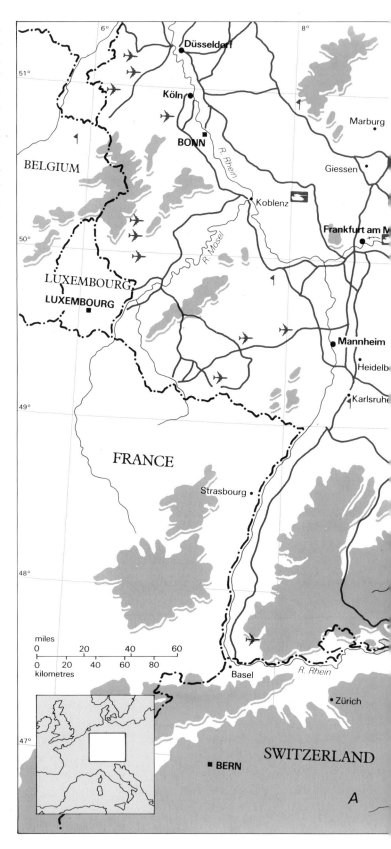

Europe: The Central Front (south)

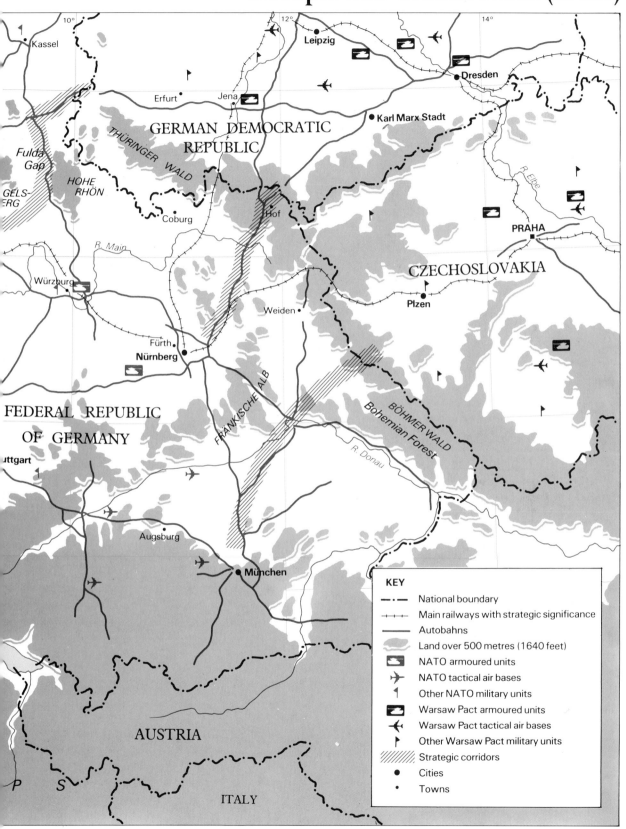

Kassel

Leipzig

Dresden

Erfurt

Jena

GERMAN DEMOCRATIC REPUBLIC

THÜRINGER WALD

Karl Marx Stadt

Fulda Gap

HOHE RHÖN

GELS-ERG

Coburg

Hof

R. Elbe

PRAHA

R. Main

Würzburg

CZECHOSLOVAKIA

Weiden

Plzen

Fürth

Nürnberg

FEDERAL REPUBLIC OF GERMANY

FRÄNKISCHE ALB

BÖHMER WALD
Bohemian Forest

uttgart

R. Donau

Augsburg

München

AUSTRIA

P S

ITALY

KEY

—·—·—	National boundary
+++++	Main railways with strategic significance
——	Autobahns
	Land over 500 metres (1640 feet)
	NATO armoured units
	NATO tactical air bases
	Other NATO military units
	Warsaw Pact armoured units
	Warsaw Pact tactical air bases
	Other Warsaw Pact military units
//////	Strategic corridors
●	Cities
·	Towns

confrontation, a status confirmed by the beginning of German rearmament in 1956.

NATO now organises the Central Front (Allied Forces Central Europe) into two Army Group areas, Northern and Central; for political reasons the topmost slice of the front, comprehending Schleswig Holstein and Jutland, is included in the area of Allied Forces Northern Europe, but local command arrangements bring it effectively under the operational control of Allied Forces Central Europe. The two Army Groups comprise eight allied corps, arranged from south to north as follows: II German, VII and V United States, III German, I Belgian, I British, I German and I Dutch; COMLANDJUT oversees the extreme north, where NATO forces consist of a German mechanised infantry division (6th Panzergrenadier) and three Danish brigades. To these forces may be added the three French divisions stationed in Baden-Württemberg, and the four other French divisions which support them in Alsace-Lorraine; but it must be noted that France, though a member of NATO's political structure, has withdrawn its forces from the military organisation.

On the Warsaw Pact side of the Inner German Border, the Group of Soviet Forces Germany comprises nineteen divisions in East Germany, organised into five armies, with headquarters at Dresden, Neustrelitz, Erfurt, Bernau and Magdeburg. They are complemented by six East German divisions. Behind the Czech frontier five Soviet divisions are stationed; the Czech army itself comprises ten divisions. There are a further six Soviet divisions in Eastern Europe, two in Poland and four in Hungary, while the Polish, Hungarian, Romanian and Bulgarian armies field a total of thirty-nine divisions at various degrees of readiness.

The obvious military imbalance between the two alliances prompts NATO to regard itself as vulnerable to a Warsaw Pact ground attack on the Central Front, a vulnerability enhanced by the conformation of the German territory it has to defend. West Germany is characterised, from a military point of view, by 'lack of depth'. The Central Front (including the COMLANDJUT Sector) is about 559 miles in length; but from the East German border it is only about twenty-five miles to Hamburg, ninety-four miles to the Ruhr industrial region and sixty-two miles to Frankfurt am Main, the principal US base area. As modern military formations have the capacity to manoeuvre at a speed of twenty to thirty miles a day, SACEUR (the NATO Supreme Commander) entertains the fear that his rear area might be overrun by Warsaw Pact formations, should they achieve surprise, within forty-eight to seventy-two hours of the inception of an attack.

By no means is the whole of the Central Front, however, equally vulnerable to attack. The North German Plain, which extends between Hannover and the Baltic, is highly 'tankable', but is constricted by the estuary of the Elbe and interrupted by the difficult going of the Lüneburger Heath.

The Harz mountains and the Teutoburger Wald, both readily defensible, divide the Plain from the territory further south, which is high and quite extensively forested. Further south again, the front is covered by the Franconian highlands and the Bohemian forest which afford a succession of good defensive positions. Strict terrain analysis is therefore generally held to reveal only five or six easy avenues of advance into West Germany from East Germany and Czechoslovakia.

The first crosses the Baltic coastal zone, through which the East Germans have built a motorway to connect with the West German road complex around Hamburg. The second is marked by the line of the Berlin autobahn to Brunswick and Hannover. The third aligns with the Kassel–Dortmund autobahn. The fourth, widely identified as the most critical since it affords rapid access to the American base area at Frankfurt, follows the Fulda Gap between the high ground of the Vogelsberg and the Hohe Rhön. The fifth runs towards Nuremberg in Bavaria, and there is possibly a sixth route via Regensburg towards Munich.

It is an unavoidable complication of NATO's defensive strategy that West Germany has a dense network of high-quality roads, more of which run east–west than north–south, and therefore facilitate penetration rather than lateral reinforcement of the front. Moreover, about 30 per cent of West Germany's population and 25 per cent of its industrial capacity, closely associated with this network, lies within sixty-two miles of the Inner German Border, a circumstance that, together with the general 'lack of depth' factor, has obliged NATO to adopt the 'forward defence strategy' that has been alliance policy since 1967.

Not all geographical factors, however, militate against successful 'forward defence'. About 29 per cent of West Germany is covered by forest, which it is believed attacking troops would avoid; another 9 per cent is urban and therefore also inimical to offensive operations. Much of this built-up area consists of vil-

lages, one of which is contained, on average, within each four-and-a-half square miles. Second World War experience encourages the view that such villages constitute excellent blocking positions, and a tactical doctrine of 'checkerboard defence', based on the propinquity of villages, now underlies NATO's forward strategy, and is believed to promise a high degree of reliability.

In the last resort, the outcome of military operations across the IGB between NATO and the Warsaw Pact turns on so much more than contingent terrain factors that their importance must be judged, however influential they may be, a secondary issue. The Pact's ability to reinforce its side of the front, from its vastly more numerous reserves, argues that a NATO defence would fail through weakness of numbers alone. The unavoidable warning signs that large-scale reinforcement would emit, ensure, on the other hand, that NATO would be given the time to make diplomatic counter-warnings, backed by nuclear threats, of such weight that a rational attacker must be deterred by them. The function of NATO's ground and tactical air forces remains, therefore, that of so adapting their deployment to the defensive advantages the terrain affords as to negate the possibility of a surprise offensive, while trusting to strategic forces to sustain the overall equilibrium.

2 Europe: The Northern Flank

Norway is, besides Turkey, the only member country of the NATO alliance to share a frontier with the Soviet Union. The frontier is short, only some sixty-two miles, running from Lake Inarijärvi to the Barents Sea on the Russian side of the North Cape. The distance from Norway's centres of population, however, the irre-

versible imbalance of force between the two neighbours and the geographical conformation of their point of contact together with its proximity to other areas, particularly maritime areas, of strategic significance, invest the frontier with acute military significance.

The juxtaposition of Russian with

Norwegian territory came about as a result of frontier adjustments imposed at the end of the Second World War. Until 1944 Finland's northern territories had extended to the Barents Sea. Following the Finno-Russian armistice, Finland ceded to the Soviet Union the strip of territory around Petsamo (today Pechenga), which cut it off from the sea and made Norway and Russia contiguous.

Finland's peace treaty of 1946 imposed severe restrictions on the size of her armed forces, while post-war Finnish governments have imposed prudent restraints on their relations with the Soviet Union, principally designed to avert any action her neighbour might interpret as provocative. Norway, though also anxious to maintain harmonious relations with the Soviet Union, is a member of NATO, to which she acceded in 1949, and pursues a policy of forthright self-defence. Although her policy forbids the stationing of nuclear weapons or foreign troops on Norwegian territory, this does not preclude the visit of NATO contingents for training purposes, and British, Dutch and United States amphibious forces, together with NATO's ACE Mobile Force, regularly exercise in the north. Norway's own armed forces maintain their principal formations in the north, at Bardufoss near Tromso, and her mobilisation plans are geared to a rapid reinforcement of the northern region in an emergency. It is a severe handicap, however, that the manpower for the eleven mobilisable brigades is almost all domiciled in the south, around Oslo and Bergen; the airlift planned to move the reserves would be a major undertaking, all the more so were it opposed.

Russia's strategic imperatives in the North Cape region are powerful and complex. The Kola Peninsula, on which stand her partially ice-free ports of Murmansk and Archangel, is the headquarters of her Northern Fleet and has been described as the largest and most strongly defended military base in the world. The Northern Fleet consists of some forty ballistic missile submarines, 140 other submarines, an aircraft carrier, eighty other major surface warships, at least 300 combat aircraft and a naval infantry brigade. Three army divisions are also stationed on the Kola Peninsula. The Northern Fleet is Russia's strongest, from which its main complement of ballistic and attack submarines are despatched into the Atlantic and the Mediterranean, where ten are believed to be normally on station. From a defensive point of view, therefore, Soviet requirements must be to dominate NATO forces in the North Cape region, hold them at the greatest distance possible from the Kola bases and secure freedom of action in the southern Arctic Ocean and North Norwegian Sea. Her positive requirements turn on a more aggressive strategy. Military analysis suggests that, in the event of NATO–Warsaw Pact hostilities, the United States Atlantic Fleet would attempt to take control of the Norwegian Sea, both to interdict Russian surface and submarine movements through those waters and to use it as a base of operations for strike missions against Soviet territory.

A NATO initiative of that nature would be severely compromised were the north Norwegian coastline to come under Russian control; a southward extension of that control would also threaten to interrupt the working of the North Sea oilfields and menace the approaches to the Baltic with a double envelopment. Free use of the Baltic, in which important Russian naval facilities are located, is believed to stand high on the list of Soviet strategic priorities. They maintain a fleet of thirty submarines and forty-five major surface vessels in the Baltic which, with a naval infantry brigade and the Polish marine division based at Gdansk, equips them with a high amphibious offensive potential. The Danish armed forces are small and weakly equipped; even with German and other NATO assistance, their capability to deny the Baltic Approaches to a concerted Warsaw Pact attack is uncertain.

NATO's principal anxiety over the security of the Northern Flank remains, however, the vulnerability of the North Cape region to a Soviet ground offensive. That might take a number of forms. The first is a direct assault over the Russian–Norwegian frontier. The difficulty of the terrain, which has been described as an 'Arctic desert', and the sharp narrowing of the front down to ninety-four miles between the Finnish border and the sea, make such a manoeuvre unlikely. It may be judged possible, therefore, that once hostilities had begun, the Soviet Union might choose to violate Finnish neutrality and attack across the top of the Finnish plateau. A particularly tempting opportunity for rapid advance is presented by the 'Finnish finger', which runs along the top of Sweden's northern frontier towards Tromso, Norway's northern headquarters. From the tip of the 'Finnish finger' to Tromso is less than sixty-two miles. It is calculated that three divisions might be deployed on that access and make rapid progress.

Severe topographical and climatic difficulties would, however, make the exploitation of such a seizure of territory fraught with problems. South of Tromso, which is joined to southern Norway by only a single road, long and deep fiords, separated by steep mountain spurs, would interrupt military movement at frequent intervals. The northernmost of these obstacles is the East Fiord, which runs from the sea to Narvik, the focus of fighting between the Allies and the Germans for control of northern Norway in the spring of 1940.

The northern indentations could be bypassed by one or both of two approaches. The Soviet Union might choose to violate Swedish as well as Finnish neutrality and institute its offensive further south. But Sweden's armed forces, based on the long-service militia principle and equipped from an advanced domestic arms industry, are powerful and well-trained. Moreover, the lie of the land, which is crossed by a succession of lakes running athwart the natural axis of advance, would make such a manoeuvre painful and time-consuming. Alternatively, the Soviet northern forces might attempt a long-range amphibious descent of the Norwegian coast, bypassing the more precipitous fiords and establishing points of control as they progressed southwards. Such an operation would demand, however, strong air and naval protection along its seaward flank, where it would be acutely vulnerable to attack by NATO ships and aircraft operating out of the Norwegian Sea, and to mining operations down the coastline.

Small and weak though NATO's presence on the Northern Flank is, close analysis suggests that its defensive strategy is encumbered by fewer difficulties than a predicated Soviet offensive strategy. The nature of the terrain works to encourage the enlargement, rather than the minimisation, of any offensive, and so to increase the dimensions of the military problem – by the drawing in of Swedish and Finnish forces – rather than to contain or reduce it. Since operations on the Northern Flank are unlikely to be conducted in isolation, but to be subordinate to hostilities across the whole zone of confrontation in Europe between NATO and the Warsaw Pact, it may be the Soviet judgment that a strategy of menace and feint would suit their overall plan better than an outright attempt at conquest, the prospects for the success of which remain in doubt.

Men can fight under the Arctic conditions of northern Norway, but not for long: too much energy has to be expended on basic survival under atrocious conditions. Nor does geography assist a potential aggressor. Few roads, deep water fiords and inland lakes, plus a chain of mountains which splits Norway from her neighbours, all impede attack. Stalemate rather than blitzkrieg is the likely consequence.

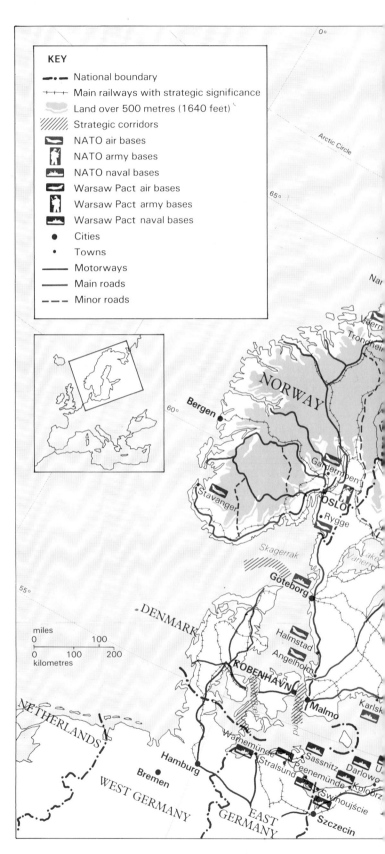

KEY
- —·— National boundary
- ┼┼┼┼ Main railways with strategic significance
- Land over 500 metres (1640 feet)
- ///// Strategic corridors
- NATO air bases
- NATO army bases
- NATO naval bases
- Warsaw Pact air bases
- Warsaw Pact army bases
- Warsaw Pact naval bases
- ● Cities
- · Towns
- —— Motorways
- —— Main roads
- --- Minor roads

miles
0   100
0   100   200
kilometres

Arctic Circle
0°
65°
60°
55°

NORWAY
Bergen
Gardermoen
Stavanger
OSLO
Rygge
Skagerrak
Trondheim
Nar...
TVaern...
Lake Vänern
Göteborg
DENMARK
Halmstad
Angelholm
KØBENHAVN
Malmö
Karlsk...
Warnemünde
Sassnitz
Darlowo
Stralsund
Peenemünde
Kołobrz...
NETHERLANDS
Hamburg
Bremen
Swinoujście
WEST GERMANY
EAST GERMANY
Szczecin

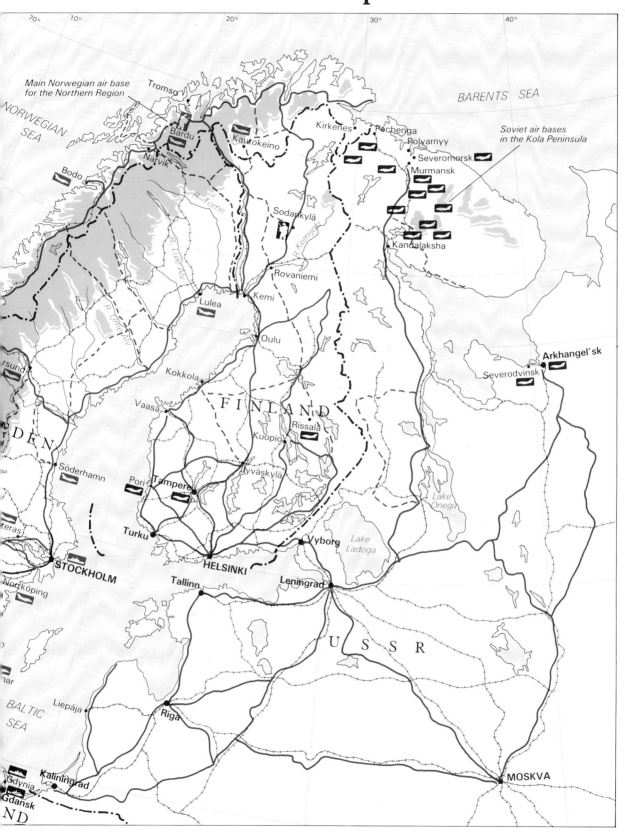

Europe: The Northern Flank

Main Norwegian air base for the Northern Region

Tromsø

BARENTS SEA

Bardu

Soviet air bases in the Kola Peninsula

NORWEGIAN SEA

Kautokeino

Kirkenes

Pechenga

Polyarnyy

Severomorsk

Bodø

Narvik

Murmansk

R. Torne

Sodankylä

Kandalaksha

R. Lule Älv

R. Ume Älv

Rovaniemi

Kemi

Severodvinsk

Arkhangel'sk

Lulea

Oulu

Kokkola

Vaasa

FINLAND

Rissala

Lake Onega

Söderhamn

Kuopio

Pori

Tampere

Jyväskylä

SWEDEN

Turku

Vyborg

Lake Ladoga

STOCKHOLM

HELSINKI

Tallinn

Leningrad

Norrköping

U S S R

Liepája

Riga

BALTIC SEA

Kaliningrad

Gdynia

Gdansk

POLAND

MOSKVA

3 Europe: The Southern Flank

The region denoted by NATO as its 'Southern Flank' comprises its member states of Italy, Greece and Turkey. Turkey shares a border with the Soviet Union, Greece with Bulgaria, a member of the Warsaw Pact, while Italy, of course, commands a dominating position in the central Mediterranean and provides the US Sixth Fleet with its most important European bases. The external security and internal stability of these three states, and the maintenance of harmonious relations between them, particularly between the second and third, is of great importance to the preservation of the status quo in the Mediterranean which may be defined as NATO's primary regional aim. Major factors threatening the status quo are Israel's unsettled quarrel with its Arab neighbours, the endemic civil war in the Lebanon and the Soviet Union's persistent efforts to extend its power and influence beyond the limits of the Black Sea; lesser potentialities for destabilisation are almost too many to enumerate.

Italy's strategic situation is the least complicated or disturbed, though its importance to NATO is perhaps the most central. From a military point of view Italy is geographically well-protected and is unthreatened by any direct military challenge. Its northern borders are encircled by some of the highest mountains in Europe, and those with France, Switzerland and Austria are either neutralised or guaranteed by alliance. The Yugoslav border, though more easily passable where the Julian Alps decline towards the Adriatic, is also geographically strong, as the static nature of the fighting there between the Italian and Habsburg armies demonstrated in 1915–18. In so far as the Warsaw Pact presents a military threat to Italy, it would arise in that direction. But the interposition of Austrian and Yugoslav territory holds such a threat at two removes; Italy's IV Corps, composed of five high-quality mountain brigades, is deployed to defend the Alpine region and its capacity to do so is estimated to be high.

The naval and air contribution that Italy makes to the alliance is also considerable. Its air force is sizeable and undergoing modernisation, and its navy includes ten submarines, a helicopter carrier and twenty modern escorts. Of equal or greater significance to NATO's strategic capability are the air and naval bases that Italy provides. There are major airfield complexes in the plain of the Po and around Foggia on the southern Adriatic coast, and well-equipped ports at La Spezia, Taranto, Ancona, Brindisi, Augusta (Sicily), Messina (Sicily), La Maddalena (Sardinia), Cagliari (Sardinia), Naples and Venice. Moreover the Italian peninsula itself constitutes a strategic position of incalculable importance. Almost exactly dividing the Mediterranean, it and its islands dominate the seaways to the east and west and command the strategic defile between Sicily and the North African coast. If maintenance of the status quo is NATO's principal strategic priority in the Mediterranean, the continued adherence of Italy to the alliance is its chief prerequisite.

The commitment of Greece and Turkey is of almost equal weight. Turkey is the mistress of the exit from the Black Sea and, though the Montreux Convention of 1936 permits the Soviet Union to pass numbers of warships of specified type through the waterway to the Mediterranean, Turkey's power to close the straits is far greater than any other state's to force and hold them open. The Soviet Union, while exercising its right to exchange units of the Fifth

(Mediterranean) Squadron through the Dardanelles, in practice maintains its strongest naval presence in the Mediterranean from the Northern Fleet. Nevertheless, the operations of all its units are severely hampered by a lack of base facilities. It makes use of the Syrian ports of Tartus and Latakia and enjoys limited repair facilities at Tivat in Yugoslavia. Its normal practice, however, is to resupply in offshore anchorages in Greek mainland and island waters.

Greece's command of wide territorial waters, extending from the mouth of the Adriatic to the Anatolian coast of Turkey, is one among many reasons that invest her membership of NATO with key significance for the alliance. Four major NATO bases are located on Greek territory: air bases at Athens and Iraklion (Crete), a communication station at Marathon and port facilities at Suda Bay (Crete), where the anchorage is large enough to accommodate the whole of the Sixth Fleet. Militarily, Greece's membership is also critical in denying the Warsaw Pact access to the Aegean shore of the Mediterranean in Thrace, which borders on Bulgaria. The Greek army, though deficient in modern equipment, is capable of defending Thrace for some time in the event of hostilities.

It is a matter for grave concern within the alliance, however, that Thrace is the principal focus of Greece's military confrontation not with the Warsaw Pact but with its NATO neighbour, Turkey. Greece and Turkey are historic enemies, Greece having won independence from the Ottoman Empire by war in the 1820s and having fought Turkey again in 1919–21. Current differences between the two countries turn not on historic quarrels, however, but on a conflict of interest in the islands of the Aegean and eastern Mediterranean. Foremost among them is the dispute over the future of Cyprus, where a unilateral attempt by Greeks of the island's majority population in 1974 to declare union with Greece prompted Turkey to invade. The island is now effectively partitioned and efforts to resolve the impasse prove fruitless. So incensed was Greece by NATO's failure to mediate judiciously, as she judged it, between the two disputing parties, that the Greek government withdrew from the military structure of NATO between 1974 and 1978.

Other disputes persist between Greece and Turkey, particularly concerning the militarisation of the Greek islands off the Turkish coast, the territorial division of the Aegean, which is believed to be an oil-bearing sea, and air traffic in Aegean waters. Demographically the Aegean is Greek, in that its islands, some of which are less than six miles from the Turkish coast, are overwhelmingly populated by Greeks. Historically, however, the Aegean has been used by both countries – and all others – as if it were international waters. Legally the Greek frontier, which follows the outer line of islands to the eastward, abuts on the landward frontier of Turkey. Turkey fears that, were Greece to exercise the prevailing customary right of extending its territorial waters from six to twelve miles, its access to the Mediterranean through international waters would be blocked, and Greek claims to control the continental shelf as far eastward as Turkish coastal waters would be considerably strengthened. Greece, in the interests of good relations, has declared that it does not intend to extend its claims unilaterally; but, equally, it will not forswear them. Moreover, it abides by its declared right to militarise its island possessions, however closely they approach the Turkish mainland.

Turkey's sense of grievance is compounded by what it feels is American inconstancy in supporting its legitimate position. Between 1974 and 1977 the

The great imponderable is whether Greeks will fight on the same side as Turks. History and a rash of current disputes suggest that the NATO treaty may be a dead letter. But neither Greece nor Turkey has much to gain from breaking up the alliance on the Southern Flank. Were Greece to leave NATO it would markedly reduce her security relative to Turkey (let alone to the Warsaw Pact). Neither side can afford a dramatic gesture.

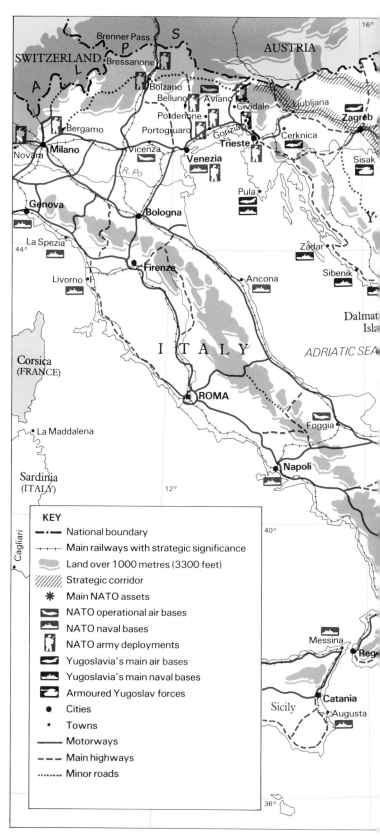

KEY

—·—·—	National boundary
—+—+—	Main railways with strategic significance
	Land over 1000 metres (3300 feet)
/////	Strategic corridor
✳	Main NATO assets
	NATO operational air bases
	NATO naval bases
	NATO army deployments
	Yugoslavia's main air bases
	Yugoslavia's main naval bases
	Armoured Yugoslav forces
●	Cities
·	Towns
——	Motorways
– – –	Main highways
········	Minor roads

Europe: The Southern Flank

HUNGARY

R. Drava

OATIA

Sombor

Danubian
Plain

Vrsac

BEOGRAD

Zemun

OSLAVIA

R. Morava

Kragujevac

Sarajevo

ostar

SRBIJA

Nis

Niksic

KOSOVO

ubrovnik

Tivat

Kotor

Titograd

Skopje

R. Vardar

MAKEDONIJA

t is used by the
et Union for occasional
irs and refits

TIRANE

Brindisi

ALBANIA

aranto

GREECE

ROMANIA

BUCURESTI

R. Danube

BLACK SEA

SOFIYA

BULGARIA

Edirne

Istanbul

THRAKI

Dardanelles

Thessaloniki

TURKEY

AEGEAN SEA

Izmir

Communication
centre

Marathon

ATHINAI

Hellenikon

Intelligence
centre

Suda Bay

Iraklion

Crete (GREECE)

R. Struma

United States imposed an embargo on arms supply to Turkey as a mark of disapproval of the Turkish invasion of Cyprus. Those years, when Greece had withdrawn from the military structure of NATO, mark the period of NATO's greatest anxiety for the integrity of its Southern Flank. Since that time, relations between Greece and Turkey, and NATO's with them, have markedly improved. It is essential that the improvement should be maintained, for the value of the region to the alliance, geographically even more than militarily, is inestimable.

Yugoslavia

Geographically, Yugoslavia is the heartland of the Balkan peninsula, bordering as it does six states – Italy, Austria, Hungary, Romania, Bulgaria, Greece and Albania – and dominating the eastern shore of the Adriatic. Politically, the country is the regional odd-man-out, belonging as it does neither to NATO nor to the Warsaw Pact, by whose member states it is regarded as a defector from the socialist camp. Internally, the country lacks homogeneity, the population comprising six nationalities and, by official reckoning, eighteen national minorities. Antipathies between several of the nationalities are ancient and intense; since the death of Tito, architect of the federal republic, the most important emollient influence has gone. The minority problem also underlies local and particular differences with Yugoslavia's neighbours, separate from the ideological dispute with the Soviet Union and the Warsaw Pact. The danger of any or all of these differences escalating into a local crisis, with wider ramifications, is enhanced by Yugoslavia's strategic geography, which leaves the country vulnerable to invasion and rapid bisection across the Danubian Plain and up the valley of the

Sava. Her vulnerability is heightened by the obsolescence of much of her military equipment, which cannot be replaced by domestic production, nor bought abroad for reasons both of economy and political scruple.

The cause of Yugoslavia's split with the rest of the Soviet world is well known. Unlike the other countries of Eastern Europe, it was neither liberated nor obliged to reverse a pro-Axis alliance by the Soviet Union, the Yugoslav partisans having fought the German occupation army close to defeat in late 1944. The heroic status his victory conferred on Tito led him from the outset to take an independent line in his dealings with Stalin and so in 1948 to a break between the two leaders, and their countries, which has never been fully repaired.

In the years immediately after the break, the fear most frequently expressed by observers of the Balkan scene was that the Soviet Union would seek to bring Yugoslavia back within the fold by force. Subsequently, and as Marshal Tito aged, the focus of anxiety shifted to the nationalities question, which it was suspected might destroy Yugoslavia from within as his power to unite his people waned. Tito was a Croat who had led a largely Serb army against the Germans. That was the secret of his unique supranational standing, for the dislike between the Catholic Croats (22 per cent of the population) and Orthodox Serbs (40 per cent) is the most disruptive in the country. It is compounded by the irredentism of the Albanian, Macedonian and Hungarian minorities, and by religious tensions between the Muslims of Bosnia-Hercegovina and their non-Muslim neighbours. Dissension between Croats and Serbs was particularly marked in the early 1970s. Yugoslavia is a federal republic and Croatia at that time chose to regard itself as disfavoured both by the central bureaucracy and the state banking system. Dissatisfaction was fuelled by nationalist fervour among the young and the fissiparous tendency was only quelled by a purge of the Croatian leadership and a strengthening of central at the expense of provincial power.

Yugoslavia's external position is complicated by disputes with its neighbours, notably Bulgaria, over the future of their minorities within her borders. Over a million Macedonians live in southern Yugoslavia and they are claimed as ethnic Bulgarians by the government in Sofia. Although the Macedonians are apparently content with their present status, it constitutes a pretext for conflict between the two neighbours in the future. Albanians number over a million in the province of Kosovo, which Tiranë regards as an irredenta. Hungary, which suffered greatly from the redistribution of territory after 1918, also seeks to reclaim the area inhabited by the Magyar minority.

Hungary's territorial dissatisfactions are directed particularly against Romania, a reason explaining the comparatively good state of Yugoslavia's relations with Bucharest. Romania does not make a military contribution to the Warsaw Pact and there are no Soviet troops stationed on her territory. Objectively, therefore, the two countries may be said to be in a similar strategic situation, a perception enhanced for both of them by Russia's intervention in Czechoslovakia in 1968.

A degree of military co-operation obtains between the two, all the more important to Yugoslavia because of its chronic state of military weakness. Its arms industry, though adequate to meet the country's needs in small and light arms, does not produce heavy artillery or armour; the aircraft industry is not in the first rank. As a result, Yugoslavia clings to something like the partisan system, through which it waged such a heroic struggle against the occupying Germans in 1942–4. The official military doctrine of the country is 'total defence', which allots a military role to every active member of society. Its aim is to create an environment of total hostility to any invader, making the country difficult or impossible to occupy.

Yugoslavia is, nevertheless, vulnerable to invasion from several directions. Though very mountainous – and the mountains have provided a refuge for resistance since Alexander campaigned against his Balkan neighbours in the fourth century B.C. – the main ranges defend the coast, and the frontiers with Greece, Austria and Italy. If Yugoslavia's present strategic predicament is posed from the east, there are few topographical obstacles that interpose in that direction. The Danubian Plain which surrounds the national capital at Belgrade is fine tank country, and the valley of the Sava which runs into it gives easy access to Zagreb, Yugoslavia's second city and capital of Croatia. Further north a third traditional invasion route runs along the valley of the Drava, while in the south the valley of the Morava leads from the Danube towards Niš and a side valley of the Struma into the defile of Vardar, heartland of Macedonia.

All these routes are open to attack and occupation by armoured forces, and control of them was indeed retained by the Germans throughout their campaign against Tito in 1942–4. Tito, though engaging the attention of twelve German divisions (of mixed quality), was constantly forced to move his headquarters and units, often over long distances and always with appalling casualties. The Germans generally managed to confine the partisans to the mountains of Serbia, Bosnia and Montenegro and at one point forced Tito to take refuge in the Dalmatian islands. The cost of the war to Yugoslavia was 11 per cent of its population, about 1.7 million, and, though many of these died in internecine fighting, between royalists and the partisans, and between Croats and Serbs, a high proportion represented deaths inflicted by the Germans by way of reprisals or in the direct course of the war. Yugoslavia's proclaimed doctrine of 'total defence' is a brave gesture; but the welfare of her population is best guaranteed by diplomacy which will not expose her open eastern frontier to invasion from the Soviet bloc.

4 Confrontation in the Caucasus

The Caucasus mountains, deemed by geographers to mark the division between Europe and Asia in the Near East, form one of the most severe military obstacles in the inhabited world. Marking in their day the easternmost frontier of the Persian, Roman, Byzantine and Ottoman empires, the Caucasus range is now NATO's longest zone of direct confrontation with the Soviet Union and its defence is therefore crucial to the security of the alliance's Southern Flank.

Because the Caucasus bars the most direct exit, between the Caspian and Black Seas, from the Central Asian grasslands, home of the nomad horsemen who were the terror of civilisation from the cavalry revolution (c. 900 B.C.) until the founding of the Ottoman Empire in the fourteenth century A.D., the region is dotted with battle sites at points where, for all the difficulty of the passage, invaders had found their way through the mountains and been forced to fight. The Hittites were the earliest recorded invaders, and their invasion was among the most successful. The Assyrians, Persians, Diadochi, Romans and Byzantines maintained permanent military frontiers in the region, and the most serious of Byzantium's setbacks is often dated to its defeat by the Seljuk Turks at Manzikert (modern Malazgirt) in 1071. Both Genghis Khan and Tamerlane crossed the Caucasus to spread terror in the Middle East and it was only with the rise of the Ottomans in the fourteenth century that a power strong enough to hold the Caucasus against steppe invaders emerged once more.

The rise and extension of Russia's power brought it and the Ottoman Empire into frequent conflict in the Caucasus from the seventeenth century onwards. Conflict grew in intensity and frequency after Russia's annexation of the mountain kingdom of Georgia in 1800. There was fighting during the Crimean War of 1854–6, during the Russo-Turkish War of 1877–8 and severe fighting during the First World War, when Russia invaded Turkey via the Caucasus in 1914–16 and Turkey Russia in 1916–18. In the Second World War the Germans, approaching the Caucasus from the north, detached forces to penetrate the region; some German mountain troops scaled Mount Elbrus, in the fore range of the Caucasus, and planted the swastika flag on its peak, the highest in Europe (18,470 feet).

Because of the severe nature of the terrain in the Caucasus, the course of the campaigns that have unrolled there over so long a period have followed a highly repetitive pattern. 'Traditional invasion route' is something of a cliché in discussions of strategic geography. In the context of the Caucasus it has unarguable force. There are, in practice, only three routes by which the Caucasus can be 'traversed' by large bodies of men in the east–west axis. The first is the coastal route along the Black Sea, a narrow corridor dominated on the landward side by ranges rising to over 10,000 feet. The second, which has two points of entry at Kars and Kagizman, leads along the valley of the River Aras (Araxes) to Erzurum. The third, which leads to Malazgirt and Lake Van, is not open throughout its length, but requires the crossing of a saddle at Diyadin. Kars, Erzurum and Malazgirt are all places of conflict, having been fought over or besieged many times over the centuries; Kars was besieged by the Russians in 1854 and taken by them in 1877, when they also besieged Erzurum. Malazgirt, scene of the disastrous Byzantine defeat by the Turks in 1071, was the focus of two Russo-Turkish battles in 1914–15, when the Russians also took Erzurum and, at the end of the Black Sea corridor, Trabzon (Trebizond, the old Greek city of Trapezus). In 1916–18 the Turks, with German assistance and following the internal collapse of the Russian army, reversed the course of the campaign and captured Tbilisi (Tiflis) in Georgia. During the course of the war the Armenian inhabitants of the Caucasus, who rose in rebellion against the Ottomans, were deported or fled in millions after ferocious reprisals against them. Today less than 40,000 Armenians remain inside Turkey.

Modern Turkey, though plagued by severe economic difficulties and beset by periodic bouts of political conflict which have twice provoked the army to take power, is a valued member of NATO, which it joined in 1952. The military reputation of the Turks is one of the highest in the world and, though the army lacks the best of modern equipment, its soldiers are hardy, well-trained, deeply patriotic and highly motivated. It is organised into one armoured, two mechanised and fourteen infantry divisions, and the Third Army, with about one-third of the army's strength, is deployed to defend the Caucasus. It would unquestionably choose to do so by holding the defiles of the 'traditional invasion routes', the topography of which would make any attempt at a deep penetration costly and time-consuming. It is a particular advantage to the defence that the conformation of the defiles necessarily keeps columns attacking along them separated while the defender, with his base in the more open territory to the west, enjoys the opportunity to reinforce his fronts as need requires. The road network, which grows progressively worse and sparser towards the frontier, also disfavours invasion, while the defender can make use of a succession of lateral spurs between the better roads to his rear, as well as of a north–south railway linking the lines to Erzurum and Lake Van. Climate also strictly limits the time of year when armies can campaign in the Caucasus. The Turks' attempt to attack Russia through the mountains in the winter of 1914 resulted in 50,000 of their 95,000 troops deserting, succumbing to frostbite or actually freezing to death. Mean temperatures at Erzurum are at or below freezing for five months of the year, while snow lies feet deep in the mountain passes.

On the Russian side of the border, the Soviet army maintains a considerable force in the two adjacent military districts, the Caucasian and Transcaucasian. It consists of thirteen motor rifle and two tank divisions, and an airborne division which is kept at Category I (fully operational) status. Communications on the Russian side of the mountains are superior to those on the Turkish. A main road and rail line run across Transcaucasia from the Caspian to the Black Seas, at a distance of 100 miles from the frontier, and both road and rail systems lead westward into Turkey. There are major airports at Baku, Kirovabad, Tbilisi and Batumi, as well as a network of military airports in the region.

During the 1970s Turkey took pains to improve its relations with the Soviet Union, without compromising its status within NATO. Since the Russian invasion

One of the great invasion routes of history, the Caucasus has always funnelled invaders from the east into Anatolia and down into the Middle East. But the mountains restrict the path that any invader can take, and with modern communications and firepower the advantage lies with the defenders, securely dug in above the valleys. Ghenghis Khan had no such problems.

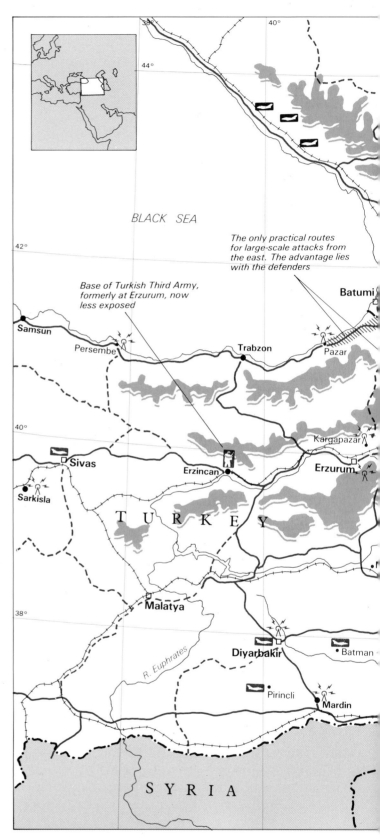

BLACK SEA

The only practical routes
for large-scale attacks from
the east. The advantage lies
with the defenders

Base of Turkish Third Army,
formerly at Erzurum, now
less exposed

Batumi

Samsun

Persembe

Trabzon

Pazar

Kargapazar

Sivas

Erzincan

Erzurum

Sarkisla

T U R K E Y

Malatya

R. Euphrates

Diyarbakir

Batman

Pirincli

Mardin

S Y R I A

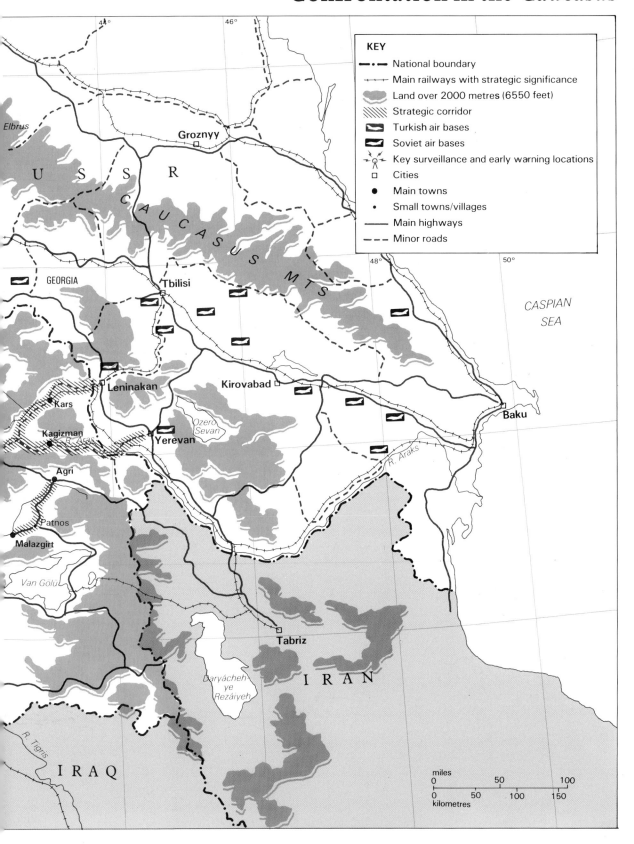

Confrontation in the Caucasus

KEY

- –·–·– National boundary
- ┼┼┼┼ Main railways with strategic significance
- Land over 2000 metres (6550 feet)
- Strategic corridor
- Turkish air bases
- Soviet air bases
- Key surveillance and early warning locations
- □ Cities
- ● Main towns
- • Small towns/villages
- ——— Main highways
- – – – Minor roads

Elbrus

U S S R

Groznyy

C A U C A S U S   M T S

GEORGIA

Tbilisi

CASPIAN
SEA

Leninakan

Kirovabad

● Kars

*Ozero
Sevan*

Baku

Kagizman

R. Aras

Yerevan

● Agri

R. Araks

Patnos

● Malazgirt

Van Gölü

I R A N

Tabriz

*Daryácheh-
ye
Rezáiyeh*

R. Tigris

I R A Q

miles
0   50   100

0   50   100   150
kilometres

of Afghanistan in 1979, however, relations have cooled. Turkey has also been troubled by the war between its neighbours, Iraq and Iran, and by the Iranian revolution itself. The revolution led effectively to the collapse of the Central Treaty Organisation, from which Turkey withdrew in 1980. These events have increased Turkey's exposure along its eastern frontier, and heightened its dependency on NATO for help with its defence. The quality of the Turkish armed forces and the intrinsic strength of the Caucasus bastion make the prospect of active operations, certainly successful operations, highly unlikely.

5 Northern Ireland: The Permeable Border

It was 'the rolling English drunkard', according to the writer G. K. Chesterton, who made 'the rolling English road'. The same chaotic hand seems to have been at work in drawing the boundary between the Irish Free State and the British province of Northern Ireland in 1921. For the most part it followed notional local boundaries, dividing one parish from another, which bore no relation either to the shape of the land or to the distribution of population. Nor did it have the logic of many artificially drawn frontiers running arbitrarily in straight lines across the map. It was produced in the belief that it would be revised in detail by a boundary commission which would resolve its more glaring anomalies, such as the village of Pettigoe which was split down its main street between the two states. But there was never sufficient political flexibility in the highly charged atmosphere between a Roman Catholic Free State and a militantly Protestant Northern Ireland to allow the commission to operate. The result was an indefensible border between two states in a condition of perpetual tension.

The lack of properly negotiated boundary lies at the root of Northern Ireland's strategic problem. At the western end it conforms better to the lie of the land than in the east. But in south Fermanagh and south Armagh, it begins to follow the line of streams and rivulets, or the line of ancient hedges. In the west the number of cross-border roads is relatively limited, but the number of crossing points increases dramatically in the east. And in addition to the minor roads which cross the border, there are innumerable footpaths and customary rights of way. While the border may have established two separate states, human contacts remain. Much of the border region is inhabited by Roman Catholics, and it is only in the Protestant heartland to the east of the River Bann that there is a substantial Protestant majority – only 20 per cent of the population is Catholic in this, the most productive part of the province. There has also been a shift in population in the border zone, with, in recent years, a more marked drift away from the border lands by Protestants. There has been a flood of borderers into the cities (and over the water to England), which is a direct consequence of the political violence. But despite these changes life on the border often ignores the frontier. There is an enormous quantity of cross-border traffic which is quite legitimate. Some farmers farm on both sides of the border (a decreasing number), and more use the markets without distinction between north and south. Towns like Dungannon and Crossmaglen have many contacts with the south, while the villages close to the border – Aughnacloy, Rosslea, Middletown – have been quick to profit from the price differentials between north and south. All the border towns and villages have smuggling as a secondary industry which has grown up since the creation of the frontier, and a consequence has been an extreme suspicion of all external authorities, whether the Gardai in the south or the Royal Ulster Constabulary in the north.

Geography, the nature of the 'temporary' border created in the 1920s, and the particular qualities of border society pose an insoluble strategic problem. Neither side can secure the initiative. The campaign which the IRA waged on the border from 1956 to 1962 proved ultimately fruitless. It made little impact on the main centres of population or on the conduct of politics. The current border troubles are also settling into stalemate. The IRA can operate across the border at will, but with increasing pressure from the authorities in the south and a new type of strategy from the authorities in the north. The idea of a physical form of defence – barbed wire and minefields – is often demanded by the more extreme Protestant politicians, but it makes no sense either militarily or politically. To make such a scheme work would involve the creation of a *cordon sanitaire* well inside the frontier, and the effective abandonment of the border villages. This is politically unacceptable to a Protestant community which has traditionally defended every inch of its territory: this was why the commission for border revision could make no headway in the 1920s.

The alternative has been a much less visible defence-in-depth based on information and intelligence. By the use of constant surveillance, of deep penetration intelligence units, and the increased use of computers to check the information and to predict patterns of infiltration, the British army and the RUC have managed to cut the war in the countryside away from the IRA campaigns in the cities. The defence-in-depth approach constrains rather than blocks incursions. It involves acceptance of a high level of violence in the border region, but it is a strategy which can be sustained over the long term and at an acceptable cost. Indeed, because the volume and quality of information becomes cumulatively more useful, it is a strategy which should progressively shift the balance of advantage to the defence.

The same techniques of control and information have been used to considerable effect in Belfast and Derry, and the security forces have discovered a strategy which allows a satisfactory rate of attrition against an enemy with relatively limited resources. It is much the most successful of all the varying approaches which have been adopted towards Northern Ireland since the rebirth of political violence in the 1970s. Yet it is a strategy of containment, not of conquest, born of a universal conviction that there can be no overwhelming and final military solution to the problems of Ireland. That, too, is sensible, for it is pointless to expect armed force to resolve social problems of the complexity of those relating to Northern Ireland.

The alternative to the die-hard approach of the extreme Ulster Unionists is a growing belief that Britain should leave Ireland altogether, and complete the process begun in 1921. The strategic position of Ireland relative to the lines of Atlantic communication to Europe cannot be ignored in the context of this argument. The British government in the Second World War was prepared to invade and occupy southern Ireland if it seemed possible that Britain's sea lanes could be threatened. The Republic of Ireland was not taken over because her neutrality was genuine, and the northern sea and air bases proved adequate. The current defensive stance depends less on the Ulster bases, with maritime surveillance based in Scotland. The value of Northern Ireland bases

Fewer people suffer death from political violence in Northern Ireland than die in traffic accidents; political violence is infinitesimal compared with the criminal violence of most North American cities. While most of the province is torpid and peaceful, there are pockets of murder and wounding. The IRA and its clones aim to make visible violence the permanent consequence of the British connection. The British aim to manage the war so as to make it unmemorable. The true war is for the attention of newspapers and television.

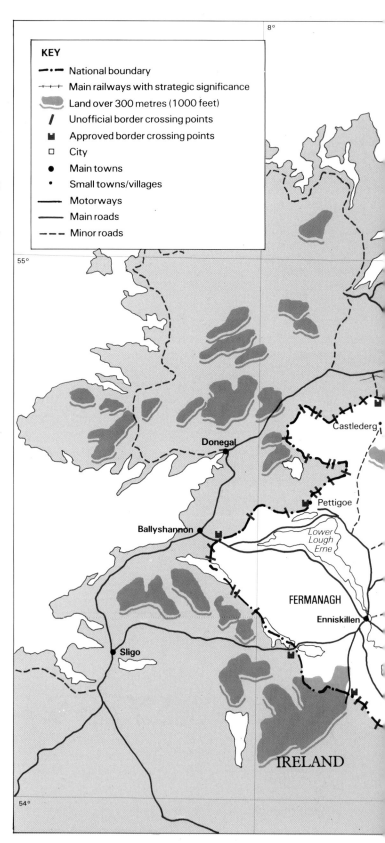

KEY

- **–·–** National boundary
- **+++** Main railways with strategic significance
- Land over 300 metres (1000 feet)
- **/** Unofficial border crossing points
- Approved border crossing points
- ▢ City
- ● Main towns
- · Small towns/villages
- —— Motorways
- —— Main roads
- - - - Minor roads

Castlederg

Donegal

Pettigoe

Ballyshannon

Lower Lough Erne

FERMANAGH

Enniskillen

Sligo

IRELAND

Northern Ireland: The Permeable Border

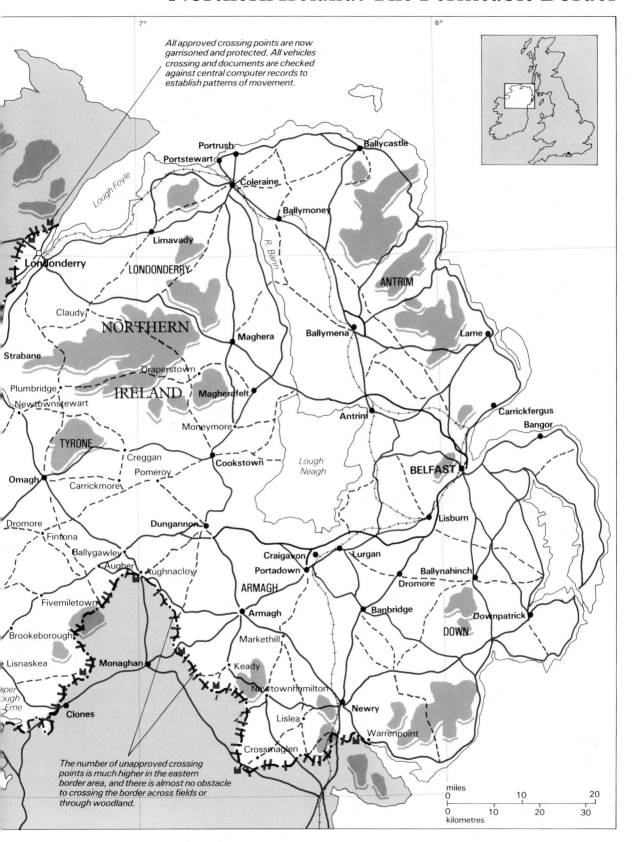

All approved crossing points are now garrisoned and protected. All vehicles crossing and documents are checked against central computer records to establish patterns of movement.

The number of unapproved crossing points is much higher in the eastern border area, and there is almost no obstacle to crossing the border across fields or through woodland.

7°

6°

Lough Foyle

Portrush

Portstewart

Coleraine

Ballycastle

Ballymoney

Limavady

Londonderry

LONDONDERRY

R. Bann

ANTRIM

Claudy

NORTHERN

Maghera

Ballymena

Larne

Strabane

Draperstown

IRELAND

Magherafelt

Plumbridge

Newtownstewart

Antrim

Carrickfergus

Moneymore

Bangor

TYRONE

Creggan

Cookstown

Lough Neagh

BELFAST

Omagh

Pomeroy

Carrickmore

Dromore

Lisburn

Fintona

Dungannon

Ballygawley

Craigavon

Lurgan

Augher

Aughnacloy

Portadown

Ballynahinch

Fivemiletown

ARMAGH

Dromore

Brookeborough

Armagh

Banbridge

Downpatrick

Lisnaskea

Monaghan

Markethill

DOWN

per
ough
Erne

Clones

Keady

Newtownhamilton

Newry

Lislea

Warrenpoint

Crossmaglen

miles
0   10   20

0   10   20   30
kilometres

in time of war hinders any policy of genuine disengagement. The proximity of Ireland to the British mainland makes it strategically difficult for the British simply to withdraw, as they did in Cyprus, with the guarantee of large sovereign base areas.

In Northern Ireland, the economy survives on the massive cash infusion which the emergency has brought. Ulster receives a degree of financial support unthinkable in other deprived British regions. Compensation from insurance claims, and even the high levels of overtime in the police and the prison service have distorted the normal shape of the economy, creating pockets of affluence amid more generalised poverty and unemployment. But Northern Ireland is much better off than the south, particularly in areas such as social security; there is a growing realisation that separation from Britain could prove economically disastrous.

The issue of Northern Ireland is not likely to lead to serious problems between Great Britain and the Republic of Ireland:

the IRA, in all its forms, is as hostile to the 'illegitimate' state in the south as it is to the 'colony' in the north. But at its height the involvement of the British army in the campaign against the IRA posed severe strains on the capacity of Britain to sustain her commitment to NATO in Germany. At the moment the IRA is pursuing a largely political strategy through backing Sinn Fein candidates at elections, while sustaining a lower level of military action, mostly in the towns and villages close to the border. If the military campaign were stepped up, the pressure on British reserves of manpower would recur. Thus, the strategic problems posed by unrest in Ireland are indirect, a 'knock-on' effect on sensitive situations elsewhere. The other consequence of The Troubles has been to make the British army outstanding in the techniques of urban warfare, and in the use and interpretation of field intelligence. This is the final paradox of the Ulster issue: the IRA have in the last decade honed the British army to a degree of efficiency unparalleled in peacetime.

THE MIDDLE EAST

6 Israel and Lebanon: The Levantine Entanglement

Israel, founded in May 1948, in fulfilment of the Zionist Movement's aspiration to create a Jewish state, occupies the central section of the land bridge linking Asia to Africa. Bounded on the west by the Mediterranean and on the east by the Arabian desert, this land bridge provides level going and a plentiful supply of fresh water over the distance of 400 miles separating the mountains of Asia Minor from the Nile delta. These properties have made it an invasion route for armies, marching north or south, since the earliest times. It has frequently also been fought over, conquered or occupied, in part because three of the world's great religions, Judaism, Christianity and Islam, claim the region as a (or the) Holy Land, an assertion over which their followers have been prepared to shed blood.

The frontiers of Israel constitute today one of the most vexed of the political problems affecting that country. Historically, however, none of its predecessor states – neither the Egyptian, Persian, Roman or Byzantine empires nor the Crusading kingdoms – maintained fixed frontiers in the area. It was not until after the coming of the Ottoman empire in the sixteenth century that administrative divisions were imposed. In 1887 these separated the 'land bridge' from the interior in a vilayet of Beirut extending from Aleppo in modern Syria to near Gaza; within the vilayet, the Mount Lebanon and Jerusalem areas formed 'special districts'. It was these administrative divisions which the British, as the power mandated to govern 'Palestine' (the Roman provincial name) by the League of Nations in 1919, inherited. International treaty determined mandate Palestine's southern boundary in Sinai with Egypt; nature the eastern boundary; agreement with the French mandatory government in Syria/Lebanon fixed the northern boundary.

Jewish immigration and the resulting conflict with the Palestinian Arab population, which resulted from Britain's fostering of the Jewish 'National Home' under the mandate, prompted efforts to partition Palestine. No arrangement acceptable to all parties had been found by May 1948, however, when Britain withdrew on abandoning the mandate. The State of Israel, proclaimed unilaterally on 14 May, was immediately attacked by the neighbouring armies of Lebanon, Syria, Egypt and Transjordan. While the latter succeeded in seizing the predominantly Arab-inhabited highlands across the Jordan (the future 'West Bank'), the other armies were almost everywhere defeated. Israel therefore retained the areas of Jewish settlement and added to them the remaining Arab districts.

Strategically, the resulting national territory was doubtfully defensible, since the boundaries almost nowhere coincided with the region's natural obstacles or barriers. Geographically, mandate Palestine consisted of three zones: a coastal plain, of which an arm extends south-eastwards from Haifa to form the Plain of Esdraeleon (site of the battle of Megiddo, the first recorded battle of history, 1479 B.C.); a hill and mountain belt to the east, in places rising to nearly 3,000 feet and, to the east again, the Jordan Valley, the northern extension of the Great Rift, here descending to the lowest point (1,400 feet below sea-level) on the Earth's land surface; the south, in all three zones, is natural desert, which extends into Sinai and reaches to the Suez Canal.

The Israeli frontier fixed by the final ceasefire of January 1949 followed the mandate frontier with Syria and Lebanon, the Transjordan frontier south of the Dead Sea and the Egyptian frontier across Sinai. The central hill zone (the 'West Bank') from Jenin to Hebron had fallen, however, to the Transjordanians, who renamed their state the Kingdom of Jordan accordingly, and a coastal strip around Gaza to the Egyptians. By desperate fighting, the Israelis had retained a route to the New City of Jerusalem. The enormous Jordanian salient of the West Bank narrowed Israel at its northern waist to nine miles, left the whole country within heavy artillery range of Jordanian, Egyptian or Syrian batteries, and exposed much of the population to terrorist raids.

The war of 1956, in which Israel temporarily occupied Sinai, did not diminish the country's insecurity. Its strategic geography was transformed, however, by the outcome of the 1967 war when Israel pre-empted mobilisation by Egypt, Syria and Jordan. The West Bank up to the line of the Jordan as well as the whole of Sinai were occupied. The Golan Heights, from which the Syrian Army had dominated northern Galilee, were captured, as too, after an epic battle, was the summit of Mount Hermon (9,232 feet) which overlooks northern Israel as far as Haifa. At a blow Israel's cities were removed from the threat of artillery attack and the start-lines of potential invaders forced back across 140 miles of desert, in the case of Egypt, and beyond a barely tankable tableland, in the case of Syria. Jordan's defeat, and the additional refugee burden that flowed from it, made its participation in future wars highly unlikely.

Other advantages derived from the 1967 victory: earlier warning of air attack and greater depth of defensive airspace; more rapid north–south communication across the West Bank; profitability of investment in fortification, particularly on the Suez Canal, where the Bar Lev Line was built (1968–9), and on the Golan. Consonant disadvantages went unforeseen; they included dangerous relaxations of alertness and force-levels, but also spatial over-extension, particularly in the Sinai. Sinai is pure desert, waterless and almost roadless, across which runs a central mountain range; the mountain passes – the Mitla and Gidi, in particular – are of crucial significance for east–west movement. Israel had always regarded Egypt's possession of Sinai as a severe strategic threat, even though it had inflicted heavy loss on the retreating Egyptians at the passes in both

1956 and 1967. It was therefore glad to occupy Sinai, and invested heavily in roads, airstrips and fortifications in the region.

Subsequent experience was to cast doubt on the strategic desirability of the occupation. The inhospitability of Sinai meant, as the Egyptians had found, that an occupying army is compelled to defend it at the front line, with little 'defence-in-depth', which conditions disfavour. If and when the front line is broken, territory then falls readily to the attacker. That had happened to the Egyptians in 1956 and 1967. In 1973 it happened to the Israelis when, on 6 October, the Egyptians crossed the Suez Canal, water-cannoned gaps in the sand ramparts of the Bar Lev Line, and captured a strip of Sinai ten miles deep. Initial Israeli counter-attacks failed and, though a foothold was subsequently gained on the Egyptian bank, forcing the imposition of a ceasefire, the Israelis were unable to recover the rest of the lost ground. Following the Camp David accords of September 1978 Israel returned the whole of Sinai to Egypt (1982), under guarantee that it should not be remilitarised. The agreement may be seen to have been as beneficial militarily as it was politically to both parties.

The Sinai settlement left Israel with other strategic difficulties unsolved, notably the exposure of its narrow northern appendix to Syrian aggression and to terrorist and missile attack by the Palestine Liberation Organisation. During the 1973 war the Syrians had very nearly broken through the defences of the Golan, fortified though it had been, and were repel-led only because Israel's enjoyment of short 'interior lines of communication' allowed that front to be rapidly reinforced. The Golan was soon recaptured and has subsequently and unilaterally been annexed to Israel. Southern Lebanon has presented Israel with a more difficult security problem. Since 1969 Lebanon had, under pressure from the Arab League States, conceded a measure of autonomy to resident Palestinians whose members had grown sharply throughout the 1970s. By 1978 the PLO had acquired and was using medium artillery against the northern Israel towns, attacks which prompted the Israel Defence Force to occupy a southern 25-mile strip between March and June 1978 (Operation 'Stone of Wisdom'). They were replaced on withdrawal by United Nations' troops (UNIFIL) but consigned key territory to a puppet Lebanese militia. Through that keyhole the IDF returned in June 1982 to wage a 'final' campaign against the PLO. Its conduct of the campaign won Israel little advantage – the PLO, twice formally expelled in 1982 and 1983, are still present in Lebanon – and much international odium. In mid 1985 its rearguards disengaged finally from the strip of territory first occupied during 'Stone of Wisdom' seven years earlier.

In strategic shorthand, Israel's problem is one of 'depth'. It has been solved by diplomatic means in the south and east, but remains unsolved in the north. It will remain unsolved as long as Israel is repugnant to its unreconciled neighbours – a political and ideological rather than a strategic circumstance.

Fourteen armies have fought over the Lebanon thoughout history: the strip of flat land between the high ground and the sea, which includes modern Israel and Lebanon, has always been a battleground. Whoever controls the high ground controls the points of access to the south. Now field fortifications, dykes and ditches are being used in a desperate attempt to insulate Israel from attack from the north. Meanwhile, Lebanon is vulnerable on all sides, except in the mountains which have defeated almost all invaders.

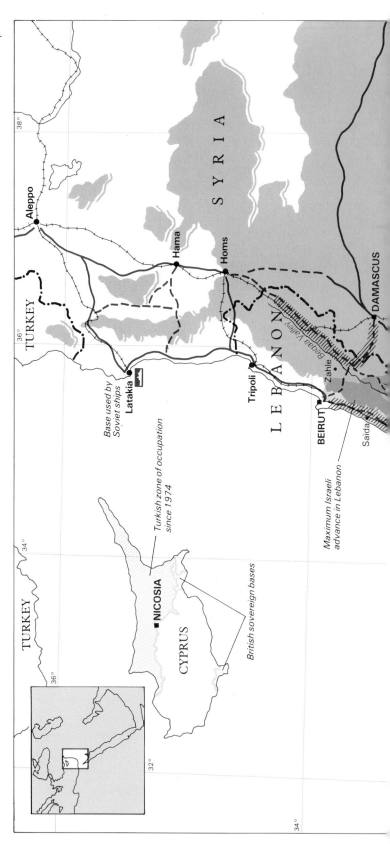

Israel and Lebanon: The Levantine Entanglement

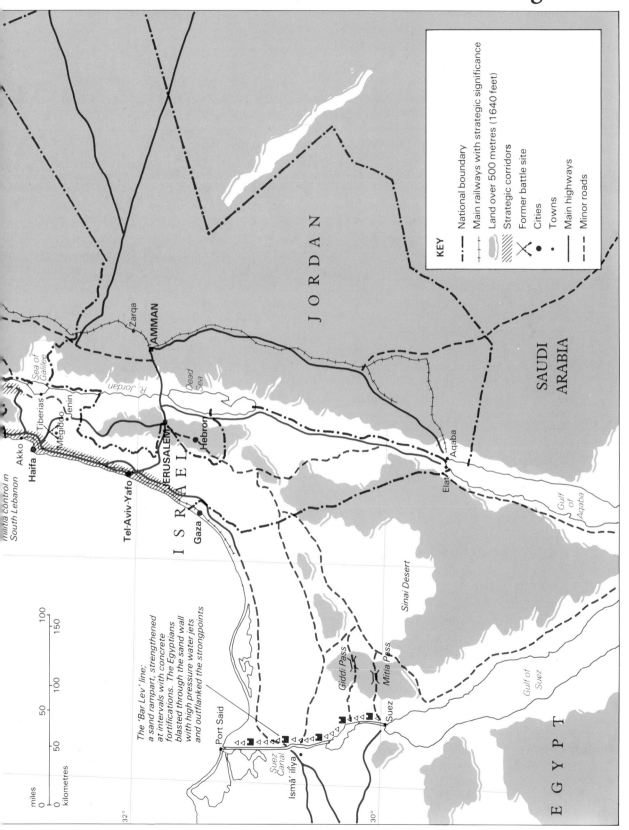

KEY

- ·—·· National boundary
- ┼┼┼ Main railways with strategic significance
- Land over 500 metres (1640 feet)
- ▨ Strategic corridors
- ✕ Former battle site
- ● Cities
- ● Towns
- —— Main highways
- – – – Minor roads

JORDAN

SAUDI ARABIA

Zarqa

AMMAN

Sea of Galilee

R. Jordan

Dead Sea

Aqaba

Tiberias

Megiddo

Jenin

Akko

Haifa

JERUSALEM

Hebron

Tel-'Aviv-Yafo

Gaza

Elat

Gulf of Aqaba

militia control in South Lebanon

I S R A E L

Sinai Desert

Gulf of Suez

Port Said

The 'Bar Lev' line:
a sand rampart, strengthened
at intervals with concrete
fortifications. The Egyptians
blasted through the sand wall
with high pressure water jets
and outflanked the strongpoints

Giddi Pass

Mitla Pass

Suez

Ismā'īlīya

Suez Canal

E G Y P T

miles
0
50
100
150

kilometres
0
50
100

32°

30°

7 Kurdistan: Millennial Antagonisms

Kurdistan is the land of the Kurds, a people without a state, who live as a minority, though often the preponderant majority of the local population, in north-eastern Iraq, north-western Iran, and south-eastern Turkey; there are also Kurdish enclaves in Syria and the Soviet Union, adjacent to the main Kurdish centres. During this century a strong national movement has taken root among the Kurds, which expresses itself in demands for, at least, local autonomy and, at its strongest, for statehood.

The Kurds, a race of warrior high-landers whose identity has been traced to 2400 B.C., have a long history both of resistance to rule by outsiders and of conflict with their neighbours – Armenians, Azeris, Turks, but particularly the Arabs. Ethnically and linguistically they are akin to the Persians, Kurdish, of which there are three main dialects, being related to modern Farsi. Religiously they belong to the Sunni branch of Islam, though their form of belief and practice differs slightly from the mainstream, and there is at least one heretical Kurdish sect. Estimates of Kurdish numbers vary greatly, between a low of 7 million and a high of 16 million. The lower figure is the safer. On that basis, it is calculated that between 1.5 and 2 million Kurds live in Iraq, about the same number in Iran, 300,000 in Syria, 80,000 in the USSR and over 3 million in Turkey. The Turkish government denies the Kurds a separate demographic identity, enumerating them for census purposes as 'Mountain Turks'. Periodically, the Turks make a concerted attack on Kurdish nationalism. In May 1983, hundreds of Kurds were sentenced to death or imprisonment after a long trial designed to deter the spirit of nationalism, backed by an attack in brigade strength into Iraqi Kurdistan through Cukurca.

Traditionally the Kurds have inhabited the valleys of the mountains that surround Lake Reza'iyeh in Iran and Lake Van in Turkey, as far west as the Upper Euphrates, as far north as the River Aras, as far east as the watershed of the Zagros range and as far south as the Iranian town of Kermanshah. The 'Kurdistan' to which Kurdish nationalists lay claim also includes the Iraqi towns of Mosul and Kirkuk in the oil-bearing region at the head of the River Tigris, and Luristan in Iran (though the Lurs themselves reject categorisation as Kurds). The total area in which Kurds form more than 50 per cent of the population is about 75,000 square miles.

Historically the Kurds have been semi-nomadic, practising 'transhumance', the seasonal movement of their grazing flocks between high and low ground. But most are now settled agriculturalists and a size-able number town dwellers, particularly in Sulaymaniyah in Iraq and Diyarbakir in Turkey. The flatlands at the fringe of the Kurdish mountains, particularly in Iraq, produce wheat of high quality and Kurdish farmers are also important growers of fruit and tobacco. Their heartland is, however, inimical to agriculture. 'Their valleys are surrounded by high rocky mountains' – 3,000 feet in Iraqi Kurdistan, but up to 12,000 further north – 'and end in narrow gorges, so that approach to them is difficult in summer and often impossible in winter, when the entire country is deeply covered in snow. There are flatlands on the slopes and sometimes on the tops of the mountains covered with grass after the thaw, but they are often bordered by chasms and precipices and only accessible by narrow tracks.' The mountains are well-watered, and warm in summer but bitterly cold in winter, the mean temperature being at freezing point in January and in the foothills.

Because the Kurds are valley dwellers, whose villages are separated from each other by high spurs and ranges, their social organisation is strongly tribal. There are some seven tribes in Turkey, twenty in Iraq and thirty in Iran. Tribal leadership is divided between hereditary chiefs, or *aghas*, and *sheikhs*, religious notables who may transmit their calling to their sons. In recent years, the authority of chiefs and *sheikhs* has been eroded by the rise of a Kurdish urban élite; but the Kurds have always produced men who make their mark beyond the mountains. The most famous of them was Saladin, the Crusaders' victorious enemy.

The chiefly class, from which Saladin came, never succeeded, however, in establishing unitary power over the Kurds, a failure that explains their modern history. Clannish, disputatious and violent, the Kurds quarrelled among themselves as energetically as they resisted outsiders, with the result that they often preferred to accept vassal status under the Persian or Ottoman emperors rather than make common cause against them. The only factor certain to arouse Kurdish resistance was any effort to reduce chiefly authority. Ottoman efforts to impose Turkish officialdom in Kurdistan in the nineteenth century provoked a series of revolts; resistance was further stimulated by the Young Turks' efforts to turkicise the Kurds after the 1908 revolution.

Because of their ethnic affinity with the Persians, it is with them that the Kurds have most easily coexisted. The proximity of the Turkic-speaking Azeris and the immigration of Christian Assyrians have been a cause of conflict in this century, however, as has Russian intervention in both World Wars, as well as efforts to centralise state power by the Pahlavi dynasty. In 1946 the Russians fostered a short-lived Kurdish 'Mahabad' Republic and armed its adherents. It did not survive the Russian withdrawal from northern Iran, though the arms then distributed were used against the Iranian army as late as 1950. Iranian Kurds continued to support their brothers' quarrels with Iraq until 1975, when the Shah agreed to restrain them as a quid pro quo to secure realignment of the Shatt-al-Arab frontier. Since the outbreak of the Iraq–Iran war in 1980, strong Iraqi security measures on the northern frontier have restricted transborder movements by the Kurds.

In Turkey, though prepared to rebel against the political authority of the Ottoman Sultan, the Kurds were always deeply loyal to his religious authority as Caliph of the Islamic community. During the First World War, which the Sultan deemed a holy war, they contributed men freely to the army and fought both Russian and Armenian incursions into their home districts. As late as 1924 many Kurds were seeking the inclusion of Iraqi Kurdistan in Atatürk's Turkey. But the abolition of the Caliphate in 1925, subsequent efforts to turkicise the Kurds, and brutal governmental repression of Kurdish resistance turned Turkey's Kurds into a dissident community. They raised revolts in 1930 and 1937, which were put down with ruthlessness. As late as 1961 there were riots in Turkish Kurdistan against the government's policy of extinguishing its tribal system. The policy, nevertheless, progressively achieved its effect and, though Kurds remain unturkicised, they no longer sustain their claim to autonomy.

Kurds had a traditional antipathy for their Christian neighbours, Assyrians and Armenians (both now displaced), as also for the Muslim Azeris. Their chief dislike, however, was always for the Arabs, and it was that dislike that motivated their efforts to avoid the inclusion of western Kurdistan in what would be British-mandated

The Kurds are different from all their neighbours; equally, they inspire fear in all of them. Over the centuries the Kurds have descended from their mountains to ravage the plains below. Their neighbours have proved incapable of united action against them, and the Kurdish problem will continue. But now the claimed borders of Greater Kurdistan include substantial oil reserves and the danger has become more acute.

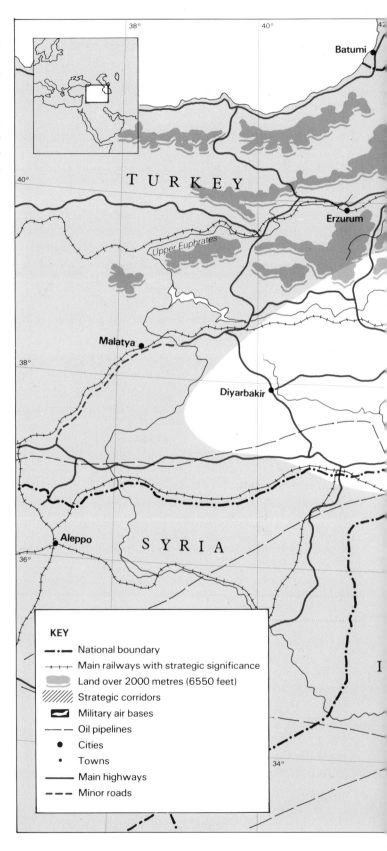

KEY

— · — National boundary

+ + + + Main railways with strategic significance

Land over 2000 metres (6550 feet)

Strategic corridors

Military air bases

— — Oil pipelines

● Cities

· Towns

—— Main highways

- - - Minor roads

Kurdistan: Millennial Antagonisms

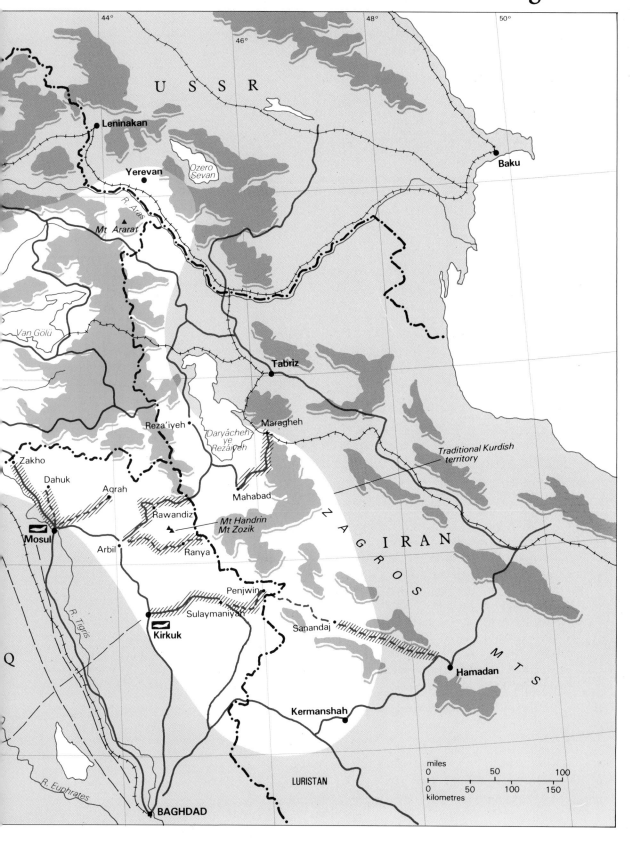

Iraq after 1918. When their hopes of self-determination foundered at Versailles, they sought alternatives in accession to Turkey or in semi-autonomy under the mandate. The British, however, found it impossible to make a binding agreement with the Kurdish leader, Mahmud Barzar of Sulaymaniyah whom they had chosen as their man. Fighting broke out in 1919 between his followers and their troops, to be revived in 1923, 1927 and again in 1930. In 1932 a new leader, Mulla Mustafa Barzani, rose in revolt against the state of Iraq, on its gaining independence from the British mandate, which he was to sustain intermittently until 1947. Exiled first to Iran and then to the Soviet Union, he returned to Iraq after the fall of the monarchy in 1958 when the new regime proclaimed a 'Republic of Arabs and Kurds'.

This effort at amity proved, however, short-lived. By 1961 the Mulla Mustafa was at war with the new regime, a war precipitated by a quarrel with old tribal enemies which supported the new government. By 1962 the Kurdish Democratic Party, representing the nationalist movement, had joined forces with Mustafa – a not untroubled relationship – and the war was to continue until 1970. It took the form of government offensives into the Kurdish mountains, which were always repelled and sometimes followed by Kurdish descents to the lower ground. The government maintained three fronts, the northern aligned along the roads to Zakho, Dahuk and Aqrah, the central towards Rawandiz and Ranya and the eastern towards Sulaymaniyah. Its offensives took the form of pushing armoured columns into the mountains, but as the terrain became progressively roadless and overlooked, these tactics proved fruitless. In 1966, during the fourth offensive, the Iraqi army, seeking to bisect Kurdish territory along the line of the Rawandiz gorge, suffered disaster at Mounts Handrin and Zozik, leaving 2,000 dead and much equipment behind. A larger effort in 1969, aimed simultaneously at Ranya, Qala Diza, Mawat and Penjwin was also turned back. Frustrated by Kurdish resistance, the government eventually offered terms in March 1970 and, in the expectation of enjoying almost complete autonomy, the Kurds settled.

In March 1974, however, following a failure to agree on the autonomy issue, the Kurds seized control of the 207 miles of frontier with Turkey and raised revolt in the Kirkuk, Arbil and Sulaymaniyah regions. The government organised in response the largest offensive yet mounted against them, cut a new road to bypass the Rawandiz gorge and made repeated assaults on Mounts Handrin and Zozik. The latter was taken on 24 October, and 130,000 Kurds fled into Iran. In March the Shah agreed to withdraw support for the Kurdish rebellion in return for a realignment of the Shatt-al-Arab frontier, and closed his borders. The Iraqi army immediately mounted a major offensive along the whole front from Sulaymaniyah to Zakho which forced the Kurdish leadership to offer a ceasefire on 13 March.

Mulla Mustafa fled to Iran and died in exile in 1979. Since that time the Kurds' revolt has been in abeyance. As long as their homeland remains in its roadless and undeveloped state, it will prove inviolable to the centralising power of the Iraqi – or any other – government. Their poverty, backwardness and physical isolation make their attainment of statehood, however, unlikely.

8 Iran and Iraq: Jihad

The modern border between Iraq and Iran, today the focus of the longest and among the bloodiest international wars fought since 1945, follows one of the most significant topographical, cultural, linguistic, racial and religious and historical boundaries in the world. To its east lies an enormous country of mountain and plateau, inhabited by the world's largest population of Shiite Muslims who, as a nation, have a tradition of empire within the Middle East which reaches back to the first millennium B.C. To its west lies the rich river valley land of the Tigris and Euphrates, seat of the world's earliest civilisation, now inhabited by an Arab population which regards its Farsi-speaking neighbours as enemies by tradition and potential oppressors by reason of ideology and religion.

Iran, often invaded though rarely conquered, has preserved its unitary identity thanks to its remarkable topography. Most notable among its topographical features is its very great size. Covering an area of 636,000 square miles, its dimensions are almost equivalent to those of the United States west of the Rocky mountains. Next in importance comes the character of its border regions. In the north it is bounded for a long distance by the shores of the Caspian Sea, in the south-west and south by the Gulf and the Indian Ocean. Following its Caspian seaboard and the adjacent land frontiers with the Soviet Union run the Elburz mountains, which rise at points to over 13,000 feet; its western boundary is found by the Zagros mountains, which touch Turkey in the north and extend as far as the narrows of the Gulf in the south. The escarpment of the Zagros is the principal military obstacle to invasion from the Arab lands. The highlands of the east are also a barrier to invasion

from Afghanistan and modern Pakistan.

But, more important as an obstacle in that region are the great deserts that cover the Iranian Central Plateau, the Dasht-e-Kavir and the Dasht-e-Lut. Because the Central Plateau is surrounded by mountains, it cannot drain outwards and, despite prevailing high summer temperatures, most surface water, the residue of vanished lakes, remains permanently trapped within it. Leaching covers these swamps with a thick salt crust, beneath which are trapped deep layers of mud and slime. In combination, the two elements make the Kavir both impassable and very dangerous to travellers; if broken, the sharp edges of the salt crust cause serious injury to man and beast, while the morass beneath threatens them with drowning. The sand and gravel wastes of the Lut further to the south are more easily traversed, but only by travellers well enough equipped to survive its waterless immensities.

A further impediment to travel in Iran is supplied by the extreme harshness of its climate. Summer temperatures in the Central Plateau may reach 50°C. (122°F.). Winter temperatures in the mountain zones average 0°C. (32°F.) and in the north-west there is frost for 130–50 days of the year. All temperatures are exaggerated by the effects of high winds which are a feature of the climate. In the south-west constant winds of over sixty miles per hour are common from May to September for days on end. Few of these winds, moreover, bring rain. The slopes near the Caspian Sea are relatively well-watered and the valleys within the mountain ranges receive sufficient rainfall to permit permanent cultivation; it is from those valleys that the population is largely fed. The Central Plateau, by contrast, receives only four inches of rain a year while the south

The roots of antagonism between Iran and Iraq lie in a murder which took place more than a millennium ago. The oppositions within Islam – Sunni Muslim against Shia Muslim – have boiled over into war. Iraq, which began the war in a moment of opportunism, now fears the effect of Shiite militancy on its own Shiite masses. Iran, fired with the image of holy war, has continuing imperial ambitions. There is no obvious point of compromise, and the terrain, now heavily defended and fortified, has all the potential for a war of attrition, like the western front in the First World War.

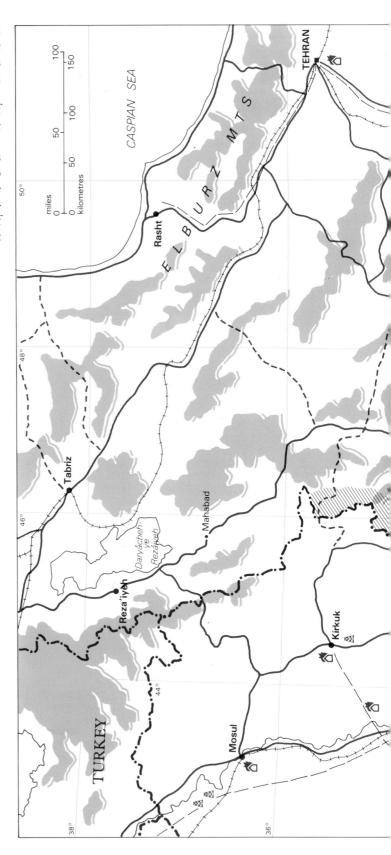

Iran and Iraq: Jihad

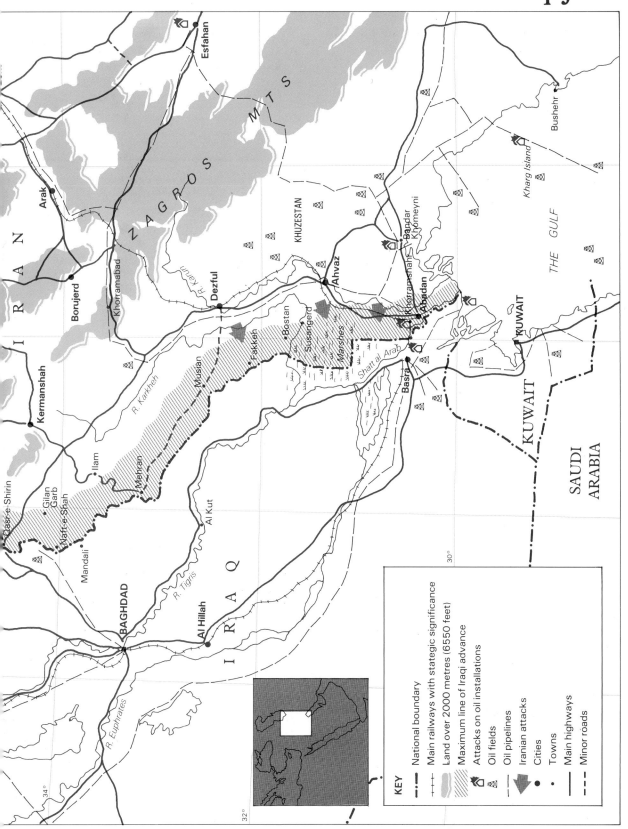

Esfahan

Z A G R O S   M T S

Arak

IRAN

Borujerd

Khorramabad

Kermanshah

Ilam

Gilan Garb

Qasr-e-Shirin

Naft-e-Shah

Mandali

Mehran

BAGHDAD

Al Hillah

I R A Q

Al Kut

R. Tigris

R. Euphrates

R. Karkheh

R. Karun

Dezful

Musian

Fakkeh

Bostan

Susangerd

Marshes

KHUZESTAN

Ahvaz

Khorramshahr

Abadan

Bandar Khomeyni

Basra

Shatt al Arab

KUWAIT

KUWAIT

SAUDI ARABIA

THE GULF

Kharg Island

Bushehr

30°

32°

34°

KEY

- National boundary
- Main railways with stategic significance
- Land over 2000 metres (6550 feet)
- Maximum line of Iraqi advance
- Attacks on oil installations
- Oil fields
- Oil pipelines
- Iranian attacks
- Cities
- Towns
- Main highways
- Minor roads

is generally dry throughout the summer.

Because topography and climate are so harsh, Iran has always been, and still is, badly provided with means of internal communication. In the sixth century B.C. Darius the Great built a Royal Road linking his capitals which was a wonder of the ancient world. But at the beginning of this century the country was still effectively without a road network, and the building of a trans-Iranian railway was not begun until 1927. Even today the eastern half of the country is largely roadless. In the west the network is denser. Paved arterial highways run parallel to the Zagros mountains on each side with interconnecting rungs, as also in the north along the Elburz range. The railway network, forming a rough T, connects Tabriz with Tehran and Meshed, its stem reaching to Abadan at the head of the Gulf. A newer branch links Tehran with the southern city of Yazd. At their extremities, the road and rail links connect with the Turkish, Afghan, Pakistani, Soviet and Iraqi systems. The first railway in Afghanistan is now being built by the Soviet Union. These connections, however, are few and there are long stretches of the frontiers not traversed even by motorable roads.

Since the outbreak of the war with Iraq on 22 September 1980, all road and rail links between the two countries have, of course, been cut, and the border has been the focus of intense fighting – particularly in the three sectors near the Iraqi cities of Basra in the south, Baghdad, the capital, in the centre, and Kirkuk in the north. But the communication systems of the two countries are, in any case, not congruent. Those of Iran are divergent, being arranged to connect its widely scattered centres of population; those within Iraq are strictly linear, following the course of the two great rivers which determine its pattern of settlement.

Iraq is essentially a lowland region.

Mountains protect its far northern border with Turkey and provide a homeland for its Kurdish population above Kirkuk. But its western reaches are level desert while its heartland is river valley land at little above sea level. Though large in extent (171,000 square miles), half the country is desert and population is concentrated in less than a quarter of the territory, around Baghdad and Basra, with significant density in the oil-bearing region of Kirkuk. A railway connects the port of Basra with Baghdad, above which it branches to Kirkuk and Mosul, from the latter place connecting with the Turkish and Syrian systems. The road network follows a similar pattern, though a trans-desert link connects Baghdad with Amman in Jordan and a southern spur Basra with Kuwait.

Of major strategic significance is the Iraqi climate. From June–July until November a dry and intensely hot summer prevails. In November the rainy season begins, raising water levels throughout the valley region and making campaigning difficult and in places impossible. Wide areas of the lowlands are, however, permanently waterlogged. Water obstacles are a particular impediment to military movement east of the Shatt-al-Arab and the lower course of the Tigris, an area which has seen much of the fighting between Iraq and Iran since 1980. During 1984 the Iraqis elaborated the water barrier by creating an artificial moat eighteen miles long by one broad, east of the lower reach of the Tigris.

Since 1982 Iraq has been on the defensive in its war with Iran, as this resort to obstacle-building reflects. At the outset, however, it was the attacker and then found the riverine topography across the Iranian border a serious impediment to progress. Its original objects – besides those of overaweing the Kurds, and defending the traditional invasion route to Baghdad via Kermanshah and Khanaqin –

were to seize ground in the Arabic-speaking province of Khuzestan and to capture the oil city of Abadan. Initially the Iraqi army made satisfactory progress. They quickly: a) isolated Khorramshahr and Abadan, b) seized the border town of Mehran to the north of Basra and cut the Iranian north–south road network on their side of the Zagros mountains and c) occupied territory around Qasr-e-Shirin which secured the protection of Baghdad from attack along the traditional invasion route.

At the end of September the Iraqis declared their territorial objectives secured; but they continued to lay siege to Khorramshahr and Abadan without making significant progress. In May 1981 the Iranians counter-attacked and in September raised the siege of Abadan and pushed the Iraqis back to the Karun river. This waterway and its tributaries, which lie athwart the strategic axis chosen by the Iraqis, had been a major obstacle to the development of their campaign. So too had been the Karkheh river, which discharges into the marshes of the Tigris; its lower course was retaken by the Iranians in November–December 1981. In March 1982 they regained more borderland west of Dezful and were then in a position to mount an attack across the Iraqi borders.

The Iranian invasion of Iraq began in July 1982 and their counter-offensive has continued intermittently ever since. But for reasons partly military and partly geographic it has made unsatisfactory progress. North of Qasr-e-Shirin the Iraqis have successfully utilised the broken terrain that leads to the Zagros chain as a defensive barrier. Further south the marshes and waterways associated with the lower course of the Tigris and the Shatt-al-Arab have proved impenetrable to the Iranian push. The obstacle they offer has been greatly improved by Iraqi defensive engineering, which has created deep and extensive trench, minefield and anti-tank ditch systems.

It now seems unlikely that Iran will find the military means to clinch its remarkable reversal of the initiative in this war. Iraq's capacity to sustain its war effort is, however, threatened by the severe economic constraint under which it has operated since 1980. The interdiction of its oil exports via the Gulf, imposed by the superior strength of the Iranian navy, has forced it to rely for foreign earnings on the capacity of its pipeline output. But its main pipeline, running to the Mediterranean through Syria, has been closed by the Damascus government, which is friendly to Tehran, while the pipeline to Turkey, though remaining open, is of small capacity. Iraq's hopes of restoring its pre-war level of oil exports rest on plans to construct new pipelines across Saudi Arabian territory to the Red Sea.

It is arresting to recall that the pretext for hostilities between Iraq and Iran lay in Iran's successful re-alignment of the common frontier on the Shatt-al-Arab achieved by the last Shah in the Algiers agreement of 1975. That returned the frontier from its alignment on the Iranian bank to the 'thalweg' in midstream. Viewed by Iraq as a potential constriction of its maritime outlet, the agreement might now be seen by Baghdad as a desirable basis on which to settle a war which has become a cultural and political conflict of an almost unbearably burdensome kind.

9 The Gulf: Permanent Flashpoint

The Gulf – known formerly as the Persian but subsequently claimed as the Arab and hence recently identified for reasons of political tact without a national sobriquet – is the body of water on to which abut the richest oil-bearing regions of the world. Saudi Arabia, Kuwait, and Iran each have, for example, greater oil reserves than the United States. In all, over 20 per cent of the oil produced and over half the oil exported in the world originates in the Middle East, of which the greater part is shipped through the ports of the Gulf. Free access to, and the security of loading and shipping from the Gulf is, therefore, of the greatest political and economic significance in the contemporary world, in which over 100 of the 160 nation states are oil importers.

The Gulf is some 475 miles long and 200 miles wide at its broadest point, but nowhere deeper than 650 feet. It is fed at its northern end and, through the Shatt-al-Arab, by the Tigris and Euphrates rivers, and by a series of short run-offs on its mountainous eastern shore. Its western shore, low-lying and almost totally desert, is effectively unwatered, fringed by coral reef and salt marsh, and interrupted by few deep-water inlets. Exceptions are the open bay of Kuwait and the Dubai creek; the harbouring facilities each provides explain the economic importance each place has attained in the region. On the eastern, Iranian shore there are major ports at Bandar Abbas, Bushire and, in the Shatt-al-Arab, the oil centre of Abadan; most of Abadan's oil-loading is, however, carried on at the partly artificial Kharg Island. Oil is also loaded at a number of terminals on the western shore, notably at Kuwait and nearby Mina al Ahmadi, the Saudi port of Ras Tannurah, Bahrain, Umm Sa'id in Qatar, Dhanna in the United Arab Emirates and at several offshore points.

The Gulf is bordered by eight states; anti-clockwise, Iran, Iraq, Kuwait, Saudi Arabia, the island of Bahrain, Qatar, the United Arab Emirates and Oman. The United Arab Emirates, formerly the Trucial States, confederated in 1971 and consist of the Sheikhdoms of Abu Dhabi, Dubai, Sharjah, Ajman, Umm al Qaiwain, Ras al Khaimah and Fujairah. Since 1981 the UAE, Qatar, Bahrain, Oman, Kuwait and Saudi Arabia have been formally associated in an economic and security grouping known as the Gulf Co-operation Council.

The strategic instability in the Gulf region derives from the historic antipathy that exists between the Iranians on the eastern shore and the Arabs on the western. This antipathy is in part racial and linguistic, since the Iranians are not Arab, and partly religious, since most Iranians are Shiite and most Gulf Arabs Sunni Muslims. Until the discovery of oil and as long as the region was dominated by an external power – the Ottomans until 1918, the British until 1971 – the antipathy was of no general significance. Since the departure of the British, however, antipathy has become tension and tension conflict, fuelled in part by existing border disputes and partly by the aggressive foreign policy of Iraq.

A number of the border disputes lie between the Arab States of the western shore – between Bahrain and Qatar over the Huwar Islands and between Iraq and Kuwait over the islands of Warbah and Bubiyan – but their recently generated solidarity makes it unlikely that such disputes will be pursued. The claims levelled by Iran on Arab territory are, on the other hand, active. Iran lays claim to the whole island of Bahrain, formerly an administrative dependency of Bushire, with a large Shiite population. And it not only claims, but now occupies, the three islands in the Straits of Hormuz, Abu Musa and the Greater and Lesser Tumbs, sovereignty over which is claimed by Sharjah and Ras al Khaimah (now states of the UAE) respectively. While the ruler of Sharjah and the former Shah of Iran agreed to the occupation of Abu Musa, the Tumbs were seized by force in 1971.

The status of these islands is particularly delicate because of the strategic position they occupy in the Hormuz waterway through which in 1980 passed one-third of the non-communist world's oil consumption. So crucial is free passage of the Straits held to be to its welfare, that in 1980 President Carter promulgated the Carter Doctrine, laying down that Soviet (and by implication all other exclusive) attempts to gain control of the Gulf would be regarded as 'an assault on the vital interests of the United States . . . to be repelled by any means necessary, including armed force'. When the Iranians declared the Gulf to be a war zone in September 1980, on the outbreak of the Iran–Iraq war, President Carter instituted moves to organise an international naval force for the defence of the Straits, which he stated to be an international imperative. The Iranians at once announced that they would make themselves responsible for keeping the Straits open and, though they have subsequently warned that they might renege if the Iraqis interfered with their own oil-exporting capabilities, they have not done so. Moreover, detailed surveys by interested parties of the practicality of closing the Straits has since revealed that it would not be simple, the channel being too deep (320 feet) and too wide (three miles) to be sealed by block-ships; mines could be swept (as the Red Sea approaches to the Suez Canal were swept by the Anglo-French flotilla in 1984) and direct fire interdiction would be countered by the intervention of western naval forces.

Partly to provide for such intervention, and partly to offset the Soviet naval presence in the region, the United States has taken steps to acquire and activate bases in the northern Indian Ocean. Its main base is at Diego Garcia in the British Indian Ocean Territory 2,500 miles south of the Straits; its forward base is the Omani island of Masirah, from which the Straits are within tactical air range. Masirah would also become the concentration point for the ground element of the US Rapid Deployment Force, created in March 1980 with the specific purpose of deploying into south-west Asia.

Since the outbreak of the Iran–Iraq war and the creation of the Rapid Deployment Force, the economic and strategic significance of the Gulf has been deliberately reduced. Iraqi attacks on tankers proceeding to load at Kharg and Iranian attacks on Arab territory (outside Iraq), as at Kuwait in November 1980, have driven oil companies to draw larger supplies from non-Gulf sources. The Gulf States themselves have found ways of exporting oil from other than Gulf outlets; Saudi Arabia, alarmed that 97 per cent of its output was formerly pumped through Ras Tannurah, has now completed a pipeline running across the desert from the Gulf oilfields to the Red Sea port of Yanbu, capable of pumping about one-tenth of Saudi Arabia's daily production (10 million barrels a day). Because, additionally, in reaction to OPEC price increases, world oil consumption has in any case declined by about 2 per cent, shippings out of the Gulf now (1985) represent only 20 per cent of non-communist oil consumption, as against 30 per cent in 1980.

The enormous oil reserves of eastern Arabia and western Iran will, however, continue to invest the Gulf, which provides the readiest means for their export,

The Gulf is the 'oil highway' of the world; most of the oil exported from the Middle East travels through it. Traditionally, the main powers in the region have had a joint interest in maintaining free passage. But the war between Iran and Iraq has brought Gulf oil into the war zone. Both Iran and Iraq ship their oil out through the Gulf, but Iran has only its Gulf terminals, making it vulnerable to Iraqi attack. But neither side has yet taken the suicidal step of seeking to block the outflow entirely. Caution still prevails, since not only would this probably fail, but it would bring the United States and the Soviet Union directly into the action.

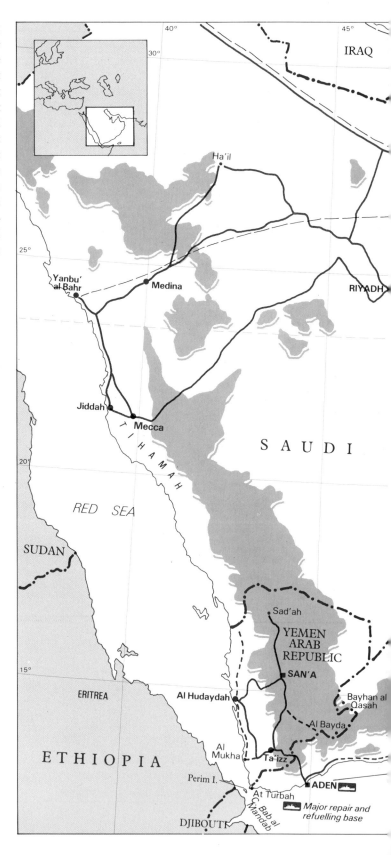

The Gulf: Permanent Flashpoint

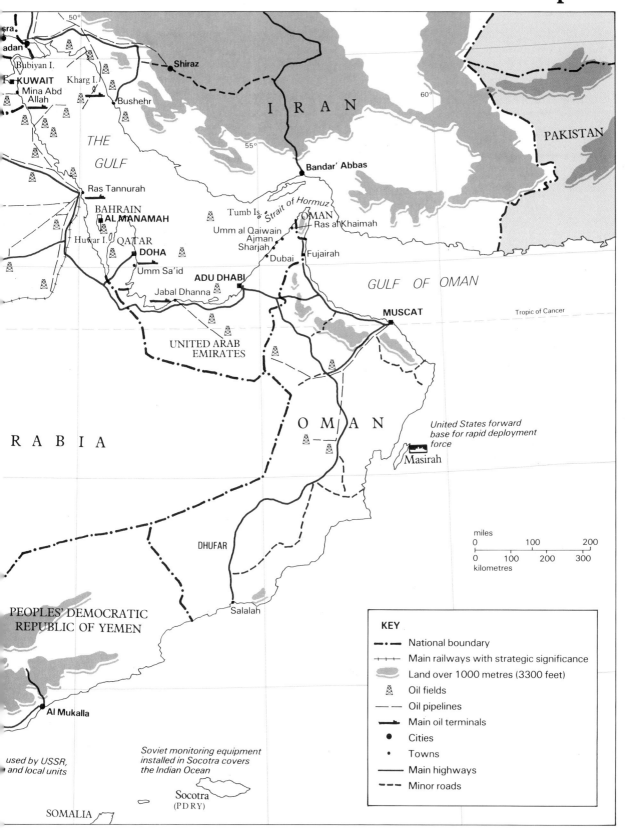

sra.
adan
Bubiyan I.
KUWAIT
Mina Abd Allah
Kharg I.
Bushehr
Shiraz

I R A N

PAKISTAN

THE
GULF

Ras Tannurah
BAHRAIN
AL MANAMAH
Huwar I.
QATAR
DOHA
Umm Sa'id
Jabal Dhanna
ADU DHABI

Bandar' Abbas

Tumb Is.
Strait of Hormuz
OMAN
Ras al Khaimah
Umm al Qaiwain
Ajman
Sharjah
Dubai
Fujairah

GULF OF OMAN

MUSCAT

Tropic of Cancer

UNITED ARAB
EMIRATES

R A B I A

O M A N

United States forward
base for rapid deployment
force

Masirah

miles
0   100   200
0   100   200   300
kilometres

DHUFAR

Salalah

PEOPLES' DEMOCRATIC
REPUBLIC OF YEMEN

KEY

–··–·· National boundary
+++++ Main railways with strategic significance
Land over 1000 metres (3300 feet)
Oil fields
Oil pipelines
Main oil terminals
Cities
Towns
Main highways
Minor roads

used by USSR,
and local units

Soviet monitoring equipment
installed in Socotra covers
the Indian Ocean

Al Mukalla

Socotra
(PDRY)

SOMALIA

with strategic significance for decades to come.

Yemen and Oman

Yemen occupies the south-western corner of the Arabian Peninsula; historically and culturally a single unit, it is now divided into the states of the Yemen Arab Republic (YAR) and the Peoples' Democratic Republic of Yemen (PDRY). Its coastline, which in the YAR forms the lower eastern shore of the Red Sea and in the PDRY half the Arabian shore of the Indian Ocean, is therefore of the greatest strategic significance; the PDRY's possession of the islands of Perim and Socotra at the Bab al Mandab, the mouth of the Red Sea, further enhances Yemen's strategic location. Its strategic importance also extends inland, both to the east where the PDRY's tribal territory overspills into the Dhufar province of oil-rich Oman, and across the YAR's undemarcated north-eastern frontier with Saudi Arabia, a country which is heavily dependent on Yemeni immigrant labour to work its industries and services. Because of Yemen's strategic significance, there has been spirited competition over the last two decades between the USSR, the USA, Egypt, Saudi Arabia and Oman for influence in the region, the last materially abetted by Britain, formerly the dominant power at the Red Sea's mouth.

Yemen occupies some 150,000 square miles of territory, much of it high plateau and all cut off from the rest of Arabia by mountains or the desert of the Empty Quarter. Except via the coastal plain of the Tihamah along the Red Sea, it is almost totally inaccessible from the interior. It is, nevertheless, the most densely populated region of the Arabian Peninsula, the YAR having 7 million and the PDRY 2 million inhabitants. The high population density is explained by the fertility of the coastal plain and the valleys cut into the plateau, which are heavily and regularly watered by the movement of the Indian Ocean monsoon. The YAR is agriculturally self-sufficient, and has traditionally enjoyed a rich export trade in coffee, the most prized grade in the world taking its name from the port, Mocha, from which it is shipped. Almost the only internal communications are provided by the roads leading down to Mocha and the other Yemeni ports, of which the most important are Hodeida in the YAR and Aden in the PDRY.

Until 1918 the territory forming the YAR was a province of the Ottoman Empire. So too, in theory, was that of the PDRY, since the Ottomans claimed suzerainty over the whole of the Arabian Peninsula; but they exercised power only patchily, and from 1839 onwards, when Aden was occupied, it came progressively under British rule. The British had occupied Aden in order to establish a coaling station there, the development of steam navigation promising to shorten the voyage to Bombay, via the Red Sea rather than the Cape, from five to two months. The opening of the Suez Canal in 1869 enormously increased the importance of the Red Sea route and led in 1881 to the subordination of Egypt to British control. That act substituted British for Egyptian influence along the Red Sea coasts, further enhanced the importance of Aden to the home and Indian governments and accelerated the growing prosperity of Aden port.

During the later nineteenth century the British extended their control of the south Arabian coast (the Hadhramaut) eastward from Aden, by bringing the rulers of the coastal tribes under their influence. These relationships were formalised in 1873–88 in a series of Protectorate Treaties. At the same time the government of India was entering into treaties with the rulers of Oman, Qatar, Bahrain and what are now the United Arab Emirates in south-eastern Arabia. A formal boundary between these two regions was defined in 1937, when Aden territory was divided into Western and Eastern Aden Protectorates, the latter adjoining the Dhufar province of Oman.

After the collapse of the Ottoman empire, the British made a half-hearted effort to incorporate parts of north Yemen into the Protectorate. Its Imam, however, already in rebellion against the Turks, succeeded in preserving his independence and until 1962 his family retained power in what was widely agreed to be one of the most backward states in the world. The army he had established to sustain his power, politicised by the Egyptian and Iraqi officers he had imported to train it, then rebelled and Egypt sent troops to assist the rebels in the Civil War that broke out between them and the followers of the Imamate. The bitterness of the war was heightened by religious differences, since the Imamate derived its support from the northern (Zaidi) tribes, which are Sunni. The southerners are Shiites, as are the tribes of Aden and the PDRY, which was also thrown into turmoil during the same period by the outbreak of rebellion against British rule.

Egyptian and British involvement ended quite suddenly in 1967, when the British transferred power to the winning faction among the Aden rebels, while the Egyptians repatriated their troops to fight in the current war with Israel. These departures did not, however, bring peace to either Yemen, civil war continuing in the north and faction-fighting in the south. Saudi Arabia, committed to the support of the Zaidi and deeply suspicious of the Marxist regime which exercised power in the PDRY, helped to sustain the war in the north; the PDRY, originally committed to assist in the struggle against the Zaidi, soon fell out with their opponents in the YAR. The breach was healed in 1972,

when the YAR and PDRY governments announced that they intended to unite. But the respective regimes, torn by frequent coups and assassinations, were too weak to realise the intention, and their conflicts of interest and foreign commitment too great to be overcome.

The YAR, connected by geographical propinquity, tradition and economic involvement with Saudi Arabia, was and has remained deeply committed to that country; the chaotic state of YAR politics has frequently shaken the relationship, but not broken it. The PDRY, on the other hand, is impelled by ideology to 'export its revolution', and to form friendships with other Marxist states. China initially succeeded in establishing some influence there; subsequently the Soviet Union came to monopolise its foreign friendships. The relationship became of particular importance to the USSR after 1977 when the outbreak of fighting between Somalia and Ethiopia, which it chose to support in the conflict, deprived its fleet of the use of Berbera as an operational port. Basing facilities were then transferred to Aden which, already in use by the Soviet Indian Ocean fleet, thereafter became its principal support centre in the region.

Ethiopia's Cuban auxiliaries were supplied exclusively through Aden, both by sea and air, via the international airport at Aden city, while the Russians simultaneously prevailed on the PDRY government to withdraw support for Ethiopia's other enemies in Eritrea.

The PDRY was simultaneously engaged in a local war against Oman. Originating as a tribal conflict in Dhufar in 1964, it intensified after 1967 as PDRY help reached the rebels who by 1973 controlled most of the province. The Sultan of Oman, with British, Jordanian and Iranian assistance, thenceforth went into the offensive and by the end of 1976 had regained control of the province, of great importance to his kingdom because of its high rainfall and consequent agricultural productivity.

The strategic importance of Yemen, isolated as it is from the Arabian interior by deserts and mountains, has always lain in its domination of its coastwise sea routes and its provision of convenient harbouring. A Yemen united under a stable and moderate government, which would attract and utilise profitably investment in its harbours and airports, would be a key power in the north-eastern Indian Ocean. The instability of government in disunited Yemen condemns the two half-states to dependency on other powers and robs both of economic and strategic influence. Russian involvement in the PDRY is a source of anxiety to the Western alliance. But the diminution in the volume of its essential maritime traffic via the Red Sea, the development of American basing facilities in the Indian Ocean and off the Oman coast, and the continuing pro-western stance of the Saudi government effectively offset the geographical advantages enjoyed by the Soviets through their friendship with the Aden regime.

SOUTH and SOUTH-EAST ASIA

10 Afghanistan: The Long War

The physical constants – terrain and climate – remain the dominant concern for any invader of Afghanistan. When Alexander the Great penetrated Afghanistan from the west in the years between 331 and 326 B.C., he faced the same strategic problems which confronted the Soviet army in the 1980s. Despite all the advances of modern technology, fighting remains an occupation of the spring and summer: between October and April, snow blocks almost all communications except on the major roads. And those roads, built over the last twenty years with the help of the Russians, Americans and Chinese, follow the course of the valleys, skirting the foothills of the great mountain ranges. The road which Alexander followed is the line taken by the modern highway between Herat and Kandahar. In Afghanistan, the invader must abandon the high ground to his enemies.

Unlike the high plateau of Tibet to the east, Afghanistan is a land of highlands and lowlands. Few tribesmen live in the high mountains, for they sensibly prefer the lusher valleys for their crops and flocks of sheep. But the highlands are used, for pasture and for the arts of war-ambush and raiding. The tribal warriors can live off the land, if their families cannot; they have by tradition taken to the hills during the war season, and lived in the villages during the cold months. This interchange of winter and summer life is also conditioned by the landscape. The landscape of Afghanistan is dominated by long mountain ranges spreading from east to west like the spreading fingers of a hand – the western extension of the Hindu Kush. The highest range is the Pamirs, in a narrow tongue of land which borders the Soviet Union, Pakistan, China and India. To the north of the Hindu Kush is a dry and largely inhospitable plain, running down to the Amu-Darya river; to the west and south-west, desert occupied by nomadic Baluchi tribesmen. Of the whole area of Afghanistan – about 251,000 square miles – only about 15 per cent is cultivated, either in areas where heroic efforts at irrigation from the rivers have produced regular crops, or in the mountain valleys.

While the mountain ranges are impassable by mechanised transport, except through the established passes, they can be

No other country offers such opportunities for guerrilla warfare, as countless invaders have found to their cost. No occupying force has mastered the huge size of Afghanistan. The current invaders, the Russians, are still fighting to secure their lines of communication, while slowly attempting to rebuild an acceptable political structure in the countryside. Both aims are likely to be frustrated, and there is no likely conclusion to the traditional pattern of raids and incursions at which the tribesmen are expert. The only possible solution would be a Domesday option, deliberately and genocidally causing famine in the countryside.

Afghanistan: The Long War

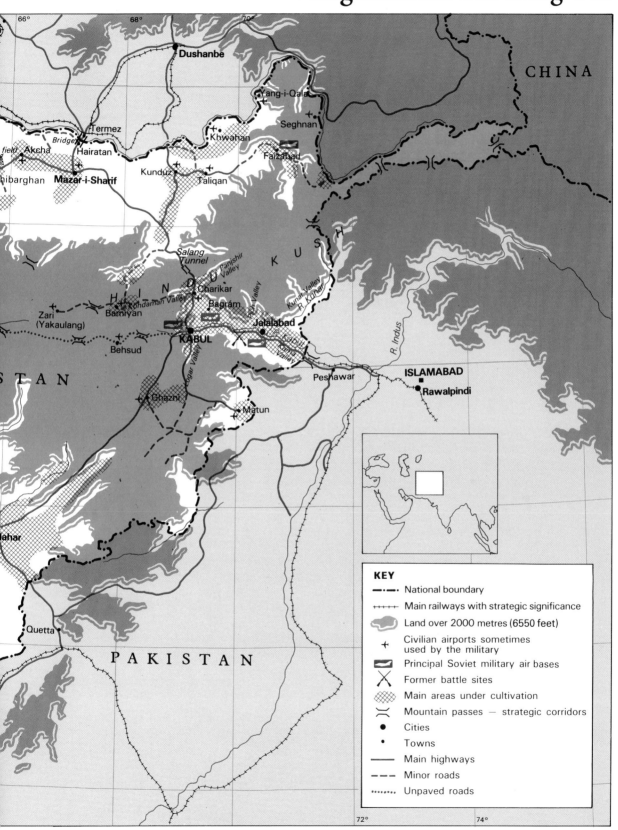

CHINA

Dushanbe

Yang-i-Qala
Seghnan
Khwahan
Termez
Bridge
Akcha
Hairatan
Faizabad
Kunduz
Mazar-i-Sharif
Taliqan
hibarghan

H   I   N   D   U
K   U   S   H

Salang
Tunnel
Panishir Valley
Charikar
Kohdaman Valley
Bagrám
Kunar Valley
R. Kunar
Zari
(Yakaulang)
Bamiyan
Kabul Valley
Jalalabad
R. Indus
KABUL
KABUL
Kama Valley
Behsud
Logar Valley
Peshawar
ISLAMABAD
Rawalpindi
Ghazni
Matun

STAN

ahar

Quetta

PAKISTAN

KEY

- ▬▬▬▬ National boundary
- ✛✛✛✛ Main railways with strategic significance
- Land over 2000 metres (6550 feet)
- ✛ Civilian airports sometimes used by the military
- Principal Soviet military air bases
- ✕ Former battle sites
- Main areas under cultivation
- ╳ Mountain passes — strategic corridors
- ● Cities
- • Towns
- ▬▬▬ Main highways
- - - - Minor roads
- .... Unpaved roads

crossed at many points on foot or on horseback. In some provinces, particularly in the east, there are forests or scrubby woodlands, and even where the hills are bare they are pockmarked with hollows and crevices. It is a land designed by the god of banditry. For this reason, no ruler of Afghanistan has ever been able to coerce the many tribes and peoples which make up the population. The various Afghan empires of history have always acted as predators on the richer lands to the south and west, and successful rulers have given their tribesmen plunder and an easy rein. No native ruler or foreign invader has ever succeeded in gaining full control over all the many tribes. Throughout history the central mountains, inhabited by the Hazara tribes, have been left alone, while the deserts and cities of the west, especially Herat, have experienced many invaders. The eastern corridor, with Kabul at its centre, was invaded twice by the British in the nineteenth century from the south-east and has now been invaded by the Soviet Union from the north. Modern communications have done little to change this pattern. All the main cities are now linked by a modern highway which runs around the central highlands. Some difficult passes, especially the Salang pass north of Kabul, have been improved: the Salang road now runs through a tunnel 1.7 miles long *under* the mountains. The national airlane also joins the main towns with a fairly reliable link, except in bad weather. There are no railways completed yet and off the main highway all transport is by foot or pack animal, as it has always been.

In the twentieth century, the rulers of Afghanistan have seen aviation as the answer to the strategic problem of the terrain. The British began the process in 1919, and bombed Kabul and Jalalabad as well as many villages along the frontier with British India. The king of Afghanis-

tan quickly learned the lesson, and negotiated a supply of aeroplanes from the newly established Soviet Union from 1920, and later, German equipment and instructors during the 1930s. The main intention behind this dramatic innovation was not to carry out some foreign adventure on the frontier, but to subdue the tribes which had previously been beyond central control. The massive expansion of all the armed forces with Soviet assistance after 1956, and with particular emphasis on air power, was stimulated partly by enmity with Pakistan. But there was an equally strong desire to use the air force for internal control, as the British had done on the North-West Frontier in the 1920s. An air strike offered many advantages. It was dramatic, a powerful symbol of technological power. It was quick, much more so than ground troops laboriously picking their way through hostile country. And it seemingly allowed the cities to dominate the hinterland, for the first time in Afghan history.

Until the Russian invasion in December 1979, all these advantages were largely theoretical: very few attempts had been made to use air power systematically, and the equipment of the Afghan air force – only two squadrons of helicopters – made it difficult to sustain a campaign. Under Russian rule, a new attempt has been made to overcome the traditional impediments of terrain and climate. Use of ground attack aircraft, helicopter attack squadrons, and air mobile infantry (as well as paratroops) in concerted campaigns have shown the limitations of war from the air. The aircraft are based at defended points located on the central ring road, and are flying at the limits of their operational range (in the case of helicopters) to attack targets in the centre of Afghanistan. Because the air is thin, fuel is used up more quickly, and the air currents off the mountains call for very skilled flying, especially at low speeds. For close support of infantry on the ground in the valleys, pilots have the unhappy experience of being fired upon from the hills above them, as well as from opposition on the ground. In practice air power has been used to support campaigning in the traditional areas – in the two corridors which centre on Kabul, and in the flat exposed desert land to the west of Herat.

For the Russians, as for the invading British from the south in the nineteenth century, and invaders from Iran in earlier periods, the terrain has imposed a defensive strategy, largely confined to protecting the roads in and out of the country. War has been taken to the enemy only in those areas which affect lines of communication – as in the Panjshir valley beyond the town of Charikar north-east of Kabul. Some attempt has also been made to control the roads and tracks south into Pakistan, but with less success. Much more hopeful, from the invader's point of view, have been successful operations against guerrillas in the flat lands to the west and south-west, around Herat and Farah. The use of air power has allowed a cheap war in terms of lives, if limited in terms of real control of territory.

In one way the land works against the defending tribesmen. So little land is productive, and what there is concentrated in areas of controlled irrigation or on the valley floors in the mountains, that it would be technically possible to interrupt or destroy the food chain. The mountains cannot support more than a tiny population throughout the winter. A scorched earth policy, carried out using pesticides and biological agents distributed from the air, is the only plausible long-term strategy for any invader wishing to do more than control the cities and the main roads. Whether it would work is anybody's guess.

This sort of apocalyptic solution is relevant only to the high mountains of the centre and east. The problems of the desert and scrub in the west of the country are of a different order. The road system south of Farah and Kandahar in theory provides an easy point of access over the deserts and hills of western Pakistan to the coast of the Arabian Sea west of Karachi. This rather elusive opportunity – 'a warm water port' – was held by some strategic thinkers to be the principal motive behind the Russian invasion of 1979: in the nineteenth century the British were always fearful that the Czars would descend through Afghanistan on to the rich prize of India. The western approach offers much more scope for the sensible deployment of modern technology, in particular armoured warfare, and sophisticated aircraft operating from Shindand and Kandahar. The traditional warrior skills of the mountaineers have dictated the battleground: most fighting in recent years has taken place in the provinces around Kabul, and up to the border with Pakistan close to Peshawar. The skirmishing around Herat has shown the devastating effectiveness of modern firepower on unsophisticated forces. In Afghanistan, while geography and the weight of population focuses attention eastwards, the real strategic significance lies in the sparsely populated and thoroughly unattractive lands of the west.

11 India and Pakistan: The Embattled Subcontinent

Drawing a new border along racial, religious, or social lines has only been attempted a few times in recent history. After the war with Greece in 1920–2, the Turks redrew the frontier along simple and brutal lines. All Greeks living in the new Turkish state were forced to withdraw into Greece: there were to be no Hellenisers in Atatürk's new society. In 1945, the Czechoslovak government decided to solve the problem of the troublesome and disloyal German minority by deporting it over the border into Germany: there was to be no Sudetenland in the new Czechoslovakia. The partition of India was designed to create an Islamic state, Pakistan, and a predominantly Hindu India, but this simple resolution could not be achieved. The minority religious groups in each country were distributed rather than concentrated in specific areas, except the Sikh community who belonged by tradition neither to the new Pakistan nor to India. Moreover, the religious division created an Islamic state in two halves, West and East Pakistan, divided by the 1,000 mile bulk of northern India. It was a messy settlement, but the best that could be achieved in the confused circumstances of 1947–8, if 'best' can be applied to a solution which involved more than a million dead and up to 15 million forced to leave their homes.

The sundering of British India was therefore a bitter and brutal business, at village level if not at the level of the political leaders. Some areas of the frontier remained particularly sensitive. In the north, to the south of the Karakoram range, the independent kingdom of Kashmir and Jammu had a Hindu ruler and largely Hindu population in Jammu, but a mostly Muslim population in the Vale of Kashmir. The decision of the Rajah of Kashmir to join India provoked a war which occupied the period 1947–9, and has subsequently proved a regular flashpoint in Indo-Pakistani relations. Kashmir epitomises the injustices of partition felt by both sides. The terrain ranges from high mountains in which only specialised 'alpine' troops can fight to much effect, down to open country around Sialkot, which is ideal for large-scale tank operations.

Pakistan faced two principal disadvantages in her conflicts with India. The long border favoured India, with her much larger army and superior logistical systems: Indian armoured attacks could be launched against the Pakistani centres of population while their own were relatively invulnerable. But with the consolidation of China after 1949, and especially after the Chinese move into Tibet in 1950, the Indians faced a much more powerful enemy across their northern frontier. The Indian army did not do spectacularly well against the Pakistani irregulars in 1947–9; they were trounced by the Chinese in Ladakh and north of the Brahmaputra river. The Chinese had limited objectives, the advantage of surprise, and troops trained for mountain warfare. The end of 1962 saw India resigned to the loss of the marginal areas on her Himalayan frontier. China had no ambitions to move down the mountains into India proper.

The Pakistanis read the events of 1962 as evidence of India's military decay. They prepared for war and began guerrilla action in Kashmir during August 1965. They then began conventional armoured warfare in the centre, and in the far south, the area of salt flats known as the Rann of Kutch, during September. Pakistan's strategy was to cut off the Indian army in

Kashmir by severing their access through Chamba and Jammu. India responded by attacking in the central zone against Lahore and Sialkot. Pakistan's counter-attacks in the centre were blocked, and both sides slugged it out in the far north and the far south. When the war ended in 1965, India held the advantage in the centre, while Pakistan could salvage some sense of pride from their dogged assaults on the extremities. Pakistan's belief that she could win against India related to psychological as much as material factors. The Pakistan army believed that it embodied the finest qualities of the old Indian Army of the British Raj. They were the 'martial races' *par excellence*. Pakistan's generals talked in terms of a dash (in the style of the Israeli armoured columns) down the Grand Trunk Road to Delhi; they were seemingly oblivious to the difficulties of attacking an enemy who possessed both numerical superiority and a much more developed support system.

If Pakistan had only a slender chance of holding the Indians on the western frontier, they had none whatever on the eastern border. East Pakistan had only religion in common with the western part of the country. The social and economic divergence became stronger year by year. In 1971 the nationalists in the east declared independence, as the new state of Bangladesh. The west responded with massacre and atrocity, in a futile attempt to preserve a united state by fear. The Pakistani army in the east found difficulty in holding the line against the Bangladeshi irregulars; once India intervened all hope of victory vanished. The Pakistan army in the west launched its traditional attacks in Kashmir and the Punjab, as well as in the deep south (Scind). But as on previous occasions these attacks never succeeded in breaking through the Indian defence lines.

The Indian army which invaded Bangladesh was faced with many natural obstacles, principally the river systems. Here, although the Indians had amphibious tanks, it was quickly discovered that it could take up to nine hours to cross the major rivers: the tanks were designed to 'swim' for no more than forty-five minutes. The Indians used airborne forces skilfully, and hopped over the major obstacles. But had the demoralised eastern Pakistan army put up a determined resistance, the Indian advance would only have been achieved at a high cost. However, the westerners had entirely alienated the local population by their savagery: it was they rather than the invading Indians who dared not venture into the jungle.

Combat experience has tightened up the Indian army. It showed it was competent in the open tank battles in the Punjab and Scind. It showed doggedness in defence in Kashmir, when the advantage of the terrain lay with Pakistan. In the war for Bangladesh, the Indians showed real tactical inspiration, adapting to unexpected circumstances. But although the antagonism with Pakistan is fairly fundamental, the Indians do not have much to fear from that direction. The exception is if Pakistan could act in concert with China. Such an alliance would leave India with a war on two fronts (like Pakistan in 1971), and an enemy (China) with effectively limitless resources. It is this threat which has locked India into a close relationship with the Soviet Union, the only effective counterweight to Chinese ambitions.

Baluchistan

The long tail of the Hindu Kush descends through the south of Afghanistan, past the town of Quetta in Pakistan to end in a range of hills just north of the Arabian Sea. To the west in Iran it is matched by another range, and between lies hot, stony desert. This land – Baluchistan – remains almost

India and Pakistan continue to spar on their frontiers; by the autumn of 1985, fighting had flared once more in the northernmost recessess, beyond Kashmir. Both countries have deliberately encouraged such religious and political hatreds in the area, so that border violence is inevitable. The trick is to ensure that it does not spread, and on occasion both governments welcome the diversion which this skirmishing provides.

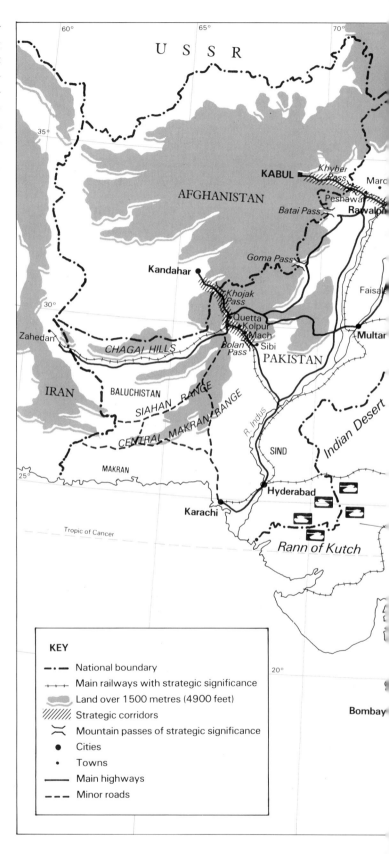

KEY

–··– National boundary

+++ Main railways with strategic significance

Land over 1500 metres (4900 feet)

///// Strategic corridors

⤬ Mountain passes of strategic significance

● Cities

· Towns

— Main highways

--- Minor roads

India and Pakistan: The Embattled Subcontinent

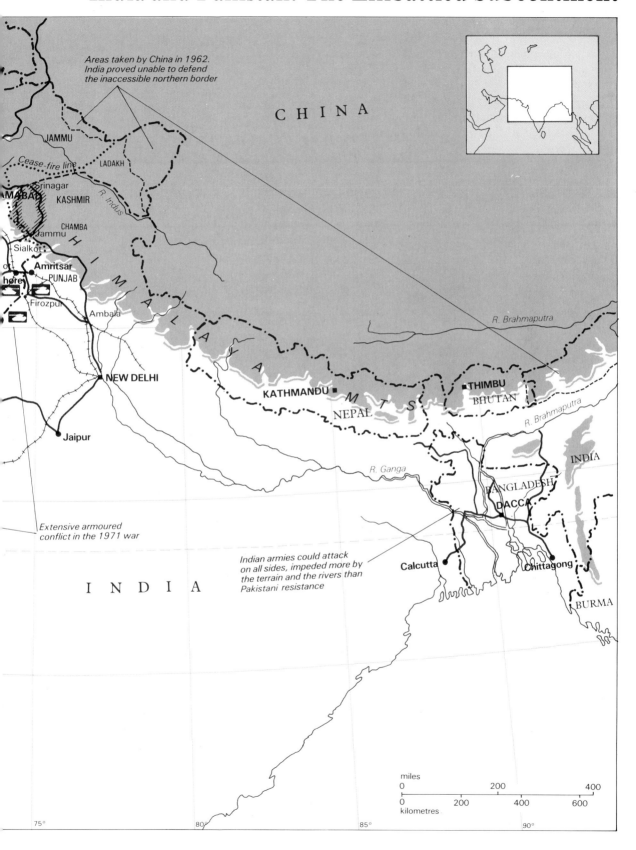

Areas taken by China in 1962.
India proved unable to defend
the inaccessible northern border

CHINA

JAMMU

Cease-fire line

LADAKH

R. Indus

Srinagar

MABAD

KASHMIR

CHAMBA

Jammu

Sialkot

H

I

M

A

L

A

Y

A

M

T

S

Amritsar

PUNJAB

hore

Firozpur

Ambala

NEW DELHI

Jaipur

R. Brahmaputra

KATHMANDU

THIMBU

BHUTAN

NEPAL

R. Brahmaputra

INDIA

R. Ganga

BANGLADESH

DACCA

Extensive armoured
conflict in the 1971 war

Indian armies could attack
on all sides, impeded more by
the terrain and the rivers than
Pakistani resistance

Calcutta

Chittagong

I   N   D   I   A

BURMA

miles
0   200   400

0   200   400   600
kilometres

75°   80°   85°   90°

as empty as it has over the centuries: the most positive comment of most travellers is 'monotonous'. It is a no man's land, administered by Pakistan, inhabited mostly by Baluchi nomads, and by Brahui fishermen along the Makran coast. There are few roads, especially in the west, and a single railway which winds up through Quetta, then along the Afghan border south of the Chagai hills to end rather abruptly in the small Iranian town of Zahedan. The link which was to have joined it to the railway network of Iran and then on into Europe was never built. Yet this empty tract has remained of key strategic and political significance as a consequence of the Russian objective of a warm water port.

This objective lies both in the political world and the realm of the imagination. The attraction of a port available winter and summer for both trade and military purposes is obvious. But advances in the techniques of clearing ice have made the distinction much less clear. Even ports on the Arctic coast of the Soviet Union now operate almost the whole year round, except in the most severe winters. The principal focus of the demand was not some location in Asia, far distant from the Russian centres of production, but Constantinople in the days of the last czars of Russia. Here nationalism, strategy, and religious zeal all united on a common objective. The same political and strategic impetus was sensed by the British in the Russian advance into central Asia in the period 1850–85: in 1885, Britain and Russia were almost drawn into war over Afghanistan. In the century since then, Western strategic thought has continued along the same line, and has, to a degree, coloured Soviet thinking.

Changes in the real world have recently helped to give new weight to this rerun of The Great Game. Afghanistan, once a death trap to any passing army because its roads were so bad, now has a good circular highway skirting the mountain core of the country. There is also a strong likelihood that the Russian railway, which at present ends at the northern border will be extended to Kabul, thereby bringing Afghanistan much 'closer', in transport terms, to the Soviet Union. And, of course, the Soviet invasion of Afghanistan in 1979 transformed a relationship of dependence into one of control. All these factors have forced attention on to Baluchistan, the natural route to the south.

Before the Soviet invasion of Afghanistan, most of the intercommunication passed along the line Kabul–Peshawar–Rawalpindi. This is the most heavily defended area in Pakistan, partly because of its proximity to the main area of Afghan resistance to the Russians, but more significantly because it abuts Kashmir and the Punjab, the most sensitive areas of the Indo-Pakistan border. Pakistan's capital is at Islamabad, which increases the importance of the region. But if the old theory of 'the rush to the sea' has any significance, then the much shorter route through Baluchistan offers a natural channel for a Soviet advance. Access to the south from Baluchistan follows the Kandahar road from the Khojak Pass via Quetta and the coal-mining town of Mach through the Bolan Pass, which is controlled by the town of Kolpur. The Bolan was seen by the British as the key to the frontier region. Bolan is the bottleneck, and the potential choke point for any army advancing south (or north). Once beyond Sibi, south of the pass, it is a clear road to Karachi, Hyderabad or on into India.

An even wilder alternative involves advancing to the west of Quetta, past the Chagai hills, through the sandy desert and salt flats, over the Siahan range and down on to the empty Makran coast. Such an approach, over the most rudimentary roads, or no roads at all, pushes this sort of geopolitical hypothesis beyond the bounds of probability. Any invader who antici-pated using the route down to the Makran should remember the observation of Mohammad bin Qusim, leading an Isla-mic army in the tenth century from Bagh-dad to Scind: 'it is a desert without any vegetation, and water is scarce and . . . if the army is small it will be wiped out; if it is large it will starve'. The logistical prob-lems have not altered over the centuries.

To see Baluchistan as some sort of Achilles' heel requires adherence to the theory of the warm water port, which in turn requires belief in a consistent Russian policy extending over a century and a half. For those who can accept both proposi-tions, then the Baluchistan problem does indeed represent a very present danger.

12 South-east Asia: Vietnam, Kampuchea, Thailand, Malaysia

Vietnam and China

The French united the three elements which made up Vietnam – the original Vietnamese state of Tonkin, the central kingdom of Annam, and the southern lands of Cochin China, which was scarcely occupied before the French arrived. The old northern kingdom, built up around the rice lands of the Red river, has always dominated the rest of the Vietnamese terri-tories, and the eventual triumph of the north after war against the French from 1946 to 1954 and against South Vietnam and the United States from 1965 to 1975, was the culmination of a long process in Vietnamese history. Two other areas of historic hostility have dominated Viet-nam's strategic position in the years since the war ended, to the north and to the south-west.

The lands which made up the other parts of French Indo-China – Laos and Cam-bodia – have always existed in an uneasy juxtaposition with their Vietnamese neighbours. The Mekong river dominates the south as the Red river dominates the north, and it links South Vietnam, Cam-bodia and Laos up as far as the falls at Khong and the impassable rapids at Khem-marat. Some river traffic takes place on the river above Vientiane, but the natural im-pediments mean that it never became the great 'fluid highway' into China that the first French explorers had hoped for. Who-ever controls the mouth of the Mekong has, historically, sought to control the lands upriver. In earlier centuries, the Mekong delta had provided the wealth of the Cambodian empire of Angkor; under the French and later the Vietnamese, the dominant position has been reversed. The three countries of Laos, Cambodia and Vietnam exist in an unbreakable, if often unwelcome, mutual dependence: the river peoples have never had much interest in national boundaries. The river itself unites the lands on either side. However, such a neat economic theory takes no account of racial and political hostilities. Over time, relations between all the river states have been seen in terms of dominance rather than co-operation.

The reunification of Vietnam under the communist north in 1975 was followed three years later by the invasion of Cam-bodia, now known as Kampuchea. The bloodlust of the victorious Kampuchean communists over the American surrogate government in 1975 made a convenient pretext, but the intervention would have taken place under other circumstances.

Vietnam now maintains an army of more than 180,000 men in Kampuchea, with annual campaigns against the remaining Khmer Rouge bases near the Thai border. In early 1985, the Vietnamese captured the base town of Ampil, but most of the Khmer fighters had by then dispersed to regroup. Attacks are also becoming more common further south as other nationalist groups begin to react against Vietnamese control. More Vietnamese soldiers (about 45,000) are stationed in Laos, in the guise of 'fraternal aid'. These commitments, which occupy almost a quarter of the Vietnamese army, assume much greater importance in the context of the tense situation on the northern border with China. The forces available for the northern front are also diminished by the need to maintain what amounts to a garrison in the former South Vietnam, where even supporters of the Viet Cong now resent the comprehensive northern monopoly in positions of power.

Vietnam and China both have very large armies, but the Vietnamese have the edge in terms of recent combat experience. During the long war for the south, Vietnam relied on the steady flow of supplies coming south from China, as well as those shipped in through Haiphong. The railway was a major target for bombing, and the harbour was mined, but the attacks reduced rather than halted the flow. The railway running north-west follows the valley of the Red river to Gejiu, often through very difficult terrain. Its building took over forty years. Tunnels were bored through the spurs of the Annamite range, and many bridges had to be built over the often flooded lands beside the river. In all there were 172 tunnels and 102 bridges – over 3,000 major engineering works. The other line, which ran up from Hanoi through much flatter country to Lang Son posed different but equally intractable problems. It ran through marshy flood plain north-east of Hanoi, and then through the outlying spurs of the Annamite range before it reached the frontier. The engineers had to contend with the annual inundation of the low-lying land, and the line was regularly washed away during the wettest part of the year. The two corridors along which the railways ran were the only sensible points of access for an invader from the north: in between lay mountains and much difficult ground which had provided a refuge for the Viet Minh in their war with the French.

The border war which broke out between Vietnam and China in 1979, like China's war with India, had a largely symbolic significance. That is not to say that large forces were not involved, with considerable casualties on both sides; however, the Chinese aim was to take the pressure off its allies in Kampuchea, and to show the Vietnamese that empire building was a dangerous path to follow. One Chinese attack took Lang Son, and could have advanced on Hanoi; others were more in the nature of border raids in strength towards Lai Chau near the border with Laos, and the hill town of Ha Giang. Neither of these attacks were much more than demonstrations of Chinese power. The Lang Son thrust was not pursued, and after having 'chastised' their enemy, the Chinese withdrew. The effectiveness of Vietnam's resistance surprised the Chinese, and they were well aware that a further advance into Vietnam would make their lines of communication dangerously extended. The Vietnamese were adept at ambush and use of the ground to engulf an enemy, as the French had found to their cost. The border settled down to a state of permanent tension, punctuated by regular artillery duels and cross-border raids. The terrain allows Vietnam the luxury of defence-in-depth, based on the capacity to retreat south and draw the enemy on. Any Chinese army advancing to Hanoi and beyond would find difficulty in getting its armour across the flood plain, while supplying a large army moving south would be a logistical nightmare. Against an army as battle-hardened as that of Vietnam, skilled in both the set piece battle and the war of attrition, a full-scale invasion would be foolhardy. The northern frontier provides too many dangers, a rough and unhelpful landscape.

Borders:
Thailand and Kampuchea
Thailand and Malaysia

Thailand was the only country of south-east Asia to avoid a direct experience of colonialism. It stood between British and French ambitions; both preferred an independent Thailand to its domination by the other. Today, Thailand forms another boundary, between communism and the non-communist world, and the refuge for minorities from the other side of its long frontiers. Thailand contains a huge number of Khmer refugees from Kampuchea, hill tribes from Laos and Burma, and a tiny Malay communist residue in the far south. But every boundary is the source of possible conflict. There is also a tradition of resistance to the military-dominated (and highly centralised) government in Bangkok. Behind Thailand stands the full support of the United States, which made extensive use of Thailand's military airfields during the Vietnam war, as well as of the varied and exotic facilities of Bangkok for 'rest and recuperation' for tired soldiers. But where the United States was supporting a feeble post-colonial government in South Vietnam, in Laos and in Cambodia, in Thailand the political institutions are solid and of long duration. The role of the Thai monarchy is crucial,

and acts as a generally respected source of political authority, with the government dominated by temporary constellations of military men around the throne. Social cohesion has allowed the military to keep subversion well under control.

Because of disputed boundaries, and the use of the border zones as sanctuaries, the Thais face regular incursions across the frontier. In the north and north-west, the highlands are inaccessible, and can be safely ignored. The southern border with Kampuchea, which is close to the capital and the economic heartland of the country, is much more threatening. There is an historic tradition of hostility between Thai and Khmer, which was suppressed during the years of French rule. Now, with the Khmer Rouge, or rather its remnants, sandwiched between the Vietnamese army of occupation and the Thai frontier, there is the constant likelihood of a major border incident. However, at present Vietnam has no real desire to engineer a confrontation with the United States, which is the inevitable consequence of hostility to Thailand. The Thais, likewise, are quite willing to accommodate their new communist neighbours, provided they do not meddle in Thai internal affairs or pursue a policy of adventurism on the frontiers. 'Leave well alone' could serve as Thailand's motto. Thus, she has been willing to accept the Malaysian communist rump in the deep south because it presents no threat to national defence. More reluctantly, she has accepted minor irregularities on the Laotian and Kampuchean frontiers, provided that these do not seem part of a concerted encroachment on Thai territory. Throughout the period of colonialism, the Thais became adept at dealing with powerful and bombastic neighbours; the same tradition provides continuity in policy and national stability in the changed but parallel circumstances of the 1980s.

France, rather vaingloriously, believed that she had resolved the petty antagonisms of south-east Asia when she created her empire in Indo-China. But the racial and political antagonisms were too deeply rooted to be stilled by the brief colonial experience. Since 1975, the imperial ambitions of Vietnam have been reborn, as have the doubts and fears of China concerning her southern neighbour. But the mountainous landscape constricts a southward advance by China, while Vietnam has no need to move north. As in past centuries, Chinese assertions of a role in Indo-China are verbal rather than practical. Where once the Khmer kingdom of Angkor Wat dominated the region, it is now the forces of a revitalised Vietnam, the principal beneficiary of France's colonial investment.

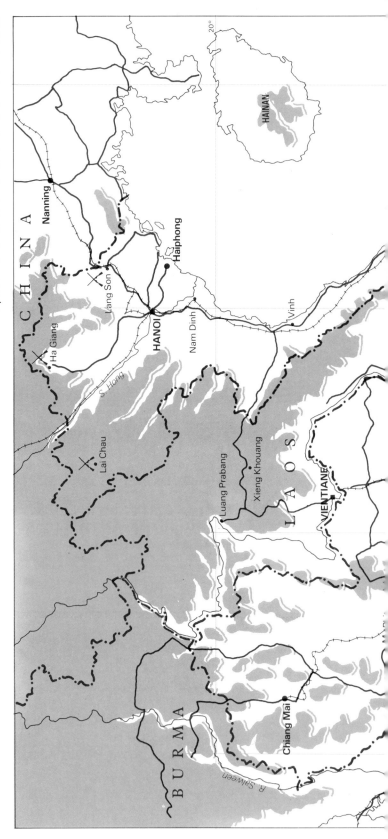

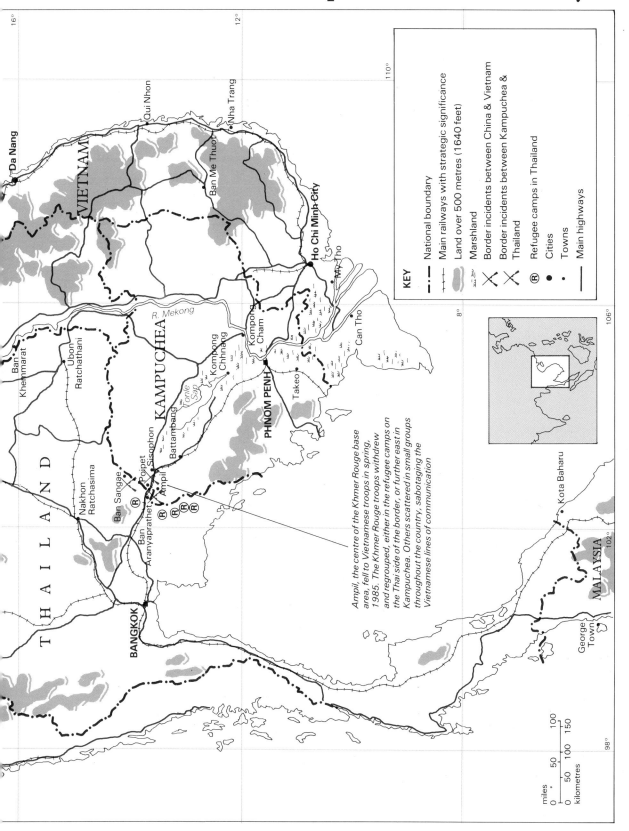

16°

12°

110°

Da Nang

Qui Nhon

Nha Trang

Ban Me Thuot

VIETNAM

Ho Chi Minh City

My Tho

8°

KAMPUCHEA

R. Mekong

Kompong Cham

Can Tho

Ban Khemmarat

Ubon Ratchathani

Kompong Chhnang

Tonle Sap

PHNOM PENH

Takeo

106°

Sisophon

Battambang

THAILAND

Nakhon Ratchasima

Ban Sangae

Poipet

Ampil

Ban Aranyaprathet

Ⓡ Ⓡ Ⓡ Ⓡ

Kota Baharu

MALAYSIA

102°

George Town

BANGKOK

Ampil, the centre of the Khmer Rouge base area, fell to Vietnamese troops in spring, 1985. The Khmer Rouge troops withdrew and regrouped, either in the refugee camps on the Thai side of the border, or further east in Kampuchea. Others scattered in small groups throughout the country, sabotaging the Vietnamese lines of communication

KEY

National boundary

Main railways with strategic significance

Land over 500 metres (1640 feet)

Marshland

✕ Border incidents between China & Vietnam

✕ Border incidents between Kampuchea & Thailand

Ⓡ Refugee camps in Thailand

● Cities

• Towns

Main highways

98°

miles
0   50   100

0   50   100   150
kilometres

THE FAR EAST

13 The Two Koreas

The divided country of Korea, on whose territory the communist and non-communist worlds fought between 1950 and 1953 the bitterest of their post-war proxy conflicts, remains an area of acute local tension and, in the wrong circumstances, might once again become a focus of high international crisis.

Geographically, the country stands at the junction point of four power spheres. On its northern border the Pacific frontiers of Russia and China meet. Its western shores close the Yellow Sea, China's *mare nostrum*. Its eastern coast forms the landward boundary of the Sea of Japan. And its territory provides the United States with both its largest and its only continental military base in Asia.

Ideologically, the two states into which Korea is divided represent extreme examples of communism and capitalism: North Korea is Stalinist, South Korea politically authoritarian but economically *laissez-faire*. Each is intensely nationalistic, regards itself as the legitimate authority over the whole country and holds reunification as its highest aim.

Economically, the two countries are complementary: North Korea is rich in mineral resources but lacks population to work its heavy industry; South Korea has a widely diversified industry and, during the years 1960–73, had the fastest growing economy in the world. It is widely spoken of as a rival to Japan in future world markets.

Politically, both states are maverick. North Korea is careful to align itself consistently neither with China nor Russia, and is therefore courted by both; South Korea, though firmly in America's camp, plays on its strategic importance to the United States to maintain an undemocratic system which is an embarrassment to every Washington administration.

Militarily, both are very powerful. Thanks to universal conscription, and a carefully cultivated atmosphere of national paranoia, the two states are able to maintain respectively the sixth and seventh largest armies in the world. Both are also well-equipped. The North Korean People's Army has Russian and Chinese equipment, not all of the latest type. The Republic of (South) Korea Army has American equipment, but now manufactures much of its own. Both countries also have sizeable aircraft inventories and effective air forces.

Socially and culturally, the two populations are now markedly opposed. North Korea has made a deliberate breach with the Confucian past and is heavily communised: over 10 per cent of the population belongs to the Workers' Party, a far higher proportion than in Russia or China. South Korea, without having explicitly abandoned the Confucian ethic, is stratifying on Western lines. It is estimated that in the cities, where nearly half the population lives, about 40 per cent belong to the new middle class.

Korea was unified as a kingdom as early as the seventh century A.D. Culturally a dependency of China, it nevertheless preserved its political independence until the thirteenth century, when it was subjugated by the Mongols. It regained its independence in the fourteenth century but, weakened by a Japanese invasion in the sixteenth century, fell under Manchu domination in the seventeenth. It remained a vassal state of the Manchu Empire of China for the next 250 years.

The decline of China at the end of the nineteenth century made Korea, geographically so important to Japan, an obvious target of the rising power's ambitions. Following Japan's victory over Russia in the war of 1904–5, Korea became a Japanese protectorate and from 1910 was ruled as a colony. Its colonial status attracted the attention of the Allies during the Second World War and it became their policy that it should be liberated, separated from Japan and re-established as an independent state. In August 1945 the United States and the Soviet Union agreed that, for temporary occupation purposes, the country should be partitioned at the 38th parallel, Russia to administer the northern half, America the southern half, until

permanent arrangements could be made for its future government.

All subsequent negotiations to that end failed, and in June 1949 the United States withdrew the last of its soldiers from the south, leaving its government in the hands of an elected assembly, led by an American-educated Christian, Syngman Rhee. The north was already governed by a local communist regime, led by a Soviet protégé, Kim Il-sung.

Relations between the two Koreas at once took a violent turn, each frequently accusing the other of border violations, of the reality of which there was no doubt. On 25 June 1950, however, the North Korean People's Army suddenly crossed the frontier in full strength and began an advance southwards. The resistance of the South Korean army rapidly weakened, and its collapse seemed certain. What saved it was the intervention of the United Nations. On 27 June the Security Council, which the Russians had been boycotting since 1950 because of its refusal to seat a Peking representative in place of the Taiwan member, called on member states to send military help to the South. America at once responded, by transferring its occupation troops from Japan to the battlefront. Other nations, including Britain, quickly followed her example.

It seemed that assistance had come too late. By 1 August the American relief force and the remnant of the Republic of (South) Korea Army were confined within a perimeter less than 100 miles deep and sixty wide around the southern port of Pusan. By 15 September the area held had been reduced to sixty miles by forty. But the appearance of imminent defeat was illusory. Douglas MacArthur, now United Nations Commander, had been using the defensive period to mount a counterstroke. On 15 September a large US Marine amphibious force landed at Inch'on, the port of Seoul, South Korea's capital, overwhelmed the defence and advanced inland. The UN forces in the Pusan perimeter simultaneously broke out northward and, as Seoul stands almost on the 38th parallel, Kim Il-sung's invaders thus found themselves threatened with encirclement far from home.

In the rapid campaign which followed much of the People's Army was indeed destroyed. On 7 October, with UN General Assembly approval, MacArthur's command crossed the 38th parallel and advanced on Kim Il-sung's capital. By late October its advance guards were approaching the Yalu river, which marks the frontier with China. It seemed that reunification by conquest, which the General Assembly had effectively sanctioned, was about to take place. On 25 October, however, the American advance patrols found themselves in contact with Chinese troops and soon afterwards it became apparent that very large Chinese formations had been committed. The Chinese government announced that all were formed of 'Volunteers', but the effect was to make China the United Nations Command's main opponent. MacArthur's forces were routed, Seoul fell again to the communists and it was not until June 1951, a year after the war had begun, that a battlefront was stabilised roughly on the 38th parallel.

There a war of attrition dragged on for another two years. The Soviet Union, whose involvement was confined to the supply of war material to the North, proposed an armistice in July 1951, and talks began, but were accompanied by persistent fighting. Terms were not finally agreed until July 1953, between the United Nations Command on the one hand and North Korea and the People's Republic of China on the other. South Korea disassociated herself from the agreement, which prescribed efforts, never undertaken, to reunify the country by peaceful means.

Korea is a country of harsh climate and difficult terrain. On average there are only 200 frost-free days and much of the summer, from June to September, is a rainy season. Only 15 per cent of the country is counted as plains, which follow the eastern coast and the valleys of the Taedong, Han, Kum, Naktong and Somjin rivers. The rest of the country is mountainous and though the mountains are not high, their extent and broken nature makes movement outside the valleys and off the major roads (which generally follow the valleys) difficult. Even in the plains, military movement off the roads is slow and laborious, because most of the area is down to paddy-field.

South Korea has an excellent road network, having doubled its length, from 15,000 to 30,000 miles, since 1960. A network of superhighways, following the main river valleys, connects the most important towns. North Korea's roads are less extensive and modern. The North is also more mountainous, the ranges confining easy movement to the western coastal plain between the border and the mouth of the Yalu. Outside the plain, northward movement is canalised into the valleys of the tributaries of the Yalu, which run north–south and along which the United Nations troops approached the Chinese frontier in the winter of 1950.

The ruggedness of Korea's terrain, and the conformation of the Taebaek range in particular, which is to the country what the Apennines are to Italy, determines that, from a military point of view, all manoeuvre must negotiate a number of well-defined 'choke points'. In the north, the most important runs between the estuary of the Taedong and the outliers of the central mountain range, where the plain is only fifteen miles wide. It gives directly on to Pyongyang, the northern capital. In the winter of 1950 the United Nations

Few states are as ready for immediate war with their neighbours as Korea: war is not merely a possibility, but the political foundation of both states. Both North and South are committed to forcible re-unification of the land of Korea, either in a capitalist or communist mould. Both the capitals are vulnerable to attack, and the border zone beyond the cease-fire line is one of the most heavily garrisoned in the world. Yet the two states are economically complementary, and in a less starkly drawn opposition they could form an im-mensely powerful economic unit, rivalling Japan.

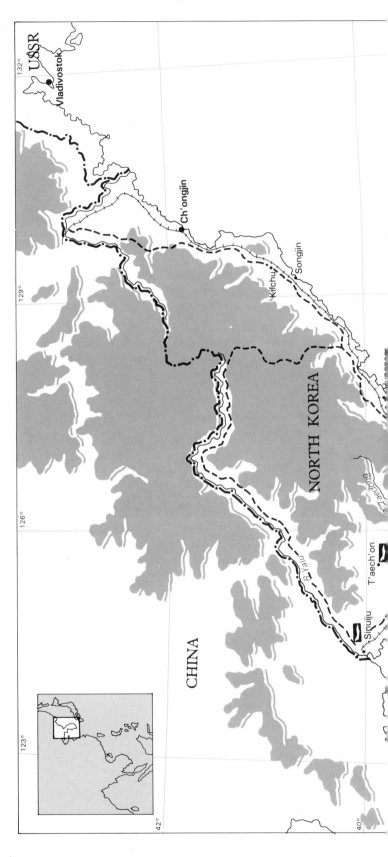

The Two Koreas

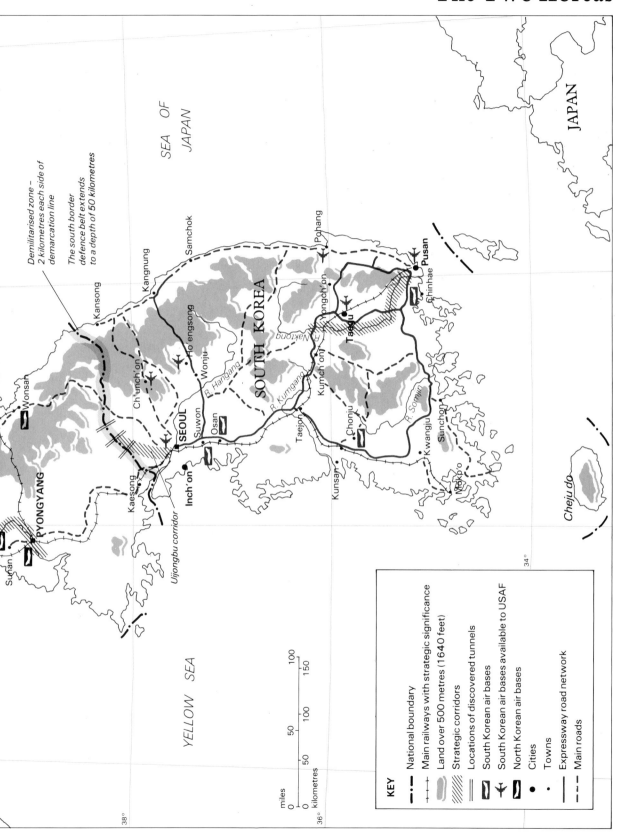

JAPAN

SEA OF JAPAN

Demilitarised zone –
2 kilometres each side of
demarcation line

The south border
defence belt extends
to a depth of 50 kilometres

Pohang

Pusan

Kansong

Samchok

Kangnung

Chinhae

SOUTH KOREA

Ho'engsong

Tongoh'on

Wonju

Taegu

Wonsan

R. Naktong

Ch'unch'on

Kumch'on

R. Hangang

R. Kumgang

SEOUL

Suwon

R. Somjin

Osan

Taejon

Chonju

Kaesong

Sunch'on

PYONGYANG

Inch'on

Kunsan

Kwangju

Mokpo

Uijongbu corridor

Sunan

Cheju do

YELLOW SEA

38°

36°

34°

miles
0   50   100
0   50   100   150
kilometres

KEY

National boundary	
Main railways with strategic significance	
Land over 500 metres (1640 feet)	
Strategic corridors	
Locations of discovered tunnels	
South Korean air bases	
South Korean air bases available to USAF	
North Korean air bases	
Cities	•
Towns	·
Expressway road network	
Main roads	

forces made their escape from the Chinese south through this gap.

Below the 38th parallel, there is another important choke point which leads from the western to the eastern coastal plain between the cities of Taejon and Taegu, and connects the valleys of the Kum and Naktong rivers. A superhighway now follows the route, which is forced to rise over an intervening mountain range connecting with the Taebaek spine. Yongch'on is at the centre of the choke point, and there was a desperate defence of this saddle of ground by the Americans in the retreat to Pusan in July 1950.

The most important of the choke points, however, is the so-called 'Uijongbu Corridor'. Uijongbu stands immediately northeast of Seoul, between an outlying spur of the Taebaek range and the estuary of the Han river, and is the knot for the north–south roads on the coastal plain. It is the 'historic invasion route' for armies entering Korea from China: both the Mongols and the Manchus made use of it in their campaigns of conquest. It was also where the North Koreans put the weight of their armour in June 1950 and it is now the most heavily defended sector of South Korea's military frontier with the North.

This frontier is now perhaps the most important feature of Korea's military topography. It follows the cease-fire line of 1953, a Demilitarised Zone just over a mile wide actually separating the armies of North and South. Outside the DMZ both sides have constructed deep defences. Those on the southern side extend for thirty miles, over a length of 151 miles from coast to coast, garrisoned by the eighteen divisions of the ROK Army. The American 2nd Division, still technically under United Nations command (the commander is an American), stands in reserve behind the front, its presence a reminder to the North that an attack will invoke American intervention. The

People's Army, twenty-two divisions strong, is believed to concentrate the bulk of its strength north of the Uijongbu Corridor.

The two Korean states remain as intransigently opposed as ever. Kim Il-sung, ruler of the North and now one of the longest-established leaders in the world, has recently rejected overtures by the South's new government for reunification talks. His son and designated successor, Kim Jong-il, is said to be 'even more radical and ruthless' than the father. In any case, the North Korean system, based on the principle of *chuch'e sasang* (roughly, political and economic self-sufficiency) is irreconcilable with any other.

The government of the South is equally unfitted to make concessions. Since 1960, when General Park overthrew the civilian regime, it has been governed effectively by the army. Park, an increasingly authoritarian and unapproachable figure, was murdered by the head of the Korean Central Intelligence Agency in October 1979 but, after a short period of civilian rule, was succeeded by another soldier. Dissent, which periodically disturbs South Korea's cities, is harshly repressed. The army is determined to maintain its grip, while transforming the country into a major economic power.

It is difficult to visualise in what circumstances the bitter hostility of the two states might break out into violence. South Korea is too dependent upon the United States for her ultimate security to risk the diplomatic consequences of initiating an attack on the North. The North, whose population is less than half that of the South's, and who no longer enjoys the superiority in equipment she had in 1950, is not placed to attack the South. Nevertheless both states are garrison societies, committed to reunification policies and highly prepared for war. South Korea is now militarily the stronger. But North

Korea, while strengthening its defences against invasion by the building of extensive tunnel systems all over its populated regions, has also applied the same technique to what appears to be deliberate preparation for surprise attack on the South. In 1975 the South Koreans and Americans discovered the existence of three large and deep tunnels, extending under the Demilitarised Zone, which would each allow passage for several thousand troops an hour to debouch into South Korean territory. Another fourteen tunnels are believed to exist; of the three located, one is in the 'Uijongbu Corridor'.

Such preparations, the high state of combat-readiness of both sides, continuing small-scale infiltration and the mutual hostility of North and South make the two Koreas one of the most highly-charged military regions of the world.

14 Sakhalin and the Kuril Islands: Eastern Redoubt of the USSR

Japan and Russia, long rivals and at times contestants for power in the Far East, to-day pursue a dispute over the possession of territory in the north-west Pacific, the outcome of which would have strategic implications far exceeding in importance the legal issues concerned. The dispute turns on Russia's title to the Southern Kuril Islands, the chain that marks the seaward boundary of the Sea of Okhotsk, the enclosed waters in which Russia maintains its Pacific surface and submarine fleet.

Russia's lack of free access to great waters is one of the best-known of all factors in world strategic geography. Despite the enormous extent of her territory, her coastline is so disposed that all her ports lie either the wrong side of choke points which remain in non-Russian hands, e.g. in the Baltic and Black Seas, or in latitudes where the ocean freezes during part or all of the winter. Archangel and Murmansk, which lie at the tail end of the Gulf Stream's reach beyond the North Cape, can be kept open only by ice-breaking; Vladivostok, in the Sea of Japan, is both ice-bound in winter (without the use of ice-breakers) and the wrong side of the Japanese island chain. Russia's only

port with unobstructed access to any ocean is, therefore, Petropavlovsk on the eastern shore of the Kamchatka Peninsula.

Petropavlovsk has, however, serious drawbacks as a major base for the Pacific Fleet, since it is connected neither by road nor rail with the main Soviet transport network; it is, moreover, extremely remote, even by air, and lies on an exposed coast which provides no sheltered water for anchorage or training. The Sea of Okhotsk, on the western side of the Kamchatka Peninsula, is exactly the sheltered water that navies require for training. It also gives on to the approaches to Vladivostok, from which it can be reached in Russian territorial waters via the southern tip of Sakhalin island, and nearby Sovetskaya Gavan; both these ports have the advantage over Petropavlovsk that they lie on the Trans-Siberian Railway.

Russia's title to Sakhalin and the Kurils is therefore of importance for reasons as much of strategic advantage as of sovereignty. The legal dispute surrounding it is, nevertheless, of considerable complexity.

Japan's case takes this form. Following its defeat in Manchuria by the Red Army in

It is a measure of the Soviet Union's strategic disadvantage that her prime naval base is at the ultimate extremity of her terrain, remote from sources of supply, with few roads, railways or other channels of access to it. Its main advantage is that it provides a convenient outlet to the Pacific, at a time when other ports are ice-bound. But more than that, it provides a practical commitment to the Soviet Union's determination to be a world naval power, strong in all the oceans of the world. From these ports, Soviet flotillas traverse the eastern seas, and submarines cruise off the western United States.

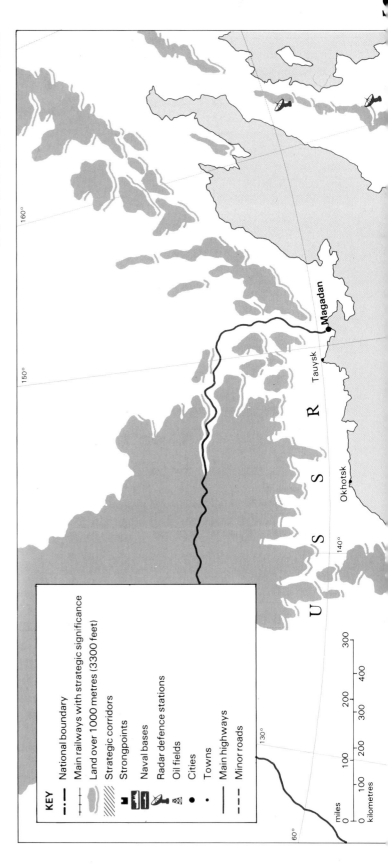

KEY

National boundary
Main railways with strategic significance
Land over 1000 metres (3300 feet)
Strategic corridors
Strongpoints
Naval bases
Radar defence stations
Oil fields
Cities
Towns
Main highways
Minor roads

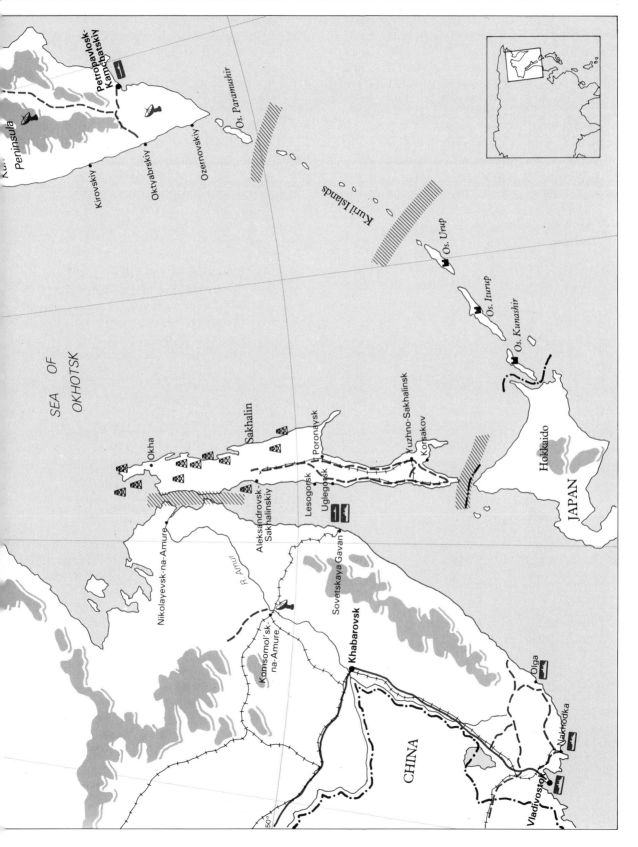

SEA OF OKHOTSK

Kamchatka Peninsula

Petropavlosk-Kamchatskiy

Kirovskiy

Oktyabrskiy

Ozernovskiy

Os. Paramushir

Kuril Islands

Os. Urup

Os. Iturup

Os. Kunashir

Hokkaido

JAPAN

Sakhalin

Okha

Poronaysk

Yuzhno-Sakhalinsk

Korsakov

Lesogorsk

Uglegorsk

Aleksandrovsk-Sakhalinskiy

Nikolayevsk-na-Amure

Sovetskaya Gavan

R. Amur

Komsomol'sk-na-Amure

Khabarovsk

CHINA

Olga

Nakhodka

Vladivostok

50°

August 1945, the Soviet Union occupied both Sakhalin, in its entirety, and the whole of the Kuril chain of twenty islands from the Kamchatka Peninsula (whose status is not disputed) as far south as the northern coast of Hokkaido. It is admitted that in 1875 Japan agreed to exchange its ownership of Sakhalin for that of the Kurils. But it is also held that the 1875 treaty only applied to the chain as far south as the island of Urup; the excluded islands of Iturup, Kunashir, Shikotan and the Habomai group remained legally Japanese. Furthermore, after the Russian defeat in the War of 1904–5, the southern half of Sakhalin was ceded to Japan under the Treaty of Portsmouth.

By agreement between the Western Allies, Britain and the United States of America, and the Soviet Union at Yalta in February 1945, Sakhalin and the Kurils were to be restored to Russia following Japan's defeat. The wording of the agreement, in the Japanese view, comprehended only the northern half of the chain, since it did not specifically mention Iturup, Kunashir, Shikotan and the Habomai, and conceded that Japan had rights in 'minor islands' beyond Hokkaido. The Japanese further interpret the San Francisco Treaty of 1951, which ended its state of war with all its enemies except Russia, Czechoslovakia and Poland, as conceding its rights to the Southern Kurils, though returning the others, and South Sakhalin, to the USSR.

The Soviet Union interprets both the Yalta agreement, the events of 1945 and antecedent negotiations between Russia and Japan in an altogether different way. By Russian accounting, Japan did not exercise sovereignty over the Kurils or Sakhalin before the beginning of the nineteenth century, by which time Russia's presence was already established on the Siberian coast of the Sea of Okhotsk. In 1875 a treaty between the two countries

arranged for Japan to give up settlements it had established on Sakhalin in exchange for the Kurils, an apportionment that persisted until 1905. Then, by the Treaty of Portsmouth, signed after Russia's defeat in the 1904–5 war, the southern half of Sakhalin was returned to Japan. During the Second World War, the Allies agreed that this territorial settlement in the Far East (by which Japan had also come to annex Korea) would be reversed at the peace in restoration of 'the former rights of Russia violated by the treacherous attack' of 1904 (Yalta Conference, February 1945).

In the post-war period Japan continued to insist that its rights in the disputed territories, now under Soviet control, remained sovereign. Nevertheless, the two countries were able in 1956 to re-establish diplomatic relations and terminate the state of war existing between them. But they were unable to agree over the future of the Southern Kurils. The Soviet Union promised that they should be returned to Japan following the signing of a full peace treaty between the two countries. Such a treaty, however, has never been signed and the current state of diplomatic (as opposed to commercial) relations between the two countries make such a settlement unlikely.

Russia's presence in the Kurils has been a precondition of the dramatic reinforcement of its Pacific Fleet, from 1970 onwards. It now numbers ninety major surface warships, including two carriers, and some thirty ballistic missile submarines. Control of the exits through the Kurils, though they are no doubt kept under close surveillance by the US Navy, is of vital importance to the operation of the submarines in particular. As a whole, however, the chain forms both a protective barrier to and an advanced position forward of the Soviet Union's Pacific coast, analogous to that formed by the

Hebrides off the British and US submarine bases in western Scotland, and its continued occupation and defence must be regarded as a vital Soviet interest.

15 China: The Zones of Vulnerability

'The Middle Kingdom', third largest and most populous state in the world, is in many ways a product of its strategic geography, which is both of great complexity and interest. In the broadest term, modern China consists of two economic and climatic regions, a southern and eastern zone traversed by great rivers in which the pattern of life is and always has been agricultural, and a western and northern zone, riverless and in parts arid, inhabited by pastoralists and nomads. Chinese history is the story of conflict between these societies of farmers and herdsmen, in which at times one, at times the other, was dominant. Historians of China associate these shifts with changes in the climatic pattern, particularly as they affect the Ordos region in the great bend of the Yellow river; in wet periods, the Ordos was penetrated by agriculturalists and the nomads pushed away from the Chinese heartland; in dry periods the agriculturalists retreated, allowing the steppe peoples to approach the settled areas and, in favourable circumstances, to dominate them. The richer dynasties attempted to regulate this cyclical pattern by the building of fixed defences, to exclude the nomads. Collectively these many lines of defence are known as the Great Wall.

The last of the nomad peoples to come to power in China were the Manchus, inhabitants of the far north, who seized the throne and established the Ch'ing dynasty, which ruled China until its fall in 1912. It was under the Manchus that China's present frontiers were defined, both at their amplest, as Chinese patriots trace them today, and at their narrower legal delineation, as they are recognised by China's twelve neighbours. China, as 'the Middle Kingdom', a rock of civilisation in a sea of inferior and barbarian peoples, regarded itself as the overlord of most neighbouring Asian peoples. Lei Pei-hua, in an official history of China published in Peking in 1954, lists the following territories as properly belonging to China: the Great North-West (parts of the Kazakh, Kirghiz and Tadzhik republics of the Soviet Union), the Pamirs, Nepal, Sikkim, Bhutan, Assam, Burma, the Andaman Islands, Malaya, Thailand, Vietnam, Laos, Cambodia, Taiwan and the Pescadores, the Sulu Archipelago, the Ryuku Archipelago, Korea, Eastern Siberia and Sakhalin, as well as Outer Mongolia and Tibet. All these territories, excluding Tibet which was occupied by China in 1951, fell outside its present boundaries, which were regulated by treaty ('the unequal treaties' to the Chinese, who regard them as dictated in a period of their weakness), between 1689 and the First World War. China's boundaries, nevertheless, now include all the lands inhabited by the ethnic Chinese (Hong Kong excepted) as well as, in the east, extensive territories thinly populated by non-Chinese peoples whom the Chinese regard as traditionally subject. The frontiers of China, a country 2,000 miles long on the north–south axis and 3,000 miles wide east–west, are very extensive, and coincide only erratically with natural features. There are 8,700 miles of coastline and 5,000 offshore islands, some, like Hainan and the irredenta of Taiwan (formerly Formosa), very large. On its landward front, China shares boundaries with Afghanistan, Pakistan, Bhutan, Burma, India, Laos, Mongolia, Nepal, North Korea, Vietnam, Sikkim and the Soviet Union, over a total distance of 12,427 miles. The frontiers with Afghanistan, Pakistan, the Himalayan states and India (the latter disputed) follow great mountain chains and are highly defensible. The frontiers with Burma, Laos and Vietnam (the latter also disputed) are marked by lower but also defensible mountain zones. The North Korean frontier, which follows the Yalu river through a mountainous region, is also strong. It is the immensely long and actively disputed frontier with the Soviet Union, and its satellite state, Mongolia, that therefore confronts the People's Republic of China with its most acute strategic problem.

The problem has three main components: imbalance of forces; topography; and distance and infrastructure. The imbalance of forces between China and the Soviet Union is very great, for although the Chinese People's Liberation Army is the largest in the world, with over 3 million men, it lacks armour and modern equipment of all types. The air force, too, is weak, and many of its aircraft obsolescent. In general, the mobility of the Chinese armed forces is low; a high proportion of the units lack the means to move out of their permanent places of garrison, where they are engaged for much of the year in public works. Their immobility is to some degree offset by the extensiveness of the fixed defences that have been built along the frontiers and in the populated regions since the foundation of the People's Republic in 1949. Labyrinthine tunnel complexes have apparently been dug as air-raid shelters under China's cities and similar labyrinths, designed to hide, house and shelter the defending forces, along the northern and western borders. Such complexes were dug by the Viet Minh and Viet Cong in Indo-China, and

presented intractable military problems to the French and American armies when they operated there. It may be, therefore, that these obstacles compensate considerably for the Chinese army's deficient manoeuvrability.

Topography also contributes notably to the defensibility of China's Soviet frontier. In the far west, the Tien Shan mountains which rise to 23,000 feet, enclose much of Sinkiang, while its two great basins, the Tarim and the Turfan, are largely desert of the most unwelcoming kind, searingly hot in summer, freezing in winter, and swept by fierce winds. A road leads through the desert to the Dzungarian Gate, which leads into Soviet Kazakhstan, but construction of the Friendship Railway that was to link the rail systems of the two countries at this point was abandoned in 1960, as a result of the Sino-Soviet split. The Gobi Desert continues from eastern Sinkiang to follow the southern border of Mongolia, through tracts that remain largely roadless, almost as far as Western Manchuria.

The immense distances, low population density, lack of water, harsh climatic extremes and absence of roads and railways combine to make China's far west and north an environment very hostile to military operations, particularly by modern mechanised forces. The country provides virtually nothing – except for nomads, who know where to look for their few needs – ensuring that an invader would have to encumber himself with supply columns which there is not the infrastructure to support.

There are, however, two zones of vulnerability in the north, which China is bound to defend and where it keeps a high proportion of its better-equipped divisions deployed. The first is on the south-eastern border of Mongolia. Though the terrain and climate are harsh and roads few, the distance from Peking (Beijing) to the border's nearest point is only 250 miles, which is well within the striking capabilities of a mechanised invading force, if its base area is adequately stocked. The second is in Manchuria, where the frontier with the Soviet Union is defined by the Amur and Ussuri rivers. The frontier here is not only disputed; because of the shifting course of the rivers it is physically difficult to delineate, a feature which has provoked a succession of border fights between Soviet and Chinese troops over the last twenty-five years. Manchuria, moreover, is an old battleground for the Russians. It was there that they fought the Japanese in the War of 1904–5 and there again that they took their revenge in the whirlwind campaign of August 1945. Attacking down the central plain of Manchuria, between the Greater and Lesser Khingan Ranges, the Soviet Army advanced a distance of 250 miles in less than two weeks, completely destroying the Japanese army that stood in its path. The blitzkrieg was complemented by a subsidiary pincer movement mounted from the Vladivostok region across the south-eastern Manchurian frontier.

For all the strength that mountains, desert, distance and lack of roads lend to China's strategic geography, the Mongolian salient and the reverse salient of Manchuria must be regarded as points of serious weakness, to which the Chinese must commit a high proportion of their military strength if they are to feel secure.

For a country with a land border extending over 12,000 miles, China is well protected by deserts and mountain chains. But the points of access correspond to areas of political or economic sensitivity. Danger is greatest in the areas which have produced successive waves of invasion, from the Mongols, through the Manchus, who ruled China as the Ch'ing dynasty until 1912, and the Soviet armies which crashed through Manchuria in 1945.

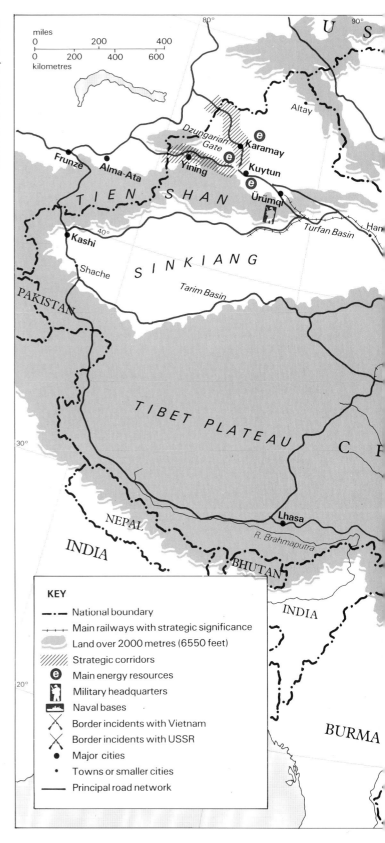

miles
0   200   400
0   200   400   600
kilometres

U S

S

Altay

Dzungarian Gate

Karamay

Frunze   Alma-Ata   Yining   Kuytun

Ürümqi

Turfan Basin   Han

T I E N   S H A N

40°

Kashi

Shache

S I N K I A N G

Tarim Basin

PAKISTAN

T I B E T   P L A T E A U

C   P

30°

NEPAL

Lhasa

R. Brahmaputra

INDIA

BHUTAN

INDIA

20°

BURMA

KEY

–··– National boundary

┼┼┼ Main railways with strategic significance

Land over 2000 metres (6550 feet)

///// Strategic corridors

ⓔ Main energy resources

Military headquarters

Naval bases

Border incidents with Vietnam

Border incidents with USSR

● Major cities

• Towns or smaller cities

── Principal road network

China: The Zones of Vulnerability

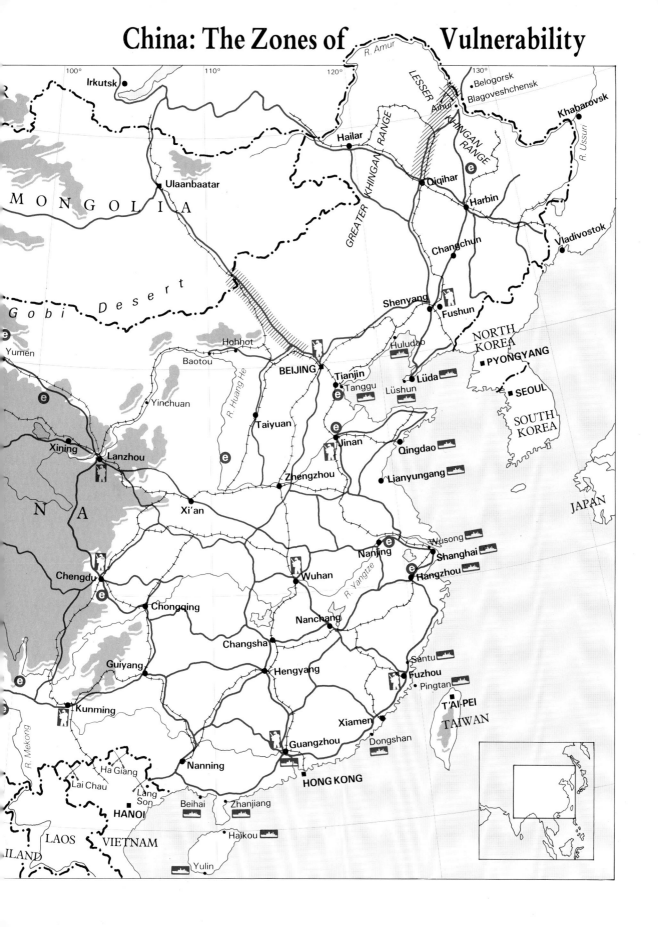

AFRICA

16 Western Sahara: War in the Desert

The endemic war in the Western Sahara, which has involved Morocco, Mauritania and Algeria in a dispute over the former territory of the Spanish Sahara, together with the inhabitants of that former colony, is one of the strangest, most obscure and yet most persistent in the world.

The Spanish Sahara, from which Spain withdrew on 26 February 1976, is a remote, bleak and poor land (though in recent years it has been found to contain important deposits of iron ore, vanadium and phosphates; the latter are under exploitation by a Moroccan state corporation). The territory was originally acquired by Spain to forestall the occupation by any other power of the coastline adjacent to the Spanish Canary Islands. Its borders were subsequently agreed with France, then the ruling power in what today are Algeria and Mauritania, which the Western Sahara adjoins, but not by the neighbouring kingdom of Morocco.

Following Morocco's recovery of independence from France, of which it had been a protectorate between 1912 and 1960, a 'Greater Morocco' policy prompted its government to lay claim to much of the Algerian Sahara (a claim which provoked a brief war between the two countries in 1963), to the whole of Mauritania between 1960 and 1969 and to the Spanish Sahara. Spain initially resisted this claim but in November 1975 agreed to withdraw from the territory and to accept its partition between Morocco and Mauritania.

Leaders of the population of the Western Sahara, the Saharawis, a partly settled but largely nomadic people, had already made their own bid for independence against Spain in 1970, but had had their resistance crushed. Subsequently a new movement, Polisario (Popular Front for the Liberation of Saguia el Hamra and Rio de Oro – the two divisions of Spanish Sahara) had come into being and on 27 February 1976, the day after Spain's withdrawal, its leadership proclaimed the existence of a new state, the Saharan Arab Democratic Republic (SADR), and it immediately took to arms against both Morocco and Mauritania. Its members were quickly to prove themselves effective and astonishingly resilient guerrilla fighters.

The environment in which they operate

Few 'desert wars' actually take place under the most rigorous desert conditions; war takes place on the fringes. But in the campaigns of the Polisario in the Western Sahara, the traditional style of desert raiding has been adapted to modern conditions. Guerrillas use the desert and ill-defined frontiers as a means of refuge, swooping to attack the towns and economic assets of the coastal zone. The defensive measures have also been updated: electronic surveillance and remote-control mines defend a sand rampart created by bulldozers. It is a far cry from 'Beau Geste'.

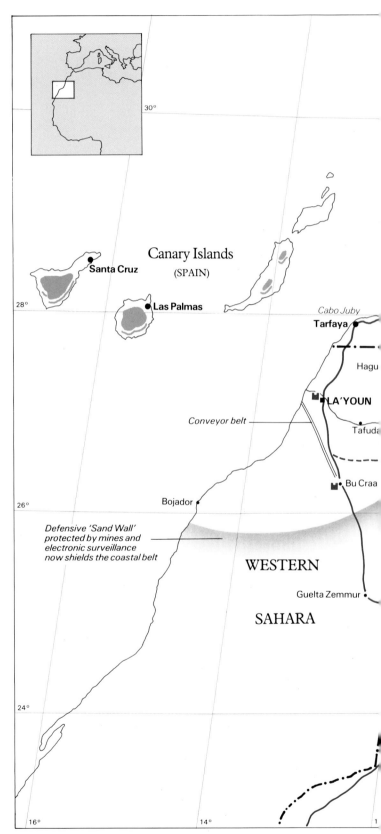

30°

Canary Islands
(SPAIN)

Santa Cruz

28°

Las Palmas

Cabo Juby

Tarfaya

Hagu

LA'YOUN

Conveyor belt

Tafuda

Bu Craa

26°

Bojador

Defensive 'Sand Wall'
protected by mines and
electronic surveillance
now shields the coastal belt

WESTERN

Guelta Zemmur

SAHARA

24°

16°   14°

Western Sahara: War in the Desert

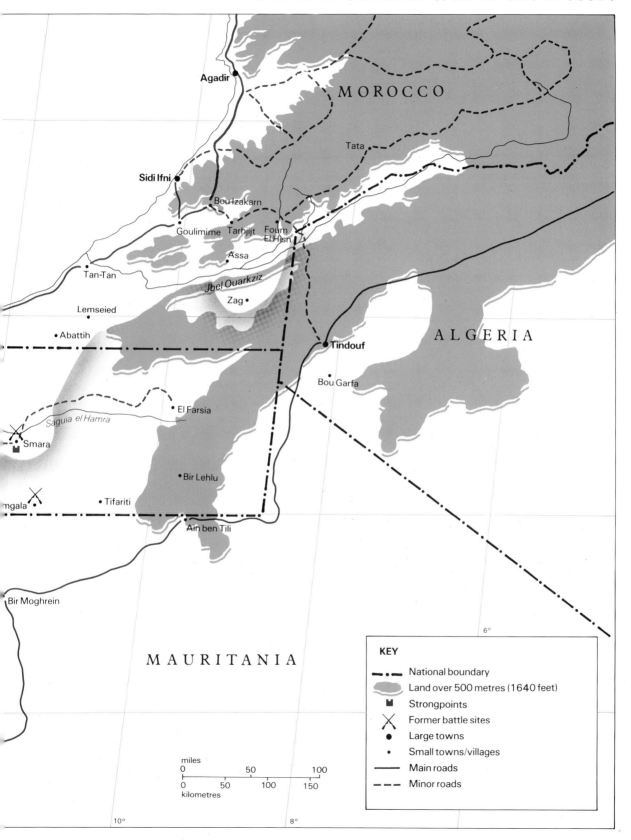

MOROCCO

Agadir

Tata

Sidi Ifni

Bou Izakarn

Goulimime Tarhjijt Foum
El Hisn

Assa

Tan-Tan

Jbel Ouarkziz

Zag

Lemseied

Abattih

Tindouf

ALGERIA

Bou Garfa

El Farsia

Saguia el Hamra

Smara

Bir Lehlu

mgala Tifariti

Ain ben Tili

Bir Moghrein

MAURITANIA

KEY

—·—·— National boundary

Land over 500 metres (1640 feet)

Strongpoints

✕ Former battle sites

● Large towns

• Small towns/villages

—— Main roads

---- Minor roads

6°

miles
0   50   100

0   50   100   150
kilometres

10°   8°

is one of the most hostile in the world. Western Sahara covers an area rather larger than Great Britain, about 103,000 square miles. Its land borders extend for 1,271 miles, of which 276 miles border Morocco, nineteen Algeria and 976 Mauritania. The coastline, 660 miles long, consists of precipitous cliffs along much of its course, backed by a line of sand dunes ten to twenty miles wide. Inland, however, the desert is of the rock and gravel variety, consisting of a succession of waterless plains which rise gradually from the coast to a height of 1,300 feet. There are two mountain regions, with peaks approaching 3,000 feet, in the centre and south-east. Vegetation scarcely exists. There are no oases, only seventeen acres of palms and even the commonest tree, a hardy acacia, covers only 6,000 acres. A little rain falls in the winter, sufficient to replace the contents of rock cisterns and to supply a seasonal flow in the only river. Otherwise the interior is constantly swept by fierce, dry winds, which drive temperatures below freezing at night in winter. Summer daytime temperatures exceed 37°C. (100°F.) in the west and 57°C. (135°F.) inland. The territory is effectively roadless, though there is a short stretch of railway which runs inland from La'youn to Bu Craa, along which phosphates are transported to the coast.

The indigenous population of the Western Sahara, which is ethnically Arab, and Muslim by religion, did not exceed 100,000 before 1976. The bulk have become refugees and are living in refugee camps in the west of Algeria, from which the guerrillas derive a measure of support.

They cannot exceed 10,000 in number, but have succeeded in winning both a considerable degree of military success and a wide measure of diplomatic support.

By 1979 they had forced Mauritania, a very poor country, which had been obliged to expand its army to 12,000 men and was spending 60 per cent of its budget on defence, to abandon the war and sue for peace. Three years later the guerrillas had gained freedom of movement throughout five-sixths of the Western Sahara. The Moroccan garrison, 80,000 strong, was confined within the coastal enclaves ('the useful triangle'), protecting the phosphate extraction area and themselves behind fixed defences and electronic surveillance devices. The Moroccan army had had to be doubled in size to meet the challenge of the war, while the military budget had quadrupled between 1974 and 1982.

The future of the Western Sahara, however, had become an international issue. By 1983 SADR had been recognised as an independent state by fifty countries in Asia, Latin America and Africa, and its admission to a seat at the Organisation of African Unity meeting at Addis Ababa in June 1983 threatened to split that body. The split was averted only by the Polisario's agreement to withdraw from the meeting.

There remains no sign that the Polisario guerrillas will give up their struggle. While they persist in it, relations between Morocco and Algeria will remain unsettled and the internal stability of Morocco will be undermined by the cost of sustaining what looks increasingly like an unwinnable war.

17 Libya and Chad: Saharan Imperialism

The former French colony of Chad, independent since 1960, occupies a strategically central location in the Central Sahara. It is landlocked, and bordered on the south and south-west by the Central African Republic, Cameroon and Nigeria, on the east by the Sudan, on the west by Niger and on the north by Libya. Libya lays claim to territory along Chad's northern frontier, has maintained a garrison inside the country since 1972 and has conducted operations in support of its nominees in Chad politics which has brought it into direct conflict with France. Libya, however, appears to regard Chad as a natural corridor of advance towards West Africa, into which region President Gaddafi of Libya entertains ambitions to extend his power.

Chad is the fifth largest country in Africa (496,000 square miles), but is largely unfertile and supports only a small population, about 4 million. North of the fourteenth degree of latitude rainfall is so sparse and erratic that the land is inhabited only by nomads, some 50,000 Tebu and Arabs. South of that line, sufficient rain usually falls to water subsistence crops and cotton. The most productive industry, however, is fishing, centred on Lake Chad. The lake is itself the centre of an inland drainage system, limited in the east by the Ouaddai and Ennedi plateaux, and in the north by the Tibesti range, in which the highest mountains rise to over 11,000 feet. The population of the south is Bantu, many of the inhabitants being descendants of fugitives from the slave trade which formerly ravaged surrounding territories.

The enormous distances incurred in travel across Chad – 2,000 miles from north to south, 1,000 from east to west – formerly combined, with its isolated location, to make it one of the least traversed regions of Africa. During the nineteenth century, however, the extension of French power southward from Algiers and the collapse of Egyptian power in the Sudan left Chad as the only open but also safe land avenue by which slaves might be brought from the interior into the Arab world. These circumstances worked to draw two major routes through the territory, passing respectively by the modern capital N'Djamena (Fort Lamy) and by Abéché, and so to attach the bleak hinterland to the coastal regions of Tripolitania and Cyrenaica.

Tripolitania-Cyrenaica remained the last directly ruled outpost of the Ottoman Empire in Africa until 1912 when, as a result of Italy's opportunistic intervention in the Balkan Wars, it passed under her rule, to emerge as the colony of Libya in 1934. In the course of their campaign of suppression, the Italians waged a long war against the Senussi sect, which dominated the Libyan Arabs until its leaders were executed or driven into exile in Chad. That territory had passed under French rule in the 1890s by the convergence of expeditionary columns which had begun their advance from the French territories in North and West Africa respectively.

Libya, which became an independent monarchy after a period of British trusteeship in 1951, has been ruled by the messianic Colonel Gaddafi since 1969. The aims of his regime are many and complex, but include strong elements of nationalism, Islamic proselytism and revolutionary anti-colonialism. A principal focus of his foreign policy, which has ramifications beyond the merely legal, has been the frontier dispute with Chad inherited from the former Italian administration.

The northern boundary of Chad with Libya was delimited by an agreement between France and Italy in 1935. Itself an

Grandiose dreams of a Saharan Empire, stretching from the Mediterranean to the heart of Africa, were a fantasy of French colonial ambitions. Libya has inherited the vision, which creates conflict with residual French concerns in the area. This clash is responsible for the fighting in Chad, with two external powers backing different ethnic and regional factions. War will continue as long as they are willing to play the game, while famine and desertification are overwhelming the country.

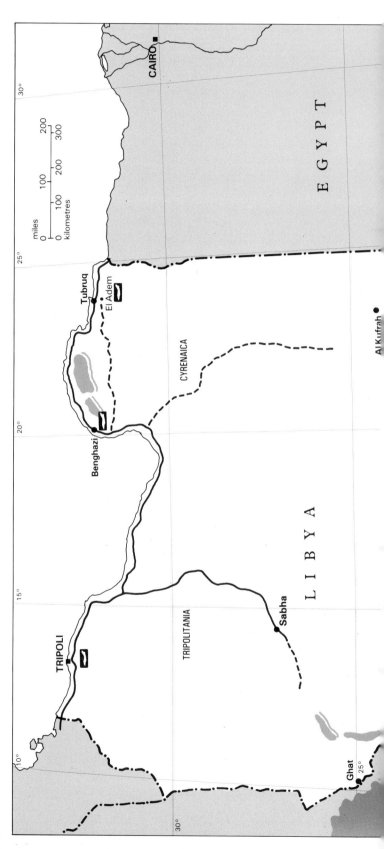

Libya and Chad: Saharan Imperialism

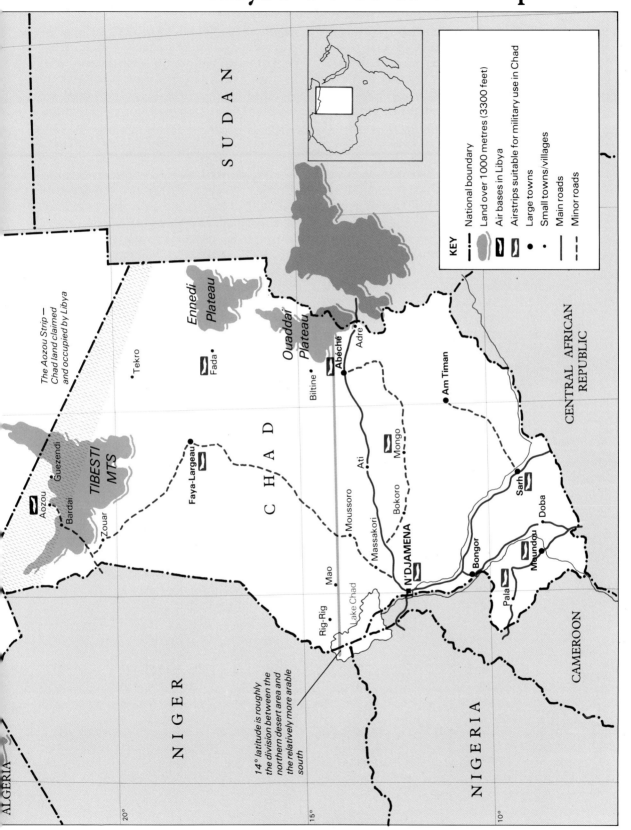

KEY

National boundary	
Land over 1000 metres (3300 feet)	
Air bases in Libya	
Airstrips suitable for military use in Chad	
Large towns	
Small towns/villages	
Main roads	
Minor roads	

SUDAN

ALGERIA

The Aozou Strip – Chad land claimed and occupied by Libya

Ennedi Plateau

Ouaddaï Plateau

Tekro

Fada

Biltine

Abéché

Adré

Am Timan

CENTRAL AFRICAN REPUBLIC

TIBESTI MTS

Aozou

Guezendi

Bardaï

Zouar

Faya-Largeau

C H A D

Mongo

Ati

Bokoro

Sarh

Moussoro

Massakori

Doba

Bongor

Moundou

Mao

N'DJAMENA

Pala

Rig-Rig

Lake Chad

14° latitude is roughly the division between the northern desert area and the relatively more arable south

N I G E R

N I G E R I A

CAMEROON

20°

15°

10°

appendix to an Anglo-French-Russian-Italian agreement of 1915, it conceded to the Italians a strip of territory, known as the Aozou Strip, some 437 miles long by ninety-four wide. Under earlier agreements between France–Britain and Italy–Turkey, however, the Strip had been recognised as belonging to Chad. Moreover, France failed to ratify the 1935 agreement, and in 1951 concluded terms with the royal government of Libya which appear to establish the Aozou Strip as Chadian territory.

Colonel Gaddafi subsequently chose to regard the 1935 treaty as the operative instrument and in 1973 occupied and annexed the Strip unilaterally. At the time this action was widely regarded as a move to appropriate territory known to contain uranium deposits, desired by Gaddafi to provide fuel for his publicly announced nuclear programme. Relations between Chad and Libya were, moreover, currently good and the move was not opposed by N'Djamena, whose power to oppose it was in any case wholly lacking. But the N'Djamena government's waning success against a northern rebellion, which Libya supported, led to a denunciation of the annexation in 1976, to stronger French intervention on N'Djamena's side and to the internationalisation of the dispute in 1978, when the Organisation of African Unity undertook to investigate Chad's and Libya's complaints against each other.

Subsequent events have spread the view that Libya's involvement in Chad is motivated by larger ambitions than the appropriation of a source of nuclear ores. After the collapse of efforts to settle the civil war by the formation of a joint north–south government in 1980, Libya increased its support for those Chadian groups which favoured 'full unity' between the two countries. Their defeat by Hissen Habré, who subsequently acceded to the presidency, allowed an OAU peace-keeping force to replace the Libyans. But Habré's overambitious effort to repossess the Aozou Strip in February 1983 brought the Libyans back in strength. By mid-summer they had occupied half the country, were restrained from further advance only by the presence of a hastily despatched French force and were causing widespread alarm in the former French colonies of Central and West Africa. An alignment arranged between Libya and Upper Volta had led the West Africans to fear that Colonel Gaddafi's long-term ambition was to open an 'Islamic Corridor' to the Atlantic.

Subsequent negotiations led to an agreement for the withdrawal of both French and Libyan troops from Chad. Though Libyans remain in the Aozou Strip, and are alleged still to be present elsewhere in the north, fears that this 'hole in the heart of Africa' offers a route of expansion southwards to any power, let alone one as militarily weak as Libya, seem exaggerated. Poor and scanty communications, harsh climate and lack of such basic facilities for travel as water make Chad a zone almost impassable to large modern armies.

18 Ethiopia, Somalia and the Sudan: The Hungry Lands

The military writer, Major-General J. F. C. Fuller first saw Ethiopia during the war between the Ethiopians and the Italians in 1935; he produced an instant, soldier's assessment: 'Strategically, Abyssinia [Ethiopia], is like a porcupine bristling with quite exceptional difficulties.' It is a land dominated, like most of east Africa, by the massive geological pressures which produced the Rift Valley. On either side of the valley are high plateaux, overlooked by still higher peaks and ranges of rough broken ground. Another correspondent in the 1935 war described how the high plateau is 'seamed with vast crevices, so that [the country] . . . stops short suddenly after several miles of travel, to go on again hundreds of feet higher or lower . . . at one point I thought we were going along a plain slightly less barren than most, but suddenly saw that a hundred yards on our right was a sheer drop of about a thousand feet to another plain, out of which a bare rock hundreds of feet high stuck up like a colossal tooth.' Only on the fringes of the high plateau does the terrain change. To the east, between the escarpment which marks the end of the northern high plateau and the Red Sea coast, is a flat dry plain, which soon becomes the Ogaden desert along the border with Somalia. On the western frontier, with Sudan, the land is also low, but changes from swamp in the southern corner near the Akobo river to dry open land in the north. The 'exceptional difficulties' which Fuller mentions come not only from the high mountainous ground, but from the great range of contrasts within the country. The land at Lake Assale is well below sea-level, while the highest point, Ras Dashan, is more than 14,700 feet above sea-level.

The rivers which cut through the plateau to the west of the Rift Valley – like the Tekeze which separates the Tigre highlands from the Gonder ranges, or the Blue Nile which cuts through the western provinces of Gwejam and Welega – make cross-country communications very difficult. Often the roads run along valleys far from the direct line to take advantage of the easier ground: the road north from Addis Ababa runs along the course of the Abbai river to Dabra Màrk'os, almost 5,000 feet below the level of the surrounding plain. Thus the geography renders Ethiopia perfect for guerrilla warfare in the highland zone. It also makes communications with the north and south extremely difficult. A single main road runs north from Addis Ababa: north of Mak'ale, the surface deteriorates during the winter, virtually cutting Asmera off from the south. Communications north of Asmera into Eritrea are virtually non-existent, and the only passable track runs through Nakfa, which has long been held by the Eritrean Liberation Front. Communications are no better into the mountains to the west of the capital. It is these difficulties which kept Ethiopia a free and independent monarchy while all the rest of Africa succumbed to colonialism.

In the nineteenth century, Ethiopia engaged in its own version of imperial expansion. The province of Eritrea and much of what became Somalia were at one time held by Ethiopia, and the claims to them have never been abandoned; these produced clashes with Great Britain under Emperor Tewodros which led to Ethiopian defeat at Magdala in 1868. But the position was reversed when the Emperor Menelik II trounced the Italians at Adowa in 1896. Thereafter, the Europeans left Ethiopia alone until the Italians attacked again (successfully) in 1935. All these attacks have tended to follow the same line, down the spine of the plateau south towards Addis Ababa. Other attacks, from the west into the mountain area around Gonder, never penetrated very far; armies landing on the Red Sea coast found the passage along the high plateau both difficult and dangerous. Banditry was always endemic in the northern provinces, and this became a patriotic duty under the Italian occupation. When the Emperor Haile Selassie recovered his throne, with

British help, in 1941, this patriotic banditry, known as 'shifmet', was transformed into a peasant resistance movement in Tigre province against control from the centre. Resistance centred on the strategic hilltown of Amba Alagi, and was only suppressed by a massive government effort in 1943. The tradition of resistance was reborn after the revolution of 1974.

The key to Italian success in the 1935–6 war was in the use of air power against an unsophisticated enemy who attempted to fight a conventional war. Towns like Mak'ale were doggedly defended, but fell to Italian artillery and bombing; tanks were used in open country against hopelessly brave Ethiopian levies. The Ethiopians had much more success with the 'shifmet' style of warfare: after 1935, the Italians held only the principal towns, and were subjected to constant harassment. Their advantage was in the mechanisms of modern war: tanks, planes, poison gas. They were notably unsuccessful in small-scale infantry actions which they avoided if at all possible. They stuck to the few roads, which meant that much of the country, especially to the south-east of Addis Ababa, was almost unaware, in any practical sense, that the Italians were in control. This changed as the Italians drove roads into the highland regions. Road communications were the key to control from the centre under the restored monarchy: Haile Selassie exerted much more effective control after 1941 than he had before, using the new Italian highways to tie the provinces to the capital. Under the post-imperial regime, power has similarly followed ease of access. But many maps are confusing. In Amharic, the principal language of northern Ethiopia, a single word *mangad* covers every form of access from a rough track to a modern highway; in the wet season between June and September many of the smaller roads were washed away. Even the modern roads, which were poorly maintained in the mountains, quickly reverted to the status of a rutted track.

The core of the traditional Ethiopian empire were the Christian northern provinces – Tigre, Welo and Begemdir. Much of the south was only acquired late in the nineteenth century: the province of Hārer was only occupied in 1887. There is a racial and religious divide superimposed upon the terrain. There is the divide between the Muslim south and the Christian north; there is a linguistic barrier, as the northern Amharic is disdained in the south; and the patterns of landholding and agriculture are also quite different. Part of the political change of the 1970s has been the rise of the southerners within Ethiopian society, and the progressive alienation of the formerly-favoured north. The pressure of the social revolution has met with armed resistance, just as more muted efforts at change by Haile Selassie in the 1940s stimulated Tigrean separatism. The conflict in the province of Eritrea antedates the revolution, but shows the continuity of Ethiopian policy despite the revolution of 1974.

Eritrea, although traditionally claimed by Ethiopia, was an Italian colony until the Second World War, and thereafter, under UN trusteeship, was administered by Britain until 1950. In 1952, Eritrea was federated with Ethiopia, and preserved a considerable degree of independence from Addis Ababa. In 1962, this was ended when Eritrea was reduced to provincial status within a unitary Ethiopia, and a movement of armed resistance began. In the south, in the debatable lands between Ethiopia and Somalia, many tribesmen of Somali origins came under Ethiopian jurisdiction: Somalia (a fusion of British and Italian Somaliland) refused to accept the boundary, as they also rejected the line between Kenya and Somalia. All the three main resistance movements have a common interest in breaking the strong central power of Addis Ababa. In Tigre there is a long tradition of provincial separatism, heightened by the belief that the revolution of 1974, which abolished the monarchy, would alter the political balance in favour of non-Christian southerners. The objective of the Tigreans is a loose form of federation rather than independence; the Eritreans look for a complete split with Ethiopia. The military problems of enforcing unity are compounded by the difficulty of communications with the north. The main road is subject to constant Tigrean attack and a convoy can take up to three weeks to reach Eritrea from Addis Ababa. But despite these logistical difficulties, the Ethiopians (stiffened by a large contingent of Cuban troops) managed to recover most of the towns in Eritrea which were lost during 1977. Outside the towns, the land is controlled by the Eritreans, subject only to regular attacks from the air, and the occasional raid by an Ethiopian column. The measure of Ethiopian weakness is the failure to recover the strategic town of Nakfa, which controls access to northern Eritrea. In repeated attacks the Ethiopians failed to regain the town: in 1982 over 30,000 Ethiopian troops were lost in fruitless assaults on Eritrea.

The importance of Eritrea is that it controls Ethiopia's sole outlet to the sea under national control at Mits'iwa. In practical terms, the railway line to Djibouti is a more convenient point of access from Addis Ababa, but it is in the territory of the Afars and the Isars, now called Djibouti. More pertinent is that the territory is claimed by Somalia, and is one of the points at which the Imperial Destinies of Ethiopia and Somalia are locked in conflict. Somalia lays claim to all the peoples of Somali origin, who are to be found in northern Kenya, in Djibouti, and in the Ogaden region of Ethiopia; Ethiopians wish to push the border further south into Somalia, justified by the imperial tradition of Menelik and Tewodros. In 1964, frontier raids became a brief full-scale war in the Ogaden, but it is difficult country for mechanised warfare, as the Italians found in 1935. War was renewed in 1976, and this time the Somali 'liberation movement' pushed through the Ogaden to the outskirts of Hārer and Diré Dawa (1977). They had pushed beyond their limit of effective support, and an Ethiopian counter-attack in 1978, aided as in Eritrea by massive Cuban and Soviet support, pushed the Somalis back across the desert regions. Two years later, a new Somali assault was defeated at Warder, and in 1982 the Ethiopians pushed forward into Somalia, establishing a strong defensive position around the town of Goldojob. Here they could dominate the only good road linking the north and south of Somalia. From that point they could strike south to Mogadiscio or north towards Hargeisa and Berbera. Northern Somalia is now very vulnerable to a sustained Ethiopian attack towards the Gulf of Aden. In the north the advantage of the ground lies with the Ethiopians; in the east it also favours them against the Somalis, always assuming the sustaining effect of Soviet support.

There are not many bright spots in Ethiopia's alternative strategies. There are now six active separatist movements operating inside Ethiopia, and several more across the borders in Sudan and Somalia which are inactive. Conversely, Ethiopia supports guerrilla movements directed against the Somali and Sudanese governments. The northern provinces are beyond the control of Addis Ababa, except during annual campaigns which are costly in terms of both cash and manpower, and never certain in their outcome. Only the provinces immediately around the capital, Shewa, Arusi and eastern Welega are securely under government control. All the main towns and cities are secure for the

All the conflicts in the region have deep, historic roots, either linguistic, religious, or racial. But central authority has never been effective in the distant recesses of Ethiopia or Sudan, or among the wandering Somali groups. Now famine is being used secretly by central governments as a means of redistributing troublesome regional populations to areas where they can be fed – and controlled – more easily.

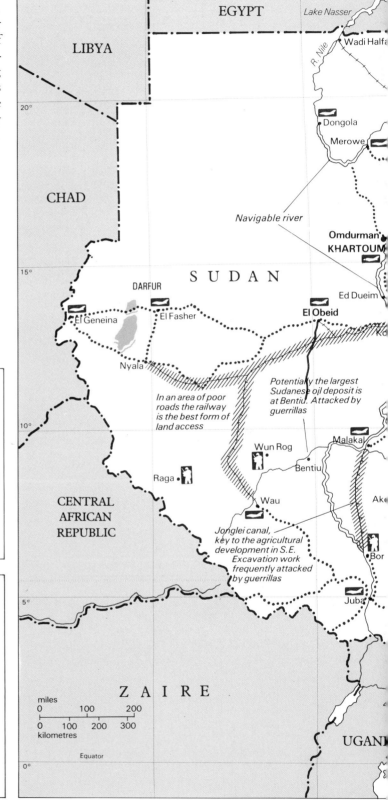

Navigable river

In an area of poor roads the railway is the best form of land access

Potentially the largest Sudanese oil deposit is at Bentiu. Attacked by guerrillas

Jonglei canal, key to the agricultural development in S.E. Excavation work frequently attacked by guerrillas

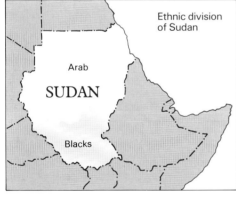

Ethnic division of Sudan

Arab

SUDAN

Blacks

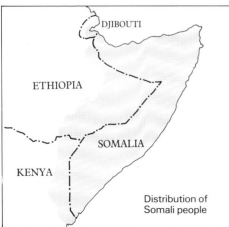

Distribution of Somali people

Ethiopia, Somalia and the Sudan: The Hungry Lands

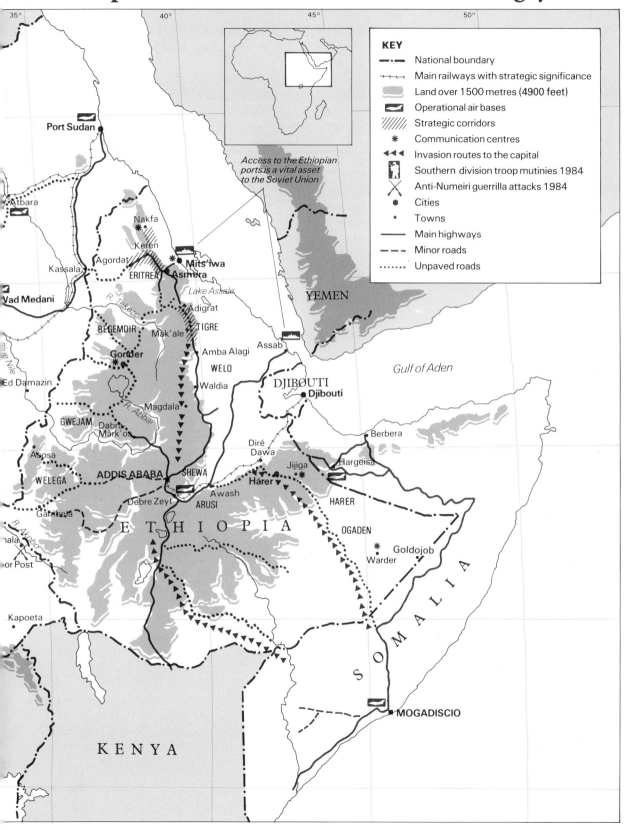

KEY

- —·—·— National boundary
- ┼┼┼┼ Main railways with strategic significance
- Land over 1500 metres (4900 feet)
- Operational air bases
- ⫽⫽⫽ Strategic corridors
- ✳ Communication centres
- ◄◄◄ Invasion routes to the capital
- Southern division troop mutinies 1984
- ✕ Anti-Numeiri guerrilla attacks 1984
- ● Cities
- · Towns
- —— Main highways
- – – – Minor roads
- ······ Unpaved roads

Access to the Ethiopian ports is a vital asset to the Soviet Union

YEMEN

Gulf of Aden

Port Sudan

Atbara

Kassala

Vad Medani

Ed Damazin

Asosa

Gambela

Kapoeta

Nakfa
Keren
Agordat
ERITREA
Mits'iwa
Asmera
Lake Assale
Adigrat
TIGRE
Mak'ale
BEGEMDIR
Gonder
Amba Alagi
WELO
Waldia
R. Tekeze
Magdala
R. Abbai
GWEJAM
Dabra Mark'os
WELEGA
ADDIS ABABA
SHEWA
Debre Zeyt
ARUSI
Awash
ARUSI
E T H I O P I A
R. AKOBO

Assab
DJIBOUTI
Djibouti
Berbera
Diré Dawa
Jijiga
Harer
HARER
Hargeisa
OGADEN
Goldojob
Warder
S O M A L I A

MOGADISCIO

KENYA

government, but the principal casualty of the war has been the rural population and the economy. The railway line to Djibouti has been repeatedly sabotaged by guerrillas, while the drought in the north has been an asset rather than a liability to the government, if a catastrophe for the rural population of Tigre and Eritrea. Constant war coupled with the lack of rain has rendered life in the villages of the north insupportable. The move off the land is the final, despairing move by communities which have abandoned hope. The government is taking advantage of the situation to break up communities still further by engaging in widespread plans for resettlement in areas which are both better able to support life, and are more closely under the control of Addis Ababa. Nature is scorching the earth, and reducing the popular base for the separatist movements.

The Sudan

Sheer size dominates every aspect of the strategic geography of the Sudan. Its vast extent − more than 967,000 square miles − and poor road communications to the west of the Nile make it virtually impossible for the central government to function effectively in the regions distant from the capital, Khartoum. The effect of distance is heightened by the social division of the country. The northern provinces are occupied by tribes of Arab origin and Muslim in religion. The southern provinces are the home of black tribes − Shilluk, Nuer and Dinka − who have quite different social, economic and political systems. The north has traditionally dominated the south, but with independence from Britain and Egypt in 1956 the southern tribes feared permanent oppression. The savage civil war which lasted from 1956 until 1972 made it clear that the northerners could never expect to hold down the south by

force alone. But the peace was little more than an armistice, which gave the south a high degree of independence; the southerners remain suspicious that the north still intends to restore central control.

The Muslim north was no more united than the south, which only managed to suppress tribal rivalries in the face of the 'northern' army. The Islamic cult of Mahdism, which looked to a charismatic religious and military leader, remains strong among the Baggara and Ja'aliyin of northern Sudan. It was these same tribes which provided the 'dervishes' who defeated the Anglo-Egyptian armies under Hicks Pasha and General Gordon between 1883 and 1885. Nor did the British victory over the dervishes at Omdurman, close to Khartoum, in 1898, defeat the force of Mahdism. Like militant Islam in Iran, it was merely dormant. In the 1970s, there were several risings by Mahdist sects, with the covert support of Libya which provided arms and money. But, like the southerners, the Islamic militants were bought off by compromise, courted by the Sudanese President Numeiri at the same time as he conceded effective self-government to the south. It was a balancing act which has lasted, precariously.

Sudan is surrounded by actual or potential enemies. Historically, the most significant is Egypt, which is forced by geography to take a positive role in the Sudan. The Nile is essential for Egyptian agriculture and Sudan controls the flow of the Nile waters. Although mutual interest at present dictates a friendly relationship, to the extent of a 'Charter of Integration' with Egypt in 1982, the greater demands which Sudan is now making on the Nile waters for irrigation projects carry the seeds of future conflict. While enmity with Egypt extends over the centuries, the hostility with Libya is of recent making. Current Libyan ambitions extend deep into Muslim Africa, in particular into Chad:

Libyan intervention in Sudan is part of the same policy. In the case of Sudan, the discovery of oil in Darfur province, which adjoins Chad, has given this aspect of 'Libyan imperialism' an economic as well as a political motive. Libya is as handicapped as Sudan by poor communications in remote regions, and while Sudan is not equipped to deal with guerrilla infiltration across the frontiers, it has strengthened both its land and air frontier on the western flank: El Fasher and El Geneina, with El Obeid to the east, are key points.

Traditionally, Sudan has been a route of invasion into Ethiopia, and Islamic militancy has been a natural point of conflict with a largely Christian Ethiopia. The progressive decline of Ethiopia's capacity to intervene outside her borders in the years after the revolution in 1974 has made serious conflict less likely. However, the war in Eritrea is of critical interest to the Sudan, because the best road to the only outlet for the Sudan, Port Sudan on the Red Sea, runs close to the Eritrean border, via Kassala. Part of the rail network runs along roughly the same line, although there is an alternative route from Khartoum along the Nile to Atbara, and then east to the coast. Great efforts have been made to improve the road which runs along the same line, which is much less vulnerable: it is this line which, significantly, the oil pipeline from the Red Sea has taken. Sudan harbours several Ethiopian groups opposing the present government, with a degree of support ranging from mere acquiescence to active aid. In the south especially there is a considerable degree of tribal spread across the border, and the various Oromo-based liberation movements operating in the southern provinces of Ethiopia move freely in and out of Sudan from the area between Kapoeta and Akobo. Similarly, Ugandan rebels lurk in the Lolibet mountains in the far south, while in the area around Kassala,

and further north, on the border with Eritrea, the refugees from the war conceal active opponents of the Ethiopian government. At one time, the Sudanese supported groups opposed to the Libyan government, largely as a reciprocal gesture against Libyan support for the extreme Muslim parties in Sudan, and for guerrillas in western Sudan. The peace between Sudan and Libya is temporary.

Wide open spaces, with scanty cover, make air power the key to the control of the ground in the Sudan, as in much of Africa outside the forest zones. Indeed, the first use of aircraft in a ground attack role in Africa south of the Sahara was in the Soba region of southern Sudan in 1919–20, where the British machine-gunned and bombed rebel villages. Today, the main role of airpower lies in the protection of the western boundary, and in the desert wastes of north-west Sudan. Air strikes are the only hope of the Sudanese in containing an advance by the much more powerful Libyan regular forces: in any advance to the Nile, the Libyan lines of communication would be extended and vulnerable. Few countries in Africa are so vulnerable to both internal fragmentation and external threats as Sudan: the others – Angola and Ethiopia – are already paralysed by civil war and foreign intervention. The fragile peace in the Sudan, which is regularly punctuated by rumblings of discontent in the army, has been preserved by a policy of constant concession backed by political manipulation. The internal enemies, both in north and south, are now riven by racial, tribal and religious factionalism, fostered where possible by the central government. The same tenderness has been displayed towards possible external threats: Numeiri avoided conflict wherever possible. The historic tie is with Egypt, and this is now being rebuilt as a counterweight to the predatory ambitions of Libya. But this merely reinforces the Sudanese sense of angry subservience, and inflames the fears of the black peoples of southern Sudan. The problem cannot be resolved, only managed. Sudan remains volatile.

The deposition of Numeiri by the army, during a convenient absence abroad in 1985, did little to alter the political and strategic position. The rebels in the south continued to raid the outlying posts of the Sudanese army, even extending their attacks into the north, and the army commanders set about dismantling the more bizarre elements of Numeiri's rule (the Islamic law code) rather than tackling more complex political issues. Numeiri himself originally emerged from a gaggle of army officers thrust into political power, and a new strong man will probably materialise. The problems transcend the personalities involved.

19 Zaire and Uganda: The Heart of Darkness

The twin elements which dominate Zaire are the great river, Congo-Zaire, and the vast equatorial forest which lies around it. It is what the novelist Joseph Conrad, who took a steamboat upriver in the first years of this century, called 'the heart of darkness'. Communication in the forest depends on the river rather than roads or railways, which have been used instead to cover the parts of the forest where the rivers cannot be navigated. Almost all the resources of the country lie around the fringes of the forest, and distant from the centre of government in Kinshasa. All these factors add up to a recipe for separatism. The greatest prize of Zaire is the province of Shaba, which borders Angola, Zambia and Tanzania, and was formerly known as Katanga. It is one of the richest mining areas of Africa, with vast resources of copper and cobalt. To the north-west of Shaba is the diamond mining zone of Kasai province, around Tshikapa and Kananga.

Despite its vast area, Zaire is an urbanised society with over 40 per cent of the population in or around the towns or cities. In the heart of the forest, the only centres are the river towns such as Kisangani and Boende; smaller places like Ikela, south of Kisangani, or Lodja, north of Kananga, are joined to the cities by roads ranging from poor to nearly impassable at the wettest season of the year. Here, the air link is a vital resource. The strategic problems of Zaire stem more from its geography and the distribution of resources than from any racial or religious divide. The movement for Katangan/Shaban independence of the 1960s and 1970s found a welcome in Angola and Tanzania after it had been expelled from the soil of Zaire. The independence movement for the north-east provinces was supported from the Sudan. External political and economic interests have always sought to abstract the best bits of Zaire for their own purposes: stability depends on a central government which is also effective on the periphery.

Independence came in a rush in June 1960. The independence regime of Patrice Lumumba held power in Kinshasa for less than three months until it was overthrown by the army led by the Chief of Staff, Joseph Mobutu, in an effort to avoid the bloodbath and national fragmentation which had been sparked off by independence. After Lumumba was murdered on the orders of Moise Tshombe, who led the separatist Katanga regime, the country fell apart. The Lumumba faction was strong in Stanleyville (now Kisangani) and in the north-east, around Wamba, Watsa, and

Bunia, all areas which repeatedly became centres of opposition to rule from Kinshasa. The control oscillated backwards and forwards, between the army under Mobutu, and Tshombe, who was backed by powerful foreign mining interests and controlled the vast wealth of Katanga. The circle was broken when Tshombe was kidnapped while trying to raise a new mercenary army in Europe to attack Mobutu, and was imprisoned in Algeria until his death in 1969. Mobutu was left unchallenged. The separatist forces of Katanga and the dregs of the Lumumbist movement had fought each other to a standstill: Mobutu, aided by the highly ambivalent role played by the United Nations 'peacekeeping force' in Zaire, has remained in power ever since.

But the country remains vulnerable. The Katangans have mounted fresh revolts in 1977 and 1978. On the latter occasion, a guerrilla war launched from Angola was successful in disturbing the mining operations at Kolwezi, and the army had great difficulty in forcing the insurgents back into Zambia. In November 1984, the town of Moba on Lake Tanganyika was briefly captured by an invading force from across the lake in Tanzania. The high ground around Moba and Kalémie, the Marungu and Mugila mountains, is rife with bandit/guerrilla fighters. While the Zaire army is being used as a peacekeeping force in Chad, many areas of Zaire itself are not under effective central government authority. While the central government can control all the major centres of population from the air – paratroops were much used during the civil wars of the 1960s and in the Belgian intervention in 1977 – it has no means to control all the rural areas. Shaba remains, and will remain, dangerously vulnerable.

Uganda

Uganda has never formed a coherent and harmonious society. It was based from its colonial origins in 1900 on a number of competing and often antagonistic traditional kingdoms united under the British Crown. Buganda with its capital Mengo, part of modern Kampala, was by far the most powerful and influential of these kingdoms, and the *kabaka* of Buganda always acted to preserve the sectional interests of his tribe, the Baganda. It was not a good foundation for an independent state, and the inner tensions of Ugandan society quickly emerged after the end of colonial rule in 1962. Milton Obote, elected as the first President of Uganda, tried to break the power of Buganda, and succeeded in allying many of the smaller tribes against the traditional enemy. His preoccupation with Buganda blinded him to the dangers of too great a dependence on the Ugandan army, led by Idi Amin. Amin, a member of the small Kakwa tribe from the far north of Uganda, was one of the many northerners in the army. He seized power in 1971, and immediately purged the army of all members of the Acholi and Lango tribes, rival northern clans. He then extended the campaign of terror throughout Ugandan society, and the Baganda, who had originally hailed Amin's coup as a liberation from Obote's oppression, realised that his successor was infinitely worse.

Under Obote, many of the regional tensions between Uganda and her neighbours had been relaxed. Zaire, Rwanda, Sudan, Tanzania, as well as Kenya, all had boundaries under dispute with Uganda. The geography of Uganda was dominated by the lake system which occupied much of the notional surface area of the country. The boundary with Rwanda ran up Lake Edward, that with Zaire through Lake Albert, while both Kenya and Tanzania

These countries have great economic resources, but inadequate political structures to sustain them. Zaire is run for the benefit of a small governing group, which has grown rich on the proceeds of power. Uganda, having fragmented into warring interest groups, is an awful warning of what could equally befall Zaire. There is seemingly no end to guerrilla war in Uganda; by September 1985 even the prized hydro-electric plant at Owen Falls was under attack. In Zaire, the violence is hidden in a vast country, but potentially equally perilous.

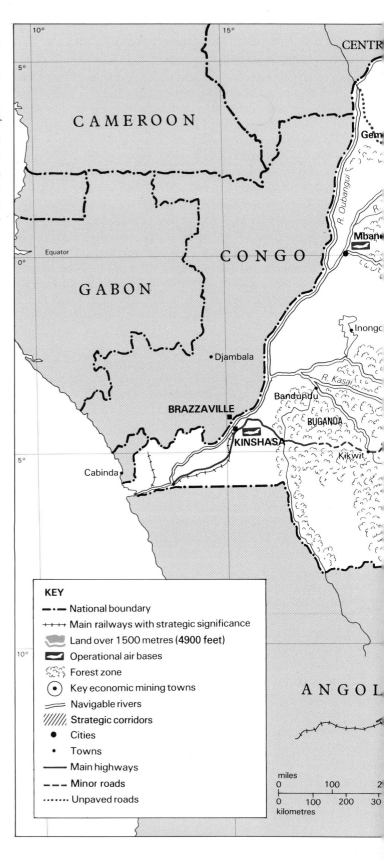

KEY

–·– National boundary

++++ Main railways with strategic significance

Land over 1500 metres (4900 feet)

Operational air bases

Forest zone

⊙ Key economic mining towns

Navigable rivers

Strategic corridors

● Cities

· Towns

—— Main highways

--- Minor roads

···· Unpaved roads

miles
0   100   2

0   100   200   30
kilometres

Zaire and Uganda: The Heart of Darkness

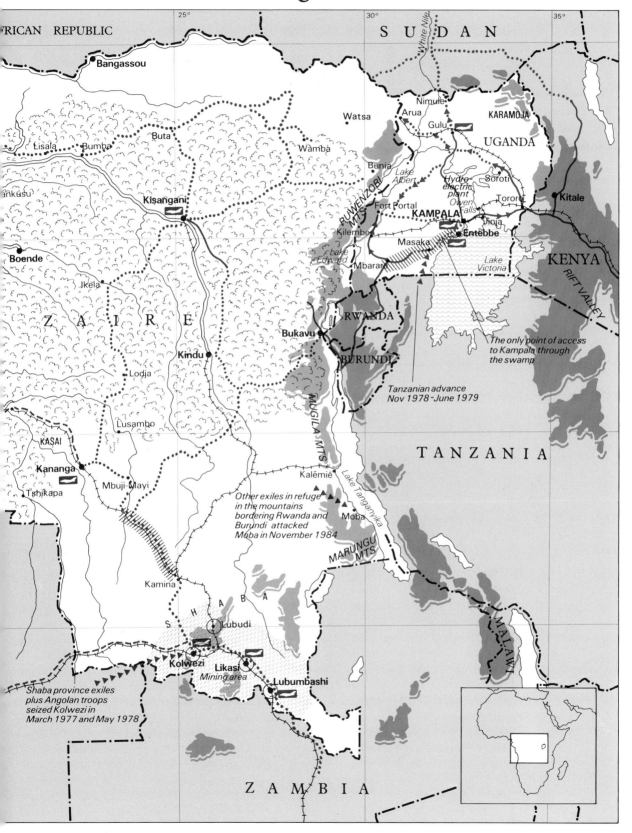

RICAN REPUBLIC

Bangassou

S U D A N

White Nile

Nimule

Watsa

Arua

Gulu

KARAMOJA

Buta

Wamba

UGANDA

Lisala

Bumba

Bunia

Soroti

Kitale

nkusu

Kisangani

Lake Albert

Hydro-electric plant

Tororo

Fort Portal

Owen Falls

KAMPALA

Boende

Kilembe

Entebbe

Jinja

KENYA

Ikela

Lake Edward

Masaka

RIFT VALLEY

Z   A   I   R   E

Mbarara

Lake Victoria

The only point of access to Kampala through the swamp

Kindu

RWANDA

Lodja

Bukavu

BURUNDI

Tanzanian advance Nov 1978-June 1979

Lusambo

KASAI

MUGILA MTS

T A N Z A N I A

Kananga

Kalémié

Lake Tanganyika

Tshikapa

Mbuji-Mayi

Other exiles in refuge in the mountains bordering Rwanda and Burundi attacked Moba in November 1984

Moba

MARUNGU MTS

Kamina

MALAWI

S   H   A   B   A

Lubudi

Kolwezi

Likasi

Mining area

Lubumbashi

Shaba province exiles plus Angolan troops seized Kolwezi in March 1977 and May 1978

Z   A   M   B   I   A

shared a common frontier with Uganda in the broad waters of Lake Victoria. The economic heartland was in the kingdom of Buganda, to the west of Kampala, producing cash crops for export; the industrial centres – Kampala and Jinja, on the northern bank of Lake Victoria – were on a small scale. Uganda remains a rural state, with over 90 per cent of the population located in the countryside: there has been nothing comparable to the urban expansion of Zaire and Kenya. The road system, which began to fall into terrible disrepair under Amin, was largely limited to the east–west line between Tororo and Kampala, and north to Soroti and Gulu. The railways assumed a key role in communications, because they linked parts of the country where there was virtually no road system.

Amin remained in power for eight years, with his rule becoming steadily more bizarre and despotic. He fell out with the Israelis, who had initially seen his regime as a point of entry into Africa, by allowing the Palestinians to land a hijacked aircraft at Entebbe. The subsequent Israeli rescue mission exposed the weakness of the self-named 'Conqueror of the British Empire'. The Palestinians now became a useful ally as Amin began to attack the Christian element of Ugandan society and to stress his Islamic faith: Palestinians and Libyans helped to purge the army after a failed revolt in July 1978. Amin renewed the border conflicts. The frontier with Kenya was closed by the Kenyan government, who put their troops on a war footing. Tanzania, which had given sanctuary to Obote and many other Ugandan exiles, was an object of particular hatred, and in October 1978 Amin invaded north-east Tanzania. The dispirited Ugandan army simply refused to fight, and retreated before an advancing Tanzanian force. Despite all Amin's bluster that he would defend Kampala to the last, he fled abroad in

April 1979. It was June 1979 before the Tanzanian forces chased the remnants of Amin's northern supporters over the border into Sudan.

The Tanzanians advanced as liberators, but they remained to reconstruct Uganda on lines they liked. In principle, this meant the restoration of Obote; in practice, it meant a return to factionalism. But the Amin years meant that violence was the dominant factor in Ugandan society. Obote was faced with the former supporters of Amin, lurking beyond the northern border but, more seriously, with all the groups in Ugandan society which had no desire to replace Amin with Obote. Where once they used political means they now resorted to armed struggle, and a guerrilla war of great ferocity began in 1980. It still continues, with a war zone to the north of Kampala.

The army expelled Obote in July 1985 and openly took power. The realities of Ugandan life were unaltered. Obote had maintained the northern predominance in the army which independent Uganda had inherited from the British; Amin's Kakwa officers were replaced by officers from the Acholi and Lango groups on whom Obote could rely. But in the six years of his rule most of the old elements of military oppression returned. Torture and random violence once more became commonplace, but the army was still quite unable to suppress the guerrilla war in the countryside. In the summer of 1985 the rebels seized Fort Portal, and it was clear that the central government had lost control. The removal of Obote changed the faces and the political rhetoric. It did little to alter the strategic problems faced by the government in Kampala.

The effect of Amin had been to destroy the prosperity of the Ugandan economy, by expropriating all available assets and handing them out to his allies. The economic chaos persisted after his downfall: the empty treasury made it impossible to re-build the basic elements of a prosperous society. This poverty was new to Uganda, since it was blessed by nature with many natural resources. It had ample power, provided by the Owen Falls hydroelectric scheme, and regular rainfall, making all except the Karamoja region on the Kenyan border highly productive. The railway system extended as far as the copper zone of Kilembe in the west and to the cotton fields of Pakwach in the north. What was good land for agriculture became the per-fect cover for guerrilla fighters: most of south-eastern Uganda is covered with tall elephant grass or thick woodland. Once war has come to Uganda, it will be hard to shift it. High wild ground covers the whole of the northern and western bor-ders: the Sudanese border zone is already a refuge for dissidents. The western zone, in the Ruwenzori mountains and the Rift Valley, has harboured refugees from the fighting in Zaire. It is likely to form a perfect base for refugees from the chaos in Uganda, if the central government is ever able to clear the war zone closer to the capital. The Pandora's box of social vio-lence, opened by Amin, cannot be closed again.

20 Angola, Mozambique and Zimbabwe: The Limits of Independence

Angola was the first point of sustained contact between Europe and southern Africa. From the beginning, in 1576 when the Portuguese built a fortress on the old treasury of the Congo kings in the lagoon at Luanda, Angola was a tapping point for the riches of the interior. The goods changed – slaves became coffee, oil, cop-per, iron ore and diamonds – but through-out Angola was split in two by the long range of hills running from the border with Zaire in the north to the frontier with Namibia in the south. To the west is the coastal plain, and the great bulk of the population. There too are almost all the economic resources of the country, and the bulk of the tarmacked roads. To the east of the hills is the 'dry zone', the arid open plains which the early Portuguese called 'the land at the end of the earth'. Roads were few, and the channels of com-munication were linked to the railways which ran inland: the most important, strategically speaking, was the Benguela railway, which was built to export the copper from central Africa.

In the last thirty years Angola has ex-perienced attacks from the north, the east and the south. The first assaults on the Portuguese in the early 1960s were mounted from across the border with Zaire into the two northernmost provinces of the country, aimed at the Bakongo population which straddled the frontier. They failed for a number of reasons. The attacks were ill-co-ordinated, and were accompanied by fruitless massacres of Portuguese farmers and their families. All they achieved was an instantaneous reaction from the large Portuguese forces in Angola, quickly reinforced by troops from Europe. There was also traditional hatred between the Bakongo and the much more numerous Ovimbundu peoples of southern and western Angola, which was a great handicap to spreading the northern revolt among all the African peoples of Angola. But the most important mistake made by the northern revolutionaries was in attacking the Portuguese at their most sensitive point. The bulk of Portugal's re-sources were concentrated in the region around Luanda, and the access by road and air gave the advantage to the defenders. The only area where the revolt held was in the Dembos mountains to the east and north of Luanda, classic guerrilla terrain where the Portuguese operated at a disadvantage.

The attack from the east was launched from Zambia after that country achieved independence in 1964. Like the northern revolt, it had a split along tribal lines. The leadership of the dominant revolutionary group in the south – the National Union for the Total Independence of Angola (UNITA) – was Ovimbundu, while the leadership of the People's Movement for the Liberation of Angola (MPLA), and the bulk of its support, came from the area around Luanda. It was much more effective to attack from the east rather than the north. The long frontier with Zambia was almost impossible to defend, and although Zaire was more willing to co-operate with the Portuguese, many revolutionary groups also found refuge in southern Zaire. The key strategic target was the railway to Benguela, which snaked across the dry plains and, unlike the Cabora Bassa Dam in Mozambique which formed a defensible *point*, was vulnerable throughout its length. Similarly, the southern railway running between Moçâmedes (Namibe) and Menongue (Vila Serpa Pinto) was constantly being sabotaged. The Portuguese defence relied on the twin pillars of anti-insurgent warfare: air power, and defended villages. In their Portuguese version, they were known as *aldeamentos*, and were no more successful or popular than they were in Algeria or Vietnam. The forward air strikes were based at Cuito Cuanavale in the south, Vila Gago Coutinho in Moxico province, and Henrique de Carvalho in the north. When they were able to find the guerrilla bands moving through the brush and scrub, they were able to achieve tactical superiority,

but there were never enough helicopters and fixed wing aircraft to maintain consistent surveillance. The ever-larger guerrilla groups were able to slip through under cover of darkness, massing against outlying barracks or isolated *aldeamentos*. By 1974, groups were infiltrating the cities.

The first phase of the war in Angola, after the false start in 1961, lasted, roughly speaking, from 1964 to 1975. At that point, the Portuguese abandoned Angola to the MPLA, who had taken the land around Luanda, and many of the industrial centres of the west coast. But a new phase of the war ensued immediately, and followed exactly the strategic pattern of the previous decade. The MPLA were sustained by massive Cuban support on the ground, and managed to throw back both the Front for the Liberation of Angola (FNLA) advancing from the north, and UNITA pushing up from the south-east. This was in November 1975. In the decade since, South Africa has served as a base and a backer for UNITA, numerically by far the most significant Angolan movement. South African support has helped to neutralise the advantage which the disciplined and skilled Cuban forces gave to the new MPLA government: UNITA now competes on more or less equal terms.

The battleground remains the same, 'the empty land' of eastern and southern Angola. UNITA now attacks the Benguela railway as the MPLA did under the Portuguese. In the south, where the Ovimbundu are the dominant population group, the MPLA have no natural support, and have never had any presence on the ground. In the centre, along the line between the capital Luanda and Malanje, and south towards Benguela, is the MPLA heartland. But even this is now being penetrated by UNITA infiltration groups: by September 1984, towns as close to Luanda as Caxito were subjected to raids. Huambo and Bie are regularly attacked.

But occasional lightning raids are a long way from conquest, and it is worth remembering that in the anti-colonial struggle the guerrillas never managed to dislodge the Portuguese from the western coastal plain, the economic heartland of Angola. Nor have the diamond mines in Lunda province, close to the Zaire border, been more than spasmodically disrupted by the guerrillas. The reality of the war with the Portuguese was that Portugal had withdrawn for domestic political reasons; the nationalists did not throw the colonialists into the sea. The cost of the war was enormous, largely because Portugal was supplying the war by air and sea over a long distance. But even the Portuguese were able to hold their own in the economically significant part of Angola. The strategic geography remains the same; the political conditions have changed.

The post-colonial government of Angola has no motherland to which it can withdraw: it must, of necessity, fight on to the end. Geography is also on its side. South Africa, while it has attacked repeatedly in the south of the country up as far as the strategic town of Cuvelai, is already waging war in Namibia at the end of a long line of communications. Prudence requires a limit to South African involvement in Angola; a political process is already being used to reduce the military strain the war imposes. Any sensible government in Angola is now prepared to accept enemy occupation of the 'empty zone', which is not worth the cost and effort of reconquest, and uses the eastern regions as a buffer zone for the western coastal plain. While the loss of towns such as Cazombo, in November 1983, was embarrassing, it made little difference, strategically speaking. None of the UNITA actions have done much to disturb mineral or agricultural production in the key regions north and south of Luanda.

Angola looks outwards, as it has done since the sixteenth century. All her resources are in the cities, towns and fertile lands of the west. Even the Benguela railway serves the needs of southern Zaire more than those of Angola. The country is more vulnerable from the north than from the east. The loss of the oil production of Cabinda could be a severe blow, and the 1961 revolt showed the vulnerability of northern farms, especially those producing the coffee crop. It is not surprising therefore that the Cuban troops stationed in Angola, the ace in the MPLA hand, are deployed to guard the key economic installations rather than hold land without strategic significance. The defensive line formed by the Cubans, roughly along the 15th parallel between Lubango and Menongue, marks the division between the war zone and the relatively undisturbed land behind it. The southern provinces have been devastated by the war; peace would transform the economic potential of the region, since the irrigation and hydroelectric projects on the Cunene river held up by the war would be a major resource for both Angola and northern Namibia. In the last years under the Portuguese Angola began a dramatic economic development; in the years of civil war since then progress has been at a much slower pace. Peace in the south is the key to future advance.

Mozambique

In the four centuries or so of Portuguese rule, Mozambique was seen as having only two real assets. The first was manpower. Slaves from Mozambique had been prime merchandise in the trade to the southern states of America, Brazil, and the Far East; after the suppression of the trade in the later nineteenth century, Mozambique supplied much of the labour for the Rand mines in South Africa. A railway was built between Johannesburg and Lourenço Marques (Maputo), which opened in 1895, principally to take the workers to the diggings. The prosperity of the port of Lourenço Marques was built on the steady flow of trade from the Rand and from the Transvaal for export. As Lourenço Marques became the coastal terminus for the Rand, so Beira to the north became the port for landlocked central Africa. A railway network was built linking the expanding industries and agriculture to the outside. The British rather than Portuguese built the railways in Mozambique, binding Bulawayo to Lourenço Marques, and the lands south of the Zambezi via Salisbury and Umtali to Beira. Thus, by the end of the nineteenth century the other asset of Mozambique was simply location: the nearest outlets to the sea for the mines and farms of southern Africa.

The colony made little sense as a unified state. Her economy was divided up between three great trading companies: by 1900, they controlled almost two-thirds of the area of Mozambique and were virtually sovereign powers within their domain. The inheritance of this tradition of divided control is that each part of Mozambique has developed on separate and distinct lines, both economically and socially. The capital is at Maputo in the far south; the commercial centre was at Beira in the centre. The provinces north of Beira – Niassa, Cabo Delgado, and Mozambique – were largely ignored. They had no great economic value, and a small population. It was an area shunned by ambitious Portuguese officials. Far distant from the centres of power, they were out of sight and out of mind. In part this was the result of poor communications. The roads in the north followed the coastal plain. There was no direct rail link to the north: a rail parcel from Lourenço Marques travelled up to Salisbury, back across to Beira, traversed Mozambique once more to

Blantyre in Nyasaland (now Malawi), and only then ran across to the Mozambique coast south of Port Amelia. Inland, there were only a few earth roads.

The best and most productive part of Mozambique lies in the south and centre of the country: the north is hillier and covered with rough grassland, rather than the lush vegetation of the southern provinces. The company which had the northern concession failed to make anything of it, and had its rights withdrawn in 1929. Thereafter, it languished. It was precisely in this neglected border region with Tanzania that social unrest grew during the late 1950s, culminating in a massacre of 500 peasants by police in the town of Mueda, in the hills a little to the south of the Tanzanian border. It provided a perfect base in which the Mozambique Liberation Front (FRELIMO) movement (founded in Dar es Salaam in 1962) could organise guerrilla warfare against the Portuguese. The lack of paved roads made land mines a characteristic weapon of the war in Mozambique. They were buried just under the surface of the earth roads and tracks, and either left to explode when the first vehicle passed over them, or used in association with an ambush. The main FRELIMO base was located at Nachingwea, just on the Tanzanian side of the border, and quite small guerrilla forces quickly established complete control of the border region shortly after operations began in 1964. By April 1971, they controlled almost all the countryside north of the Montepuez river. But they failed to take any of the coastal towns, linked by road and by air to the cities of the south. Cabo Delgado province around Mueda was the first 'liberated zone', followed by Niassa, but they failed to make any significant impact on Vila Cabral, the provincial capital of Cabo Delgado. Nor did they succeed at any point in the war in halting the building of the Cabora Bassa Dam, a huge hydroelectric project and the only target of real significance north of the oil pipeline which ran from Beira to Rhodesia.

The advance into Tete province, where Cabora Bassa was located, had, however, considerable strategic significance. Until 1972, the threat was a fairly marginal one. The guerrillas had had an effect on communications and some impact on agriculture, but they were still an acceptable irritant. The extension of the war to Tete province, bordering on Rhodesia, gave the Zimbabwean nationalists a base close to the most important regions of Rhodesia, and one which was relatively secure. By August 1973 guerrillas were launching regular attacks on Vila Paiva de Andrada, and infiltrators were working around Vila Pery, on the crucial Beira–Umtali–Salisbury railway line. When in January 1974 the first attacks were launched on the rail link, and on the oil pipeline which runs close to it, the strategic initiative passed decisively to the guerrillas. The 20th parallel marks the division, more or less, between northern and southern Mozambique, between the grasslands of the north and the much more profuse woodlands of the south. With the guerrillas pushing across the railway into Manica e Sofala province, and threatening to isolate Beira by cutting the main road to the south, the war quickly became unwinnable in the eyes of public opinion in Portugal. The revolution in Lisbon, which lead to the winding-up of the African empire, gave victory to FRELIMO before they had had to fight a serious battle to secure it. The capture of the south would have posed a very different problem.

Even before the final Portuguese collapse, opposition was growing to the nationalist movement. A counter-guerrilla force was built up in the Serra da Gorongosa, inland from Beira, which quickly became adept at sabotaging the FRELIMO forces. And the support for the nationalists was much less enthusiastic in the south than in the north, partly for tribal reasons, and partly because the south was inextricably tied up with the South African economy. The pattern of events since the independence of Zimbabwe shows how the advantages of the terrain work against any central government in Mozambique. Where FRELIMO mounted a guerrilla war from the sanctuary of Tanzania, the RENAMO forces opposed to the new nationalist regime were supplied from South Africa. Where FRELIMO had considerable popular support in the north, so the counter-revolution has considerable support in the south. And in both campaigns, the oil/rail link to Beira has been the key strategic issue, as well as the oil storage resources in Beira itself. Even more vulnerable were the pylons and power distribution lines which ran south from Cabora Bassa. By 1985, not one of the power networks was operating properly, and Mozambique, which had been earning hard currency from selling power to South Africa, lost a major source of revenue.

At the time of independence it was seriously suggested within the liberation movement that the capital should be moved from Lourenço Marques, renamed Maputo, to Beira. It was turned down on political and symbolic grounds, but it would have made considerable strategic sense. The dangerous proximity of Maputo to South Africa has been demonstrated vividly by South African air and commando attacks on guerrilla bases in and around the capital.

The realities of Mozambique have not been changed by independence. The south still sends men to the mines in South Africa; Beira is still the vital channel into central Africa from the east; the countryside is still isolated and now, after famine, even more depopulated than before. The analogy with Vietnam, frequently made in

All the countries of southern Africa are locked together by both mutual interests and antagonisms. The balance of power changes constantly, as all participants use allies and surrogates to attack each other. In the space of a few months in 1985 South African-backed UNITA forces in Angola shifted from attacking deep into the heartland of Angola to being themselves forced back into their core zone, sustained only by South African support. In this context new equipment – Soviet ground attack aviation – can dramatically alter the tactical balance. The strategic issue is unchanged.

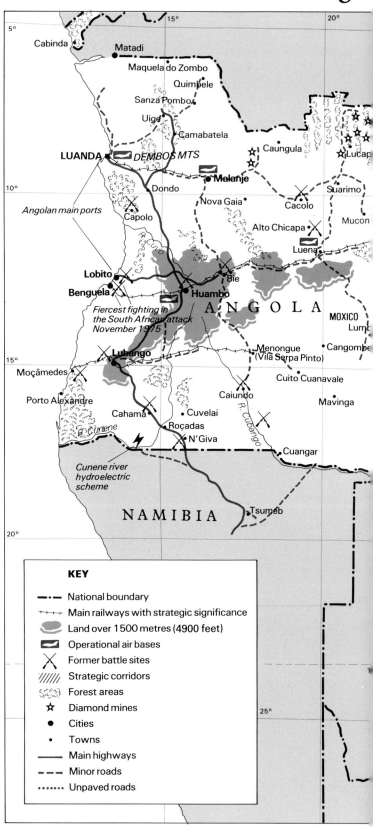

KEY

—·—·—	National boundary
++++++	Main railways with strategic significance
▬	Land over 1500 metres (4900 feet)
▭	Operational air bases
✕	Former battle sites
/////	Strategic corridors
🙜	Forest areas
☆	Diamond mines
●	Cities
•	Towns
——	Main highways
---	Minor roads
······	Unpaved roads

ozambique and Zimbabwe: The Limits of Independence

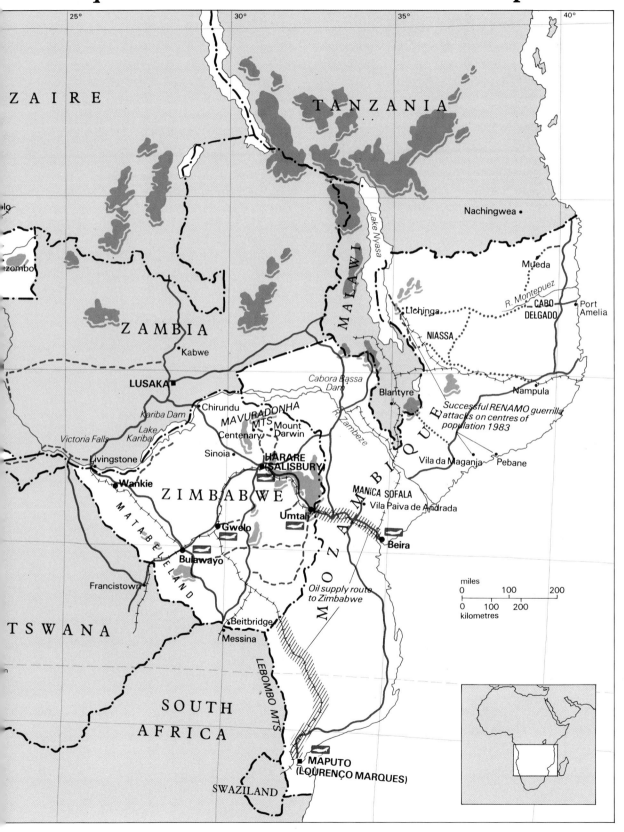

ZAIRE

TANZANIA

Nachingwea •

Mueda

zombo

ZAMBIA

Kabwe •

Lake Nyasa

MALAWI

Lichinga

R. Montepuez

CABO DELGADO

Port Amelia

NIASSA

LUSAKA ■

Cabora Bassa Dam

Blantyre

Nampula •

Chirundu •

Kariba Dam

MAVURADONHA MTS

Mount Darwin

Centenary •

Successful RENAMO guerrilla attacks on centres of population 1983

Victoria Falls

Lake Kariba

Sinoia •

R. Zambeze

Livingstone •

HARARE SALISBURY

Vila da Maganja •

Pebane •

Wankie

ZIMBABWE

MANICA SOFALA

Umtali

Vila Paiva de Andrada

Gwelo

MATABELELAND

MOZAMBIQUE

Beira

Bulawayo

Francistown •

Oil supply route to Zimbabwe

miles
0   100   200

0   100   200
kilometres

TSWANA

Beitbridge
Messina

LEBOMBO MTS

SOUTH
AFRICA

MAPUTO
(LOURENÇO MARQUES)

SWAZILAND

the last stages of Portuguese occupation, is an apt one, because there is a geographical and social parallel. The north and the south are virtually two countries, not one, and their unity, as in so much of Africa, is the product of European governments drawing lines on the map. The difference is that Mozambique exists in the shadow of much stronger and richer states, and consequently remains, and will remain, their client.

Zimbabwe

The lands between the northern border of South Africa and the Zambezi river were taken over by the British South Africa Company in the hope that they would produce gold in vast quantities. They did not; nor did they have the huge copper reserves of the lands just north of the Zambezi, which became Northern Rhodesia (now Zambia). Lack of one dominating and profitable resource may have disappointed the mining men, but it forced Southern Rhodesia (Zimbabwe) to develop a flexible and balanced economy. Cash crops such as tobacco, energy from the coal mines at Wankie, cattle raising (which flourished in country outside the region affected by the deadly 'rinderpest'), and many mining and manufacturing enterprises made the Rhodesian economy closer to that of South Africa than to that of its neighbours to the north.

Although the economies of Northern and Southern Rhodesia were closely linked, with the output of the northern Copper Belt travelling south on the railway to the coast, and the coal from Wankie powering the mines north of the Zambezi, all Southern Rhodesia's effective linkages were with the south. The best roads ran south and south-west; the Zambezi was only bridged at Victoria Falls, and Chirundu. For the rest of its length, the whole north-

ern boundary of Southern Rhodesia, it was both a commercial and a strategic barrier. It was the only clearly defined natural frontier which the country possessed. The boundary with Mozambique to the east lay beyond the Zambezi escarpment, in an ill-defined and sparsely populated area of dense bush and scrub. The division between Bechuanaland (now Botswana) and Southern Rhodesia was merely a matter of cartographic and political convenience: in the space of sixty years it had shifted backwards and forwards, sometimes running through small villages, sometimes bypassing them. On the ground, it was a vast area of near desert with few roads and little to relieve the dreary flatness. The same terrain continued further south along the boundary with South Africa until Mozambique, South Africa and Southern Rhodesia all met in the foothills of the Lebombo mountains.

The greatest strength of Southern Rhodesia was not her strategic geography, but the resilience of her economy. In 1963 it was put to the test. A government dedicated to permanent white supremacy was elected in Southern Rhodesia, and after seemingly endless arguments with the British Government, which sought to protect the interests of the majority black population, ended the diplomatic debate by declaring UDI. This unilateral declaration of independence not only added a new word to the vocabulary of statesmanship, but was the first major use of economic warfare since the Second World War. Britain and the United Nations declared the new rebel state of Rhodesia to be a pariah, and economic sanctions were to be applied by all member states of the UN. The British Prime Minister declared that Rhodesia would be brought to her knees in 'weeks rather than months'. Sanctions failed partly because they were tacitly or directly disregarded by all the principal parties. The oil pipeline from Rhodesia to

Beira continued to operate: the Portuguese wanted to support the rebels, and the British, who hoped to bring them back to settlement talks, preferred not to sever the jugular vein. The Rhodesian economy was reorientated from a leaning towards South Africa to a total dependence. The Zambezi frontier was closed, and Northern Rhodesia, now the black state of Zambia, became the principal base for attacks on the rebellion.

The northern and western frontiers were defended by broadly similar means. South Africa provided technical support and trained manpower from the outset, garrisoning the key points along the Zambezi. River patrols were organised, and a rudimentary form of electronic surveillance was complemented by an elaborate intelligence network run by the Rhodesian police. It was remarkably effective. Guerrillas tried to infiltrate across the river close to the Victoria Falls, but all were intercepted by the defending forces. One group made it as far as the outskirts of Wankie in July 1967, where they were surrounded and all killed. The focus of attention shifted further along the Zambezi to Lake Kariba and beyond, to the boundary with Mozambique. But even there only a few guerrillas managed to penetrate the security net. The northern frontier held. The group organising the attacks from Zambia, the Zimbabwe African People's Union (ZAPU), led by the dominating figure of Zimbabwean black nationalism, Joshua Nkomo, tried to open a second front along the long frontier with Botswana. This made both political and strategic sense. The area on the Rhodesian side of the frontier was known as Matabeleland, where Nkomo had much of his personal following, and attacks across the frontier would threaten the key industrial zone around Bulawayo as well as the crucial road and rail links to South Africa.

In the north, protected by the Zambezi,

the Rhodesians played a waiting game, and intercepted the guerrillas as they crossed the river. But in the south, where the whole frontier was easy to cross, they turned to the offensive. Regular attacks were launched against the ZAPU command structure inside Botswana, and informers were infiltrated into the training camps and the resistance movement inside Rhodesia. Any successful guerrilla groups were ruthlessly suppressed by combined South African and Rhodesian operational groups. In both west and north, a massive intelligence effort combined with powerful and well-directed attack groups were used to keep the enemy at bay.

In both areas the advantage of the terrain lay with the defenders. There was very little cover, and all the African villages were separate and easily supervised. The eastern frontier was quite different. The many rivers and streams which flowed down the escarpment in the wet season broke up the ground and provided good cover. The dense bush made aerial reconnaissance more difficult, and paradoxically, because much of the land beyond the poor frontier area had been cleared for European settlement, it was harder to use the African villages as an (unwilling) intelligence network. There was also remarkable complacency. The very success of the security operations against the ZAPU guerrillas in the north and west led the authorities to leave the eastern frontier only lightly guarded. The Zimbabwe African National Union (ZANU) guerrilla groups followed the Chinese model of warfare, and spent many months invisibly consolidating their position in the hills north of the white farms of north-east Rhodesia. Here the ground favoured the guerrilla rather than the defender. The Mavuradonha mountains were the highest point in a chain of hills which ran down to the capital, Salisbury (now Harare), and beyond. It was not the economic heartland of Rhodesia, but it was, politically, a most vulnerable point. The defenders reacted with new tactics. Helicopters and counter-strike forces were based on Centenary and Mount Darwin; on the ground, wide-spread use was made of counter-guerrillas and small reconnaissance groups. From early 1974, they also attacked ZANU bases in Zambia and Mozambique, both by bombing and by commando assaults. As FRELIMO took over more and more of Mozambique, the area of guerrilla in-filtration extended gradually southwards, until it extended over the whole of the eastern frontier. The oil pipeline from Beira, and the oil tanker trains from Lourenço Marques came under attack.

The Rhodesians were handicapped by shortages of manpower and aircraft suit-able for close support and reconnaissance. More and more operations after 1975 were mounted against ZANU bases deep in Mozambique, as well as some spectacular attacks against the ZAPU commanders in the heart of the Zambian capital, Lusaka, and in Francistown in Botswana. But these operations were a confession of strategic failure. The Rhodesians could not prevent infiltration over the long eastern border as they could in the west and north: they could not know where to strike. Oper-ations were mounted against the main training camps: the guerrillas split their forces among smaller camps, or into bases heavily defended by FRELIMO regulars. Attacks were launched against the railways and the main roads. The guerrillas moved along the back roads. And they continued to move into Rhodesia in increasing num-bers so that by 1978 they dominated almost half the country.

It was the threat of withdrawal of South African support rather than military defeat which forced the Rhodesian government to new negotiations in 1979. They could not prevent the inflow of guerrillas, but they continued to hold all the cities and the industrial/mining heartland. The war was still at a stage where ZANU ruled by night and the Rhodesians by day, and the Rhodesian army was still capable of defeat-ing the conventional invasion planned by ZAPU via Victoria Falls and Chirundu but never executed. But if the lifeline to the south were severed, Rhodesia could no longer remain viable. When the black government under Robert Mugabe took power in 1980, the same realities prevailed. The anti-South African rhetoric dimi-nished, and Zimbabwe, as Rhodesia had become, did not form a base for penetra-tion by black South African nationalists. Instead, Zimbabwe faced a guerrilla movement in Matabeleland supported by South Africa, who neatly exploited tribal and political differences within the black nationalist movement.

Zimbabwe is vulnerable, by her geo-graphy, on all frontiers except the Zam-bezi to the north. Security depends on the friendship or enmity of her neighbours and, crucially, on the regional Great Power to the south. From its first colonis-ation, Southern Rhodesia/Rhodesia/ Zim-babwe was conceived as a northern exten-sion of the Rand and the mining economy of the south: history has not altered that basic dependence.

21 South Africa and Namibia: Flaws in the Carapace

There are two equally valid ways of looking at southern Africa. In the first, the dominant image of the continent is the flat-topped mountain which towers 3,000 feet above Cape Town. Although it seems to soar up from the small coastal plain, its summit is lower than much of the vast high plateau which makes up the major part of southern Africa. This is high, dry, mostly flat country, desert to the west and hills and mountains to the east. The other way of seeing southern Africa is down the continent looking south. Beyond the high plains and the small coastal fringe is a seemingly infinite ocean; the nearest land is Antarctica to the south, South America to the west and Australia due east. In this perspective view, southern Africa is a promontary jutting out into the ocean, dominating half the sea lanes of the world. From the underground communications complex at Silvermine by Cape Town it is possible to monitor all the shipping and air movements in an arc stretching from North Africa, via South America and Antarctica, to the Bay of Bengal.

The uniting factor in the two very different strategic concerns is distance. The land and coastal frontiers of South Africa and her neighbouring states are enormously elongated. Natural boundaries, except for a few great rivers and the occasional mountain range, are infrequent. The boundary between Botswana and Zimbabwe, for want of any better line of division, had to be drawn in 1899 to run down the centre of a highway, splitting villages in two. (It has since been moved deeper into Botswana.) The same electronic technology which can sweep the seas from Cape Town is much less effective on the great inland areas of southern Africa, where there is too much life, human and

animal, that confuses the picture. All these theoretical concerns would not matter much if the political context of southern Africa was tranquil. It is not. In the space of the last decade, since the Portuguese abandoned their historic role in Angola and Mozambique in 1975, and Zimbabwe was created out of the former white bastion of Rhodesia in 1980, the strategic position in southern Africa has been drawn in much stronger primary colours. At the southern tip of the continent, coloured white, is the republic of South Africa, to the north, coloured black, the 'front line' states, dedicated in theory and by alliance to the overthrow of the white *laager*. The reality is much greyer and more uncertain. While the enmity between the white and black states is undiminished, both Zimbabwe and Mozambique depend economically on South Africa, and both are vulnerable to guerrilla campaigns funded and supported from the south.

War on the high plateau has been altered in its range and scope by modern technology, not always for the better. South Africa divides neatly into two segments. East of a line running north from Port Elizabeth (approximately 26° of longitude) is the best land, the bulk of the population, and almost the whole of the road network. Cape Town is almost an island, isolated beyond the Great Karroo range. In the area between Pretoria and the border with Zimbabwe, the country again becomes rougher, with fewer roads, and begins to drop down to the coastal plain of Mozambique. This is the area – the North Transvaal – where the last stages of the Boer War were fought in 1901–2, and where the war against infiltration of guerrillas is being waged at the moment. The British technique at the turn of the century was to break up the country into sections, using long barbed wire fences and simple block-houses to control the land in between. The idea was that the Boer *kommandos* would be corralled by the fences, or would, at the very least, betray their movements where they cut the fences. British field intelligence would then plot their routes, and send a flying column out in pursuit. The Boer leader, De Wet, scornfully described it as a blockhead rather than a blockhouse policy, and pointed out that it absorbed large resources both of money and man-power, without effectively inhibiting the *kommandos*. In the 1980s the British role is being played by the Afrikaner descendants of the *kommandos*. Their approach is more sophisticated, but essentially the same.

The fences of the 1980s are invisible-electronic rather than tensile steel, but the principal gain, as in the past, is intelligence. The blockhouses have been replaced by trained reservists, fit young farmers required to maintain a radio net reporting all movements to a central control point by regular transmissions: each farmer has a set area to survey. The flying column is now more likely to be transported by helicopter, or armoured personnel carrier, than on horseback. But helicopters are noisy, and armoured vehicles more easily bogged down than a horse or a man on foot. In many cases, close surveillance requires the trapping skills and the element of surprise which marked the most successful anti-guerrilla operations of the Boer War. But the extent of the ground to be covered has made it impossible to block all points of access, especially in the eastern Transvaal where the Kruger National Park provides almost an open border with Mozambique. The temporary solution to the guerrilla problem is to cut off their attacks at source. The front line states have been threatened with immediate reprisals if their territory is used for infiltration, and South African forces have

already attacked guerrilla bases deep in Mozambique. The fruit of this tough policy was a reluctant agreement between Mozambique and South Africa in 1984: Botswana, Lesotho, and now Zimbabwe have already been cowed.

The plain fact is that no combination of surrounding nations can muster even a small fraction of South Africa's military power. The real danger is that even a limited breach in the aura of invincibility might upset the fragile political balance within South Africa. In the same way that the frontier policy is designed to filter out all threats before they can reach the centres of population, internal policy too has a strategic logic to it. All the African townships are designed for ease of control. Where possible they are built on low ground, and with a pattern of access roads which allows rapid deployment of police and army vehicles. All 'unofficial' settlements are being systematically uprooted, and the policy of transferring as much as possible of the urban black population to the 'black homelands', scattered on the fringes of the republic, is intended to reduce the possibility of subversion. Effective internal control in the core area east of an arc drawn from Cape Town–Kimberley–Johannesburg is made much easier by efficient surveillance on the system of main roads, but these controls cannot operate in the crowded conditions of the cities and the townships. It is a system of 'social defence-in-depth', beginning with the settler-soldiers of the outlying regions, through the movement control system of observation and pass books, to political attempts to fragment the non-white opposition. The present danger is evident in the long war for Namibia (South-West Africa), and South African involvement in Angola.

In military terms, South Africa is winning in the war for Namibia, and in doing so is demonstrating the type of forward strategy implied in her threatening gestures towards Mozambique and Zimbabwe. It involves air raids over much of southern Angola, support for internal rebel movements (UNITA) in Angola, and the capacity to intervene in considerable force on the ground as necessary. Within Namibia itself the war has been waged on classic counter-insurgency lines. But this is an unpopular campaign waged very much at the farthest extremity of South African control. The principal means of supply is along a corridor from Upington to Windhoek, which contains the original railway and a highway built alongside it, while the main supply route to the Caprivi Strip and the Zambezi runs through Botswana, along a new road from Francistown to Kazungula. The Kalahari provides a block which is difficult to traverse, and all the roads across it are unsuitable for anything except light traffic. The terrain in much of Namibia is unfriendly towards tracked vehicles, and the South African army relies principally on wheeled rather than tracked armoured vehicles. The value of Namibia is economic as well as strategic, with large mineral deposits on the 'hard veldt', which shows as higher ground on the maps; the output of diamonds from the south is huge. But despite the supply problem, much of the success in the war can be attributed to the factor of distance. Windhoek is further from Johannesburg than Harare, the capital of Zimbabwe, and it is almost entirely cut off from prying eyes by an extensive security zone. It is much easier and more politically acceptable to wage this style of war on the periphery rather than close to the heartland. A forward strategy in Zimbabwe or Mozambique is perhaps technically easier, given better communications, but it is very close to home.

The strategic logic of southern Africa is that the Republic of South Africa needs to dominate the whole area to the line of the Zambezi and its imaginary extension to the west. Until the collapse of Portugal and the white regime in Rhodesia/Zimbabwe, that need was reflected on the ground, with a bloc of buffer states (in South African eyes) protecting the core. That logic has not altered: South Africa still needs to dominate the high plateau, and has the military capacity to do so. The war of confrontation being fought in Namibia and southern Angola is part of that logic. Beyond the economic advantages of possessing Namibian resources, which are considerable, and the advantages of at least a buffer zone to the west of the Republic, it also points to the devastating consequences which would befall Mozambique and Zimbabwe if they were to confront South Africa. Since 1978, when the South African government took powers which allowed it to establish a six mile security zone along the whole of the 1,300 mile border, the central preoccupation of strategic thinking has been the prevention of infiltration: the lessons of the guerrilla war in Zimbabwe were well learned. On this principle, the dangers in the east and centre, of saboteurs entering through Zimbabwe, Mozambique, and Botswana, take precedence over the much more open conflict in Namibia and southern Angola. South Africa could reach a settlement in Namibia, and improve security by shortening her frontier considerably. Then the Kalahari would become a nuisance to an invader rather than a blockage in the logistic chain feeding the troops in the north. Domination can be achieved by means other than occupation. The crude confrontation in Namibia/Angola is already being replaced by an attempt to provide a permanent solution to the problem posed by the 'loss' of Mozambique, Angola, and Rhodesia/Zimbabwe. That solution consists of a firm and defensible frontier for the republic, and a willingness to strike against any attempt to

South Africa's problem is war on too many fronts. There is a draining conflict for the protection of Namibia, battles to preserve an economy over-reliant on the gold price, a constant need to police an increasingly unworkable racial policy, and a never-ending struggle to preserve contacts – personal and commercial – with an increasingly hostile outside world. Fighting on all fronts, she is winning on none; problems which are containable in isolation become insuperable in combination. The root cause is the ceaselessly rising tide of internal violence, which calls into question the capacity and wisdom of the political leadership. It is also the most difficult problem to cure.

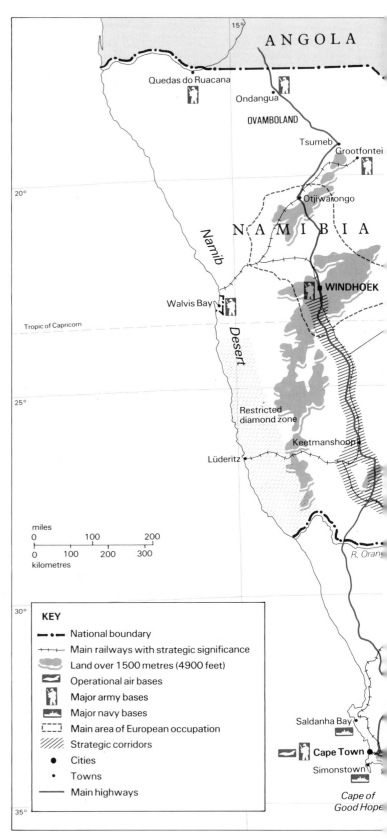

15°

ANGOLA

Quedas do Ruacana

Ondangua

OVAMBOLAND

Tsumeb
Grootfontei

20°

Otjiwarongo

N A M I B I A

Namib

WINDHOEK

Walvis Bay

Tropic of Capricorn

Desert

25°

Restricted
diamond zone

Keetmanshoop

Lüderitz

miles
0   100   200

0   100   200   300
kilometres

30°

R. Orang

KEY

National boundary
Main railways with strategic significance
Land over 1 500 metres (4900 feet)
Operational air bases
Major army bases
Major navy bases
Main area of European occupation
Strategic corridors
Cities
Towns
Main highways

Saldanha Bay

Cape Town

Simonstown

Cape of
Good Hope

35°

South Africa and Namibia: Flaws in the Carapace

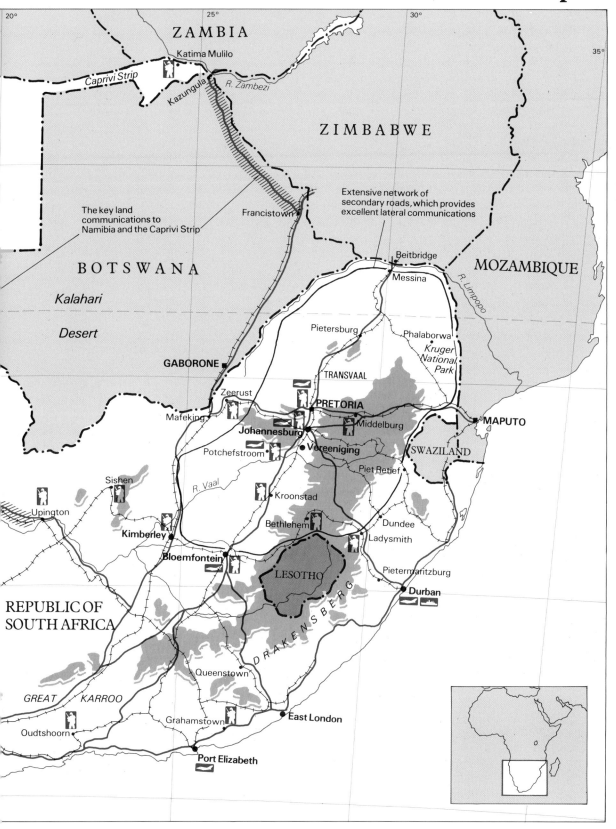

ZAMBIA

Katima Mulilo

Caprivi Strip

Kazungula

R. Zambezi

ZIMBABWE

The key land
communications to
Namibia and the Caprivi Strip

Francistown

Extensive network of
secondary roads, which provides
excellent lateral communications

Beitbridge

Messina

MOZAMBIQUE

B O T S W A N A

Kalahari

Desert

R. Limpopo

Pietersburg

Phalaborwa

Kruger
National
Park

GABORONE

TRANSVAAL

Zeerust

PRETORIA

Mafeking

Middelburg

MAPUTO

Johannesburg

Potchefstroom

Vereeniging

SWAZILAND

Piet Retief

Sishen

R. Vaal

Kroonstad

Upington

Dundee

Bethlehem

Ladysmith

Kimberley

Pietermaritzburg

Bloemfontein

LESOTHO

Durban

REPUBLIC OF
SOUTH AFRICA

D R A K E N S B E R G

Queenstown

GREAT   KARROO

Grahamstown

East London

Oudtshoorn

Port Elizabeth

use neighbouring states as a sanctuary for African revolutionary fighters. Devotees of the British Empire in India will recognise it as merely a new variant of the 'North-West Frontier' approach to defending the indefensible.

Namibia

Few colonies can have seemed less attractive to the German traders who established German South-West Africa in 1884. Barren waste and scrub inland, desert along the coast, the initial significance of the colony was strategic rather than purely economic. South-West Africa was a foothold in southern Africa, a presence on the developing sea lanes around the Cape of Good Hope. The three decades of German rule were marked by wars of extermination waged against the Herero tribes of the inland areas, and the only bright spot was the discovery of rich diamond fields in 1908. The climate on the higher ground inland from the coast was more suitable for Europeans; the natives were killed or expelled and the capital, Windhoek, established. By the end of the First World War, the country had settled into its present economic shape. The central core around Windhoek is the most productive and attractive part of the country; to the south, vast herds of sheep are raised on the poor ground bounded by the coastal Namib desert to the west and the Kalahari desert to the east. The high ground is the best land. To the north and along the border with Angola, Europeans have made few attempts at settlement. The Ovimbundu peoples, who dominate much of Angola, occupy most of northern Namibia. Neither the Germans, nor the South Africans, who took up 'trusteeship' of Namibia in 1915, have done much to disturb them.

In 1966, the South African trusteeship was revoked by the United Nations, acting as the successor of the old League of Nations which had granted it. The South African government could not accept the prospect of a hostile black government in Namibia, and refused to withdraw. Immediate steps were taken to strengthen South African control. The garrison was increased, especially after 1971 when the International Court of Justice finally declared the South African occupation unlawful. The South-West African People's Organisation (SWAPO) was first formed in 1959, and after 1966 turned to a rather ineffective guerrilla warfare, infiltrating the Caprivi Strip (the narrow strip of land which gave Namibia an outlet on to the Zambezi) from Zambia. The South Africans easily defeated the guerrillas and used the pretext of the invasion to round up the political leadership of the movement in Windhoek late in 1968. The Caprivi Strip was reinforced with new bases and, because the border with Zambia was so short, it was easy to defend. The remnants of SWAPO retreated into a shadowy existence in Zambia and Botswana, while the South Africans pushed ahead with a comprehensive 'apartheid' structure for Namibian society.

The strategic situation was transformed by the collapse of the Portuguese in Angola in 1975. The UNITA nationalist group in southern Angola was, like SWAPO, mostly composed of Ovimbundu, whose traditional lands straddled the border. Although the turmoil of Angolan revolution eventually brought UNITA into an alliance with South Africa, in the two years before 1975 SWAPO was able to build up a strong base in the lands on the Angolan side of the border. Their position was made even stronger after the Portuguese withdrawal in 1975. A guerrilla movement striking anywhere along the lengthy border was impossible to contain in the same way as the early incursions into the Caprivi Strip. SWAPO achieved some striking successes in the north, and even began to send sabotage and assassination groups into the white areas of the centre and south. The South African response was to take the war deep into southern Angola, striking at the SWAPO bases from the air and on the ground. Furthermore, by reaching an agreement with UNITA against the MPLA, the victor in the civil war within Angola, it managed to remove the SWAPO presence from the eastern area of the border.

The balance of forces should have been strongly in South Africa's favour, except for the presence of a large and well equipped Cuban contingent acting to support the MPLA government in Luanda. Cuba was fighting a war at the end of a long supply line across the Atlantic, but South Africa was also handicapped by geography. Communications with Namibia were either along the railway which ran up through Upington, or along the road from Cape Town. Most of the supplies were shipped along the main road which ran close to the railway, and passed through Windhoek to the northern operational areas. The Caprivi Strip was largely supplied along the road which ran through Botswana from Francistown to Kazungula. The Kalahari desert, which occupied most of the eastern border of Namibia was, for all practical purposes, impenetrable. Air supply was correspondingly very important, especially for the outlying posts in the north which were inaccessible by road; the army bases at Ondangua in Ovamboland and Katima Mulilo at the eastern end of the Caprivi Strip were the main staging points for the airlift.

To date, South Africa has won the war for Namibia, and the forward zone in southern Angola. Attacks on the SWAPO bases have been costly, especially the battles for the strategic centres of Caiundo, Cuvelai, Lubango and Cahama. But what the South Africans cannot cope with is the change in the tactical balance which comes with the changing seasons. In the spring the dry lands of the border become lush with vegetation, while the spring rain and low cloud makes aerial surveillance much more difficult. This is the time of year when the guerrillas filter across the border, and try to work their way through the defensive zone set up in Ovamboland. The defence line is patchy, which is why the South Africans have preferred to break up the SWAPO concentrations inside Angola. The security of the frontier depends more on the precarious balance of forces in the Angolan civil war than on the strength of South African arms. Almost all the eastern frontier is effectively secured by the presence of the UNITA army; the South Africans concentrate their attention on the zone west of Cuangar. Any change in the Angolan situation which meant that the South African Defence Force had to defend the whole length of the frontier could transform the strategic position.

AMERICAS

22 North America

The territory of the modern United States and of Canada was, in the century between the Seven Years and the American Civil Wars (1756–1865), an arena of keen strategic conflict, both external and domestic, in which the key events turned on possession or dominance of a cluster of geographical features: in the years of conflict between France and Britain (the latter aided by its colonists but later opposed by those who became independent Americans), the valleys of the Hudson and St Lawrence rivers, together with Lakes Erie and Ontario, the waters and estuaries of Chesapeake Bay, and the delta of the Mississippi. During the American Civil War, the delta and Chesapeake Bay retained their great strategic importance, but control of the Mississippi itself became a crucial strategic concern, together with that of the Chattanooga–Atlanta gap in the Allegheny mountain chain and of the more northerly Shenandoah Valley.

Since the end of the Civil War, however, internal geographic features have lost their strategic significance, so complete is the military dominance that the United States have established over their own land mass

and surroundings, and so amiable are the relations that prevail between them and neighbouring Canada. External geographic factors, always important in determining the context in which North America has conducted its relations with Europe and Asia, have grown greatly in importance. The first of these is that of oceanic isolation. The North American continent is separated from Europe by 3,000 and from Asia by 4,000 miles of open sea. These expanses guarantee it a degree of immunity from external interference enjoyed by no other region of the world; during the nineteenth century this condition encouraged the government of the United States to proclaim a fixed policy both of disengagement from non-American affairs and of active hostility to foreign intervention in the western hemisphere. Known as the Monroe Doctrine (1823), it derived its force initially from the benevolent protection of the Royal Navy, London sharing Washington's judgment that the interests of the Anglo-Saxon Atlantic States were not served by the involvement of other powers in that oceanic area. After the rise of American

Two great oceans, a tranquil relationship with Canada, and a containable problem from the states to the south give the United States a sense of basic isolation and security. It is also a country which is almost completely self-reliant; faced with a loss of all external supply, the USA would 'come through'. No major war has been fought on her soil for more than a century, and she exercises influence by economic more than by military means. The problems of being a world power still run against many of the basically solitary impulses of the United States, and often produce seemingly bizarre shifts in policy. Isolation is both a strength and a weakness.

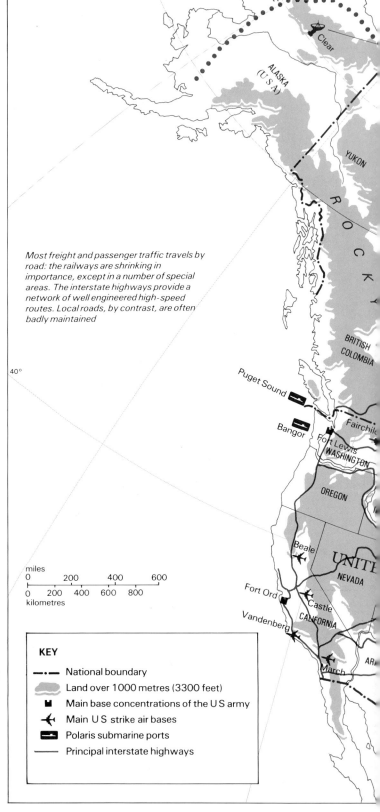

Most freight and passenger traffic travels by road: the railways are shrinking in importance, except in a number of special areas. The interstate highways provide a network of well engineered high-speed routes. Local roads, by contrast, are often badly maintained

miles

| 0 | | 200 | | 400 | | 600 |

| 0 | 200 | 400 | 600 | 800 |
kilometres

- ■ Cities with more than 1,000,000 people
- • Cities with more than 250,000 people

KEY

—·— National boundary

Land over 1000 metres (3300 feet)

■ Main base concentrations of the U S army

✈ Main U S strike air bases

Polaris submarine ports

—— Principal interstate highways

North America

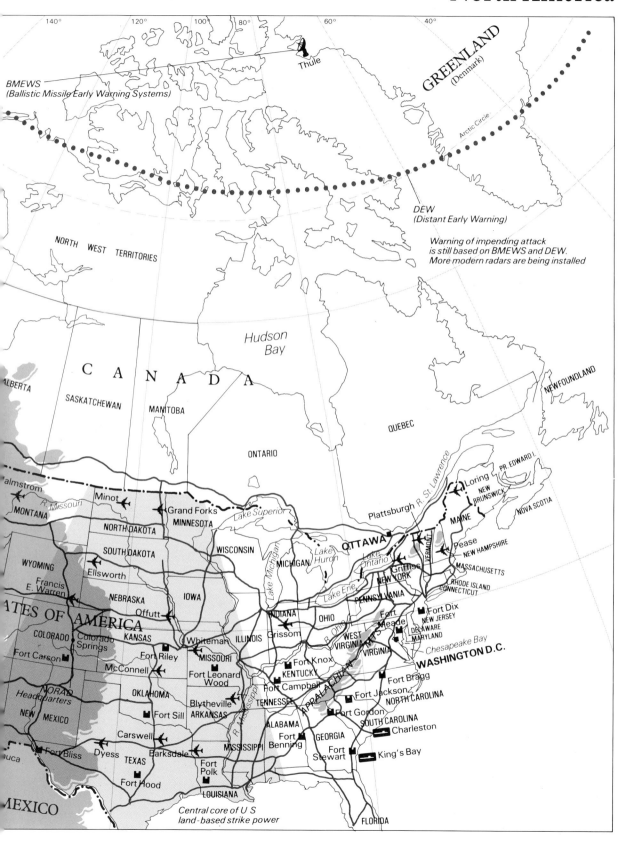

BMEWS
(Ballistic Missile Early Warning Systems)

GREENLAND
(Denmark)

Thule

Arctic Circle

DEW
(Distant Early Warning)

Warning of impending attack
is still based on BMEWS and DEW.
More modern radars are being installed

NORTH WEST TERRITORIES

Hudson
Bay

C A N A D A

ALBERTA

SASKATCHEWAN

MANITOBA

ONTARIO

QUEBEC

NEWFOUNDLAND

PR. EDWARD I.

NOVA SCOTIA

NEW BRUNSWICK

Loring

Plattsburgh   R. St. Lawrence

MAINE

Pease

NEW HAMPSHIRE

almstrom

R. Missouri

Minot

Grand Forks   Lake Superior

MONTANA

NORTH DAKOTA

MINNESOTA

WISCONSIN

Lake Michigan

Lake Huron

OTTAWA

Lake Ontario

Grimes

NEW YORK

VERMONT

MASSACHUSETTS

RHODE ISLAND

CONNECTICUT

WYOMING

SOUTH DAKOTA

Ellsworth

IOWA

MICHIGAN

Lake Erie

PENNSYLVANIA

Francis
E. Warren

NEBRASKA

INDIANA

OHIO

Fort
Meade

Fort Dix

NEW JERSEY

Offutt

WEST
VIRGINIA

DELAWARE

MARYLAND

ATES OF AMERICA

COLORADO   Colorado
            Springs

KANSAS

Whiteman   ILLINOIS

Grissom

VIRGINIA

Chesapeake Bay

WASHINGTON D.C.

Fort Carson

McConnell

Fort Riley

MISSOURI

R. Ohio

Fort Knox

KENTUCKY

Fort Bragg

NORAD
Headquarters

OKLAHOMA

Fort Leonard
Wood

Fort Campbell

APPALACHIAN

Fort Jackson

NORTH CAROLINA

NEW MEXICO

Fort Sill

Blytheville

ARKANSAS

TENNESSEE

R. Mississippi

Fort Gordon

SOUTH CAROLINA

Carswell

Charleston

uca

Fort Bliss

Dyess

Barksdale

MISSISSIPPI

ALABAMA

Fort
Benning

GEORGIA

King's Bay

TEXAS

Fort
Polk

Fort
Stewart

Fort Hood

LOUISIANA

MEXICO

Central core of U S
land-based strike power

FLORIDA

naval power in the 1890s, the United States were able to provide the required force to lend teeth to the Monroe Doctrine on their own account.

Neither in the First nor Second World Wars was the sovereign territory of the United States threatened by extra-hemispheric military action; neither was that of the Latin American republics over which the USA had cast the protective cloak of the Monroe Doctrine. America's Pacific possessions, protectorates and allies, Hawaii and the Philippines most notably, however, suffered Japanese attack in the Second World War; the Philippines underwent Japanese occupation for three years, and were liberated only by a major American amphibious effort. It was largely because of the consequences of this Japanese assault on its hemispheric interests that, after 1945, America abandoned its traditional posture of aloofness from non-hemispheric politics and embarked on its still prevailing policy of active involvement in the worldwide balance of power.

The oceanic factors retain, even in the nuclear age, the determining importance in the making of American strategy that they have had since the founding of the republic. The seas still protect America from threat of invasion; they have also been, since the adoption of a strong and then a 'two' (Pacific and Atlantic) navy policy in the period 1890–1920, the medium through which American power is transmitted. America has traditionally shunned the acquisition of overseas possessions for reasons of national ethos; some external territory was acquired none the less in the period 1890–1900, notably Hawaii and Puerto Rico. These, together with a chain of facilities leased from or made permanently available by the governments of Japan, Italy, Greece, Great Britain, the Philippines and other countries provide the United States Navy with

a system of support sufficient to sustain worldwide operations. It must be noted, however, that the development of the 'fifteen carrier group' navy under President Reagan's administration, and the attempt to establish its presence strongly in the central and north Indian Ocean, has been hampered by a lack of strategic 'reach'; despite the well-developed American practice of independent cruising and replenishment at sea, lack of bases in the most distant of the oceans has proved a restraint on capability in the region.

The navy and its supply ships provide most of the means through which America's large overseas army is supported. Traditionally, for isolationist and anti-imperial reasons, the United States has not maintained troops abroad (with exceptions in the Caribbean between the Wars). Since 1945, however, its victorious occupation armies in Europe and Asia have been transformed into detached garrisons, stationed on foreign soil by agreement or treaty; the most important concentrations are in West Germany (five divisions), South Korea (one division) and Japan (Okinawa – one marine division). A main achievement of President Reagan's defence policy has been to create a strong army intervention force (the Rapid Deployment Joint Task Force), with an associated tactical air arm, to supplement the power of the overseas garrisons and extend their reach. The force has exercised regularly in Egypt, Arabia and the Indian Ocean and will have a forward base in Oman; its main operating base is at Diego Garcia in British Indian Ocean Territory.

American isolationism has never meant disinvolvement from the affairs of Latin America, which, after a period of quietude in the immediate post-war period, are coming to have increasing strategic significance for the United States. The military importance of the Panama Canal, built by American effort on land acquired from the

Republic of Panama in 1903, has diminished since the defeat of Japan. But security in the Caribbean, where Russia has had an ally in Cuba since 1959, and in Central America, is of growing significance. The American defence establishment rightly fears that the Caribbean Islands might provide temptingly convenient air, sea and missile bases for foreign powers; the Cuban missile crisis of 1962, between the USA and the USSR, was provoked by precisely such a threat. In a broader sense, however, the whole of Central America is now viewed by Washington as a region of potential instability threatening the security of the southern United States. It is anxious to see the left-wing government in Nicaragua and the opponents of the government of El Salvador defeated; it is yet more anxious to see preserved the stability and prosperity of Mexico, illegal immigration from which country is now helping to transform the settled ethnic pattern in the United States.

America's overriding post-war strategic concern remains, however, in the realm of air – and now space – power. The ultimate guarantee of American security derives from the deployment of its 'triad' of submarines, aircraft and land-based intercontinental missiles, all armed with nuclear warheads. America's forty-one strategic submarines, of which some twenty-five are usually on station, operate in deep waters around the Soviet coasts (including the Arctic coast, where the ice-cap provides valuable protective cover), and at ranges of up to 4,000 miles from it. The Strategic Air Command, whose prin-

cipal equipment is the ageing but serviceable B-52 bomber, maintains main bases in the continental United States, and the Pacific island of Guam. The land-based missiles, of which the Minuteman remains the most numerous, are deployed in a chain of armoured silo complexes, of which the largest concentration is in the State of North Dakota.

Underpinning these strategic forces, and essential to their effective operation, is the largest and most complex military surveillance and communication system in the world. Many of its elements, both surveillance and communication, are now space-based, in stationary or orbiting satellites. The earliest of early-warning, against missile attack, for example, would now be provided by satellite-mounted sensors, capable of detecting missile ignition, news of which would be transmitted to North America Air Defence Command (Colorado Springs) via radio satellite. But the land-based warning system remains large and elaborate: its chief elements air stations in Greenland, Alaska and Yorkshire, the Distant Early Warning Line along the north Alaskan and Canadian coastline and eight coastal stations aligned to detect missile launchings in the Atlantic and Pacific.

Ultimately, therefore, America may be judged to remain a sort of island in the strategic world, extending its power through alliances and detached forces, but counting upon distance and time to protect it against serious and direct attack. Its geographic isolation is both its greatest strength and greatest weakness.

23 Central America

There is no more obvious strategic 'choke point' in the world than the narrow strip of land which joins North America to South America. All land traffic between north and south passes along a single traffic artery – the Pan-American Highway – as

Like angry scorpions, the small states of Central America have a capacity for social violence built into their structures. The pattern extends back to the days of Spanish rule and beyond: blood sacrifice has a long and ghastly history. The United States has superimposed its power on all these states in the past and continues to do so, but with only the most cursory interest in their history, and little understanding of their political heritage. In consequence, it has made many mistakes and will make more. In Nicaragua the fortunes of the CONTRA forces on the northern and southern border ebb and flow with the weight of the government attack. But in neither area can the insurgent threat be eradicated.

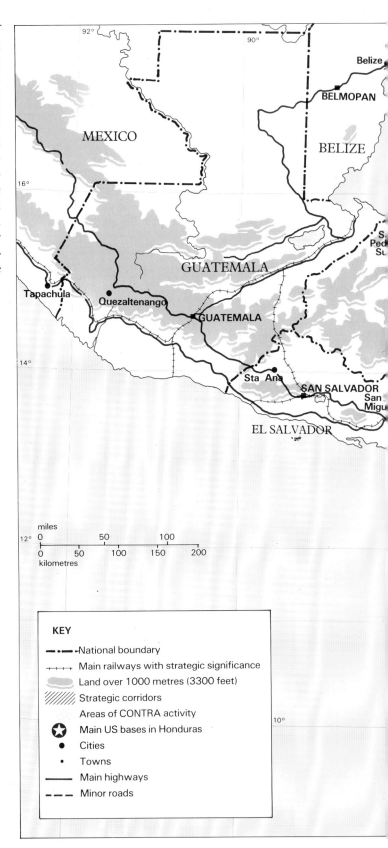

KEY

—·—·— National boundary

+++++ Main railways with strategic significance

Land over 1000 metres (3300 feet)

///// Strategic corridors

Areas of CONTRA activity

⭐ Main US bases in Honduras

● Cities

· Towns

—— Main highways

- - - Minor roads

Central America

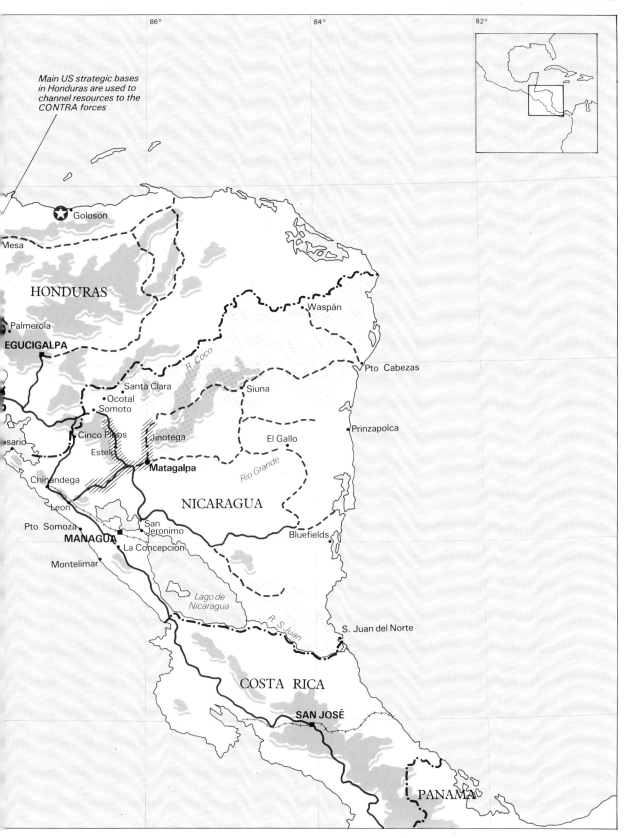

86° 84° 82°

Main US strategic bases in Honduras are used to channel resources to the CONTRA forces

Goloson

Mesa

HONDURAS

Palmerola

EGUCIGALPA

Santa Clara
Ocotal
Somoto

Cinco Pinos

sario

Esteli

Jinotega

Matagalpa

Chinandega

Leon

Pto Somoza

MANAGUA

La Concepcion

Montelimar

San Jeronimo

NICARAGUA

Waspán

R. Coco

Pto Cabezas

Siuna

Prinzapolca

El Gallo

Rio Grande

Bluefields

Lago de Nicaragua

R. S. Juan

S. Juan del Norte

COSTA RICA

SAN JOSÉ

PANAMA

there is no rail link; even more important is the east–west link provided by the Panama Canal. There is no convenient sea route between the Atlantic and the Pacific other than through the Canal, as the southern route via Cape Horn is difficult even for large ships and imposes a penal addition to the length of any journey. The use of the Canal still figures prominently in United States military thinking, although less in terms of troop movements and warships. There is now a careful balance preserved between Pacific- and Atlantic-based fleets, which means that each should be self-sustaining in the event of war, while men (being light and compressible) are ideal subjects for movement by air. What the Canal still provides is an invaluable short-cut for bulk transport, which will be essential for any sustained war effort.

The interest of the United States in the region is irreducible, although its outward shape has altered over the years. In 1903, the USA provided the support and leverage for the feeble independence movement in Panama to seize control from Colombia and to allow the Canal to be built. The treaty vested control of the Canal Zone in the USA, which maintained a garrison; the treaty of 1977–8 revised the arrangements to take account of Panamanian nationalist feeling. The new treaty only provided for the return of the Canal to Panama by 1999, while various emergency provisions allowed the USA to intervene if free access through the Canal seemed likely to be threatened. Beyond a direct strategic interest, the United States has a complex of financial and commercial interests in the region: the term 'banana republic' was coined of those states in Central America where the United Fruit Company dominated both the politics and the economy of these tiny societies. The USA has intervened militarily, removed governments and implanted others; Nicaragua in particular has suffered in this way throughout the twentieth century.

In the last two decades, new economic and political patterns have been imposed on this traditionally imperial role played by the USA in relation to her southern neighbours. Mexico and Ecuador have become major oil producers; Venezuela continues to produce on a huge scale. The structure of defensive pacts in the region, principally the Organisation of American States, has been weakened as individual states argued about boundaries and the allocation of natural resources. Most disruptive of all have been the tremors in the frozen social structures of the Central American republics. The extreme inequalities in El Salvador and Guatemala have generated violent unrest in the countryside on a huge scale. The armed forces of the republics have always proved adequate to control the towns and cities, but the control of the countryside has been seen as the responsibility of the landowners. In the marginal areas, on the frontiers, and in the highlands of El Salvador in particular, it has proved almost impossible to eradicate popularly based revolutionary movements. In the area around Chalatenango, and stretching north towards Metapan, the guerrilla core remains solid, while attacks are launched towards the principal cities – Santa Ana and San Salvador. El Salvador is densely populated throughout its lowland region, which makes the traditional type of search and destroy mission very costly in civilian lives – and unacceptable in terms of international public relations. The border with Honduras has become much tighter during 1984–5, but mainly because Honduras is unwilling to accept an inflow of Salvadorean citizens into her border regions. Illegal Salvadorean immigration during the 1960s was the prime cause of the war which broke out between El Salvador and her neighbour Honduras in 1969.

The interests of the United States require a collection of politically harmonious governments in all the small states in Central America. The reality is that many of the states in the region have long-standing grievances and boundary disputes with their neighbours. Nationalism is the dominant ethos of all the republics, and they distrust each other as much as outside powers. Guatemala has had governments dominated by the army since 1944, and the anti-communist credentials of the Guatemalan military leadership are beyond question. Yet the aid and military supplies from the United States are accepted not because the American line on regional solidarity has been absorbed, but because they serve short-term nationalist aims. The model for solidarity in the area was Nicaragua under the Somoza government, kept stable under Anastasio Somoza and his sons between 1934 and 1979. The defeat of the Somoza regime in 1979 and its replacement by an opposition inspired by the memory of Augusto Sandino, an enemy of the Somozas in the 1930s, dealt a double blow. It unlocked the increasingly fragile alliances in Central America, which were only held together by strong pressure from the United States, and it introduced the creeping peril of peasant revolution in the region. None of the existing societies could, in the estimate of the United States, absorb radical land reform, and preserve their stability. Costa Rica, which is aptly named, is secure, by contrast, simply because it does not have this fundamental social problem. Yet even Costa Rica has been drawn into the turmoil which has followed the revolution in Nicaragua.

Nicaragua has now equalled Cuba in the demonology of the United States as a wild, maverick force for international disruption, like Cuba in the early 1960s. The argument is not so much about arms supplied to guerrillas in El Salvador or the build-up by the Sandinistas, although these are convenient demonstrations of the evil intentions of the Nicaraguans. The very existence of the Nicaraguan revolution is seen as *essentially* destabilising, and encouraging, by force of example alone, local forces of disruption throughout the region.

Nicaragua is vulnerable because of her geography. There is a long coastline on both the Atlantic and the Pacific, and in the swamplands between Puerto Cabezas and El Bluff, an easy point of access beyond the surveillance of the central government. The Indians along the Honduran border, who have been persecuted by the Sandinistas, provide aid to the American backed CONTRA guerrillas, who are led by remnants of Somoza's National Guard, and disgruntled former Sandinistas: the key city of Matagalpa is now a front-line town. Managua itself is dominated by high ground, while the twin lakes – Managua and Nicaragua – channel communications along the roads to the west of the lakes. All these are vulnerable to attack from the sea. Finally, the roads to the north are channelled through the town of Esteli, and to the north-east through Matagalpa. Both are vulnerable to attack. The Sandinistas can be squeezed on three sides.

Much of the pattern of threat and counter-threat is pure military posturing. Threatening manoeuvres by United States forces have continued for more than eighteen months along the border between Honduras and Nicaragua; tanks have even been deployed as a conscious counter to the much larger Nicaraguan tank force. The fact that the mountainous terrain makes large-scale tank warfare unlikely is irrelevant. More seriously, harbours have been mined, and regular air sorties are made into Nicaraguan airspace. The Sandinista command for their part have cleared a free-fire zone along much of the border and prepared the defences of the cities for street fighting.

The traditional United States intervention in Nicaragua has been a limited occupation of the coastal cities, and support for an 'internal solution' which favoured United States interests. The support of the CONTRA movement follows this pattern. There is no precedent, however, for the United States waging war in Central America, especially against a well-armed population. The terrain of Nicaragua makes invasion easy, but it also makes conquest and consolidation difficult. Moreover, direct United States military intervention would release the barely suppressed anti-Americanism of other Central American states. Under these circumstances communism might seem less of an immediate danger than the 'Yanquí'. The continuing interest of the USA is for political harmony in the region. Paradoxically, an attempt to lance the Nicaraguan pustule would probably spread infection to the entire region.

24 Argentina and Chile: Conflict in the Andes

The crossing of the Andes by the small army of General San Martin in 1817 is one of the epics of military history. It is also an awful warning to both Argentina and Chile to avoid a war in the Andes. San Martin's men arrived ragged and exhausted through the high passes. They took the Spaniards entirely by surprise, and liberated the lands which became the republic of Chile. Had the passes been defended, the epic would have become a catastrophe. Today, the state of veiled (and, sometimes, open) antagonism between the two states means that the passes are guarded on both sides of the frontier.

The communications across the Andes are less perilous than they were in San Martin's day, but they are still not easy. A main road and railway line runs from Mendoza across the frontier, with another snaking up through the high pass of San Francisco between Tinogasta in Argentina and Copiapo in Chile. The pass on the route between Salta and Antofagasta at Volcan Socompa is higher still at almost 14,000 feet. Yet neither country has been able to lower its guard: during the war with Britain in 1982, Argentina was forced to maintain a high state of readiness on the Andean frontier. Chile, with a sense of history, sees the proximity of the capital Santiago and all the main population centres – almost 80 per cent of all Chileans live in the zone between Concepción and Coquimbo – to possible attack through the Andes. In reality, the real danger of war lies far to the south, far distant from either the Argentine or Chilean centres. Neither country has done much more with its southern provinces than exterminate the native Indians in the late nineteenth century and, in the case of Argentina, to allow scattered settlement. More recently, with the discovery of oil at the southern tip of the continent, and the undoubted (if inaccessible) mineral wealth of Antarctica, both countries have had something serious to quarrel over.

Today, the southern lands are dominated by the presence of the military. The communications are more difficult for the Chileans than for the Argentines, since the road network does not extend much further than Puerto Montt. Indeed, the landward access to southern Chile is from the Argentine side of the frontier. The Chilean naval base at Punta Arenas is supplied either from Argentina, or by sea from Valdivia more than 1,000 miles away. By contrast, Rio Gallegos and Ushuaia – which are the equivalent Argentine strongpoints – have good communications to the north. The developed oil resources lie on the Chilean side of the frontier, very vulnerable to any Argentine military adventure, while the Chileans do not pose an equal threat to Argentina's oilfields in the area of Comodoro Rivadavia. In the jockeying for position which has continued ever since the arbitration by the British monarch in 1902 was supposed to have settled the border question, the advantage of geography has been Argentina's. Where once it was merely a question of theoretical sovereignty over a few sheep and some sickly Indians, it is now a dispute over ownership of strategic minerals in huge quantities. Moreover, the control of

the passage around Cape Horn – in particular the submarine channel – is of vital strategic concern. All recent attempts to settle ownership of a number of islands in the Beagle Channel, even arbitration by the Pope, have gone against the Argentine view of the matter, but they have refused to accept the decision. The Falklands adventure was a catastrophe for Argentina, since she faced an infinitely more competent adversary who was in a position to cut her lines of communication. In the dispute with Chile, she faces a probably inferior enemy, while all the logistic advantages lie with Argentina. The temptation for any Argentine government to impose a military solution in the south is almost irresistible, given the frustration of the disaster in the Falklands.

25 Peru, Ecuador, Bolivia, Paraguay: The Dangers of Opportunism

Peru – Bolivia – Chile

War has been the exception rather than the rule in South America. Arbitration by third parties has often settled disputes where nothing more than the sense of national pride was at stake: the potential hostility between the two greatest states of the continent – Brazil and Argentina – has been resolved in this way. The decision to go to war has always had some clear economic or strategic cause. Paraguay engaged in a war with Brazil, Argentina and Uruguay between 1865 and 1870, which cost the lives of 80 per cent of her male population. The prize was the domination of the central tract of South America, and the rivers which provide access to the coast. In an area where overland transport remains difficult the rivers are a vital channel of access. Thus the war between Chile,

Peru and Bolivia between 1879 and 1883 was a conflict over communications and mineral resources.

For most of the nineteenth century, the best source of agricultural fertiliser was natural nitrates. In the 1850s a number of small islands off Callao were found to be some thirty feet deep in seabird droppings – an immensely rich source of phosphates and nitrates for the farms of Europe and North America. Chile had no equivalent natural asset. But in the 1860s vast resources of nitrates were discovered under the Atacama desert. In value and potential they far exceeded the declining Peruvian supplies. The third party with an interest in the region was Bolivia, who claimed the lands as her natural channel to the sea. In fact, access was largely notional since at that point there was no reasonable route between the *altiplano* and the coast.

The Andes provide an almost absolute barrier between Argentina and Chile: even today the passage over the Andes is a taxing journey. Hostility between them has been constrained by the facts of geography. But now real interests are at stake at the southernmost extremity of each country. Oil has been found, and there are mineral traces in the Antarctic areas claimed by both states.

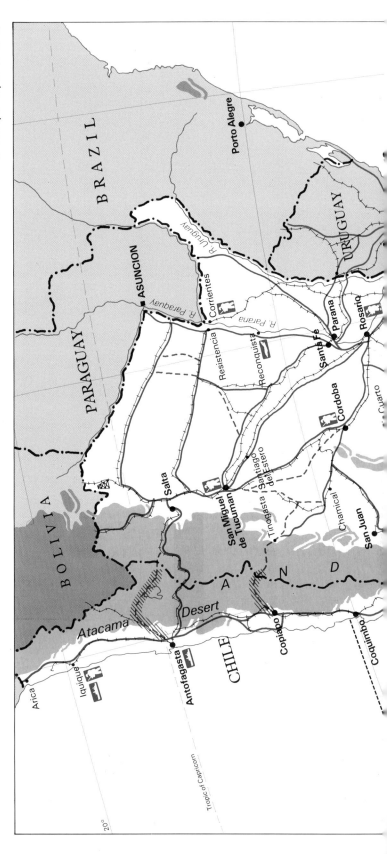

Argentina and Chile: Conflict in the Andes

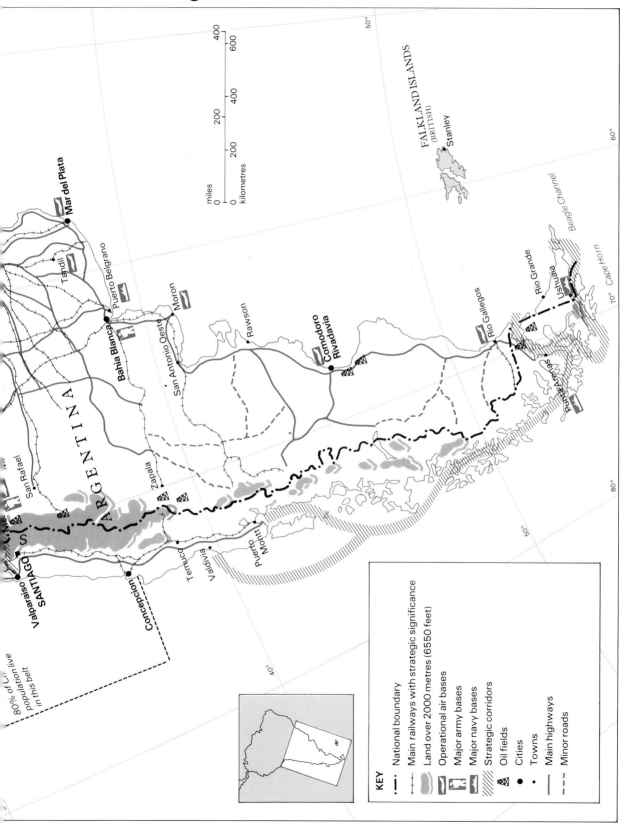

miles

kilometres

0   200   400   600

50°

60°

70°   Cape Horn

80°

50°

40°

FALKLAND ISLANDS
(BRITISH)

Stanley

Beagle Channel

Mar del Plata

Tandil

Puerto Belgrano

Bahia Blanca

Moron

San Antonio Oeste

Rawson

Comodoro
Rivadavia

Rio Grande

Ushuaia

Rio Gallegos

Punta Arenas

Zapala

Temuco

Valdivia

Puerto Montt

Concepcion

SANTIAGO

Valparaiso

San Rafael

A R G E N T I N A

80% of Chile
population live
in this belt

KEY

┼	National boundary
	Main railways with strategic significance
	Land over 2000 metres (6550 feet)
	Operational air bases
	Major army bases
	Major navy bases
/////	Strategic corridors
⚔	Oil fields
●	Cities
·	Towns
│	Main highways
╎	Minor roads

In the 1870s, however, a railway was built to the nitrate fields from Antofagasta, and Bolivia saw a chance to secure the whole of the mineral concessions for herself. Chile was likewise eager to end the situation whereby, while she controlled the mineral exploitation, Bolivia officially administered the region: Bolivian control of Antofagasta was considered an affront. Peru had a long-standing dispute with Chile over her southern boundary, and the nitrate fields were a considerable lure.

In 1879, Bolivia lined up with Peru against Chile. Bolivian troops were exposed in the coastal strip with little hope of reinforcement, and in 1880 were forced to surrender at Tacna. Peru, although protected from the south by the impassable Atacama, lost control of the sea and was subjected to invasion by a Chilean force which landed near Lima. The capital was taken in 1881, and a rather feeble guerrilla war was carried on from the interior until 1883. In the subsequent peace, Chile achieved all her war aims. The principal loser was Bolivia, now cut off from her former outlets to the sea. The handicap was notional rather than real because the Chileans extended the railway by stages from Antofagasta up to the Bolivian cities of the *altiplano*. By 1913 another line was built linking La Paz to Arica on the coast.

The dispute over the ownership of the land between the coast and the highlands remains, in Bolivian eyes, still open. Peru has never accepted the loss of the lands south of Arica, although these were never effectively under Peruvian control. The treaty signed in 1929, which was supposed to resolve all the issues in question, failed to quench the irredentist aims of both Bolivia and Peru. The resulting sense of insecurity is reflected in the military dispositions of all the states in the region. Much of the Chilean army is deployed along the Andes, against both Argentina and Bolivia, while the Chilean navy main-

tains a naval presence at Iquique to guard against a Peruvian attack. Although roads now criss-cross the Atacama, the main highway runs through the coastal belt and provides a risky prospect for any advancing force which could easily be cut off from its base. The key to the control of the north remains the sea, as it was in the late 1870s.

The new dimension is the use of the air, but no state has such superiority as to guarantee protection in the event of war. The tensions between Peru and Ecuador balance the potential for conflict between Chile and Peru. Chile is constrained by the knowledge that Argentina could take advantage of any involvement in the north to achieve a forcible resolution of the Beagle Channel question. On the principle that 'my enemy's enemy is my friend', Chile has close relations with Ecuador over military and naval training, while Peru actively supported Argentina during the Falklands dispute. The strategic balance in the region is maintained by a complex of mutual antagonisms. All the Andean states are equally vulnerable to their neighbours.

The condition of historic hostility, often stretching back more than a century, has, rather bizarrely, preserved peace. The flashpoints on the frontier between Peru and Chile have failed to ignite because the strategic geography made a quick and certain victory impossible. Peru could take the provinces, but could not hold them. Bolivia, which still smarts under the loss of the coastal provinces, had a more recent failure against Paraguay in the Chaco War of 1932–5 as a source of humiliation. Moreover, the economic significance of the coastal provinces has been outstripped by the potential of the Amazonian frontier of both Peru and Chile.

In Amazonia neither country has the capacity to exploit its potential resources in the area, especially in the face of the massive force of Brazilian expansionism. The real preoccupations of the Andean powers other than Chile, which has no contact with the interior, are now in the east. Thus, while the strategic geography of the coastal plain remains frozen in its traditional pattern, a new situation is developing in the heart of the continent. Chile likewise is looking south rather than north, and seeing Argentina as her competitor for strategic resources. While the linkages have not altered, the economic opportunism which lay behind them has shifted its direction.

Peru – Ecuador

Uncertainty has dominated the relationship between Peru and Ecuador since the first moments of their freedom from Spain in the 1820s. There is no 'natural' frontier between them to the west, in the land between the mountains and the sea, or in the east, in the emptiness of northwestern Amazonia. Peru is the larger, richer, and more powerful of the two, and Ecuador has for more than a century existed as the victim of Peruvian ambitions. In 1941, while the rest of the world was preoccupied with the triumph of German armies in Europe, Peru attacked both in the region south of Guayaquil, which was undisputed Ecuadorean territory and, more significantly, in the jungle no man's land east of the Andes. The Ecuadorean defence was handicapped by the lack of good roads in the south, and by Peru's command of the air. Peruvian paratroops captured Puerto Bolivar, by the first military use of airborne force in the continent: Ecuador could only hope to contain the disaster by concession and diplomacy. The 'unequal treaty' – the Rio Protocol of January 1942 – resulted in the loss of almost 55 per cent of Ecuador's previous area and exclusion from the complex of

rivers which gave access to the Amazon around Iquitos. In fact, only the pressure of the major powers in the region (notably the USA) stopped the Peruvians making even more extravagant demands.

Naturally, the settlement settled nothing. Ecuador regarded the 1942 agreement as a national affront, and a blow to her feeble economy. The lure of access to the Atlantic along the Amazon, a 'psychological outlet to the east' as it was described at the time, became infinitely more seductive with the opening of Amazonia by Brazil. Even more potent was the discovery of oil in the disputed lands east of the Andes. Vast oil reserves were also discovered north of the border to the west of the mountains, which enabled Ecuador to become one of the principal oil producers of South America. The dispute has now moved from the largely emotional to the economic level. The consequence has been an active renewal of hostilities both east and west of the mountains. Ecuador's national radio broadcasts the slogan 'Ecuador has been, is, and will be an Amazonian country'; this was used on the nation's postage stamps in 1961, and was prominently displayed all over the national capital, Quito. Since the oil began to flow in the 1960s, much of Ecuador's newfound wealth has been used to re-equip the army and air force, in preparation for the day of revenge against Peru. Border conflicts broke out in June 1976 and January 1977; a border incident in the winter of 1981 almost led to all-out war. Peace was only maintained by the heavy-handed intervention of the Organisation of American Unity in an effort to preserve the status quo. Despite the continuing disparity between the size of their armed forces, certain advantages now lie with Ecuador. Her northern frontier with Colombia is settled and secure, and relations have traditionally been good. Peru, on the other hand, has an unresolved antagonism with Chile and a

Few South American armies have done much fighting, and their experience of war has been generally unfortunate. Bolivia has come off worst, against Chile to the west and Paraguay to the east. Many wars have been opportunistic and have created long-term hostility. As natural assets become ever more valuable to poor states, wars of advantage are increasing rather than diminishing.

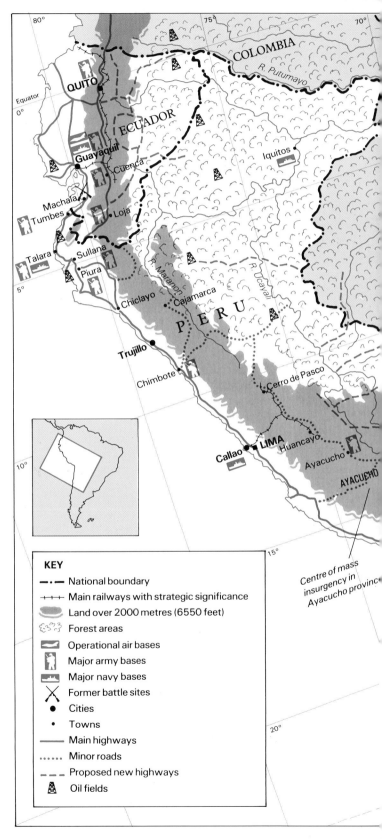

KEY

- –·– National boundary
- ++++ Main railways with strategic significance
- Land over 2000 metres (6550 feet)
- Forest areas
- Operational air bases
- Major army bases
- Major navy bases
- ✕ Former battle sites
- ● Cities
- · Towns
- — Main highways
- ····· Minor roads
- – – – Proposed new highways
- Oil fields

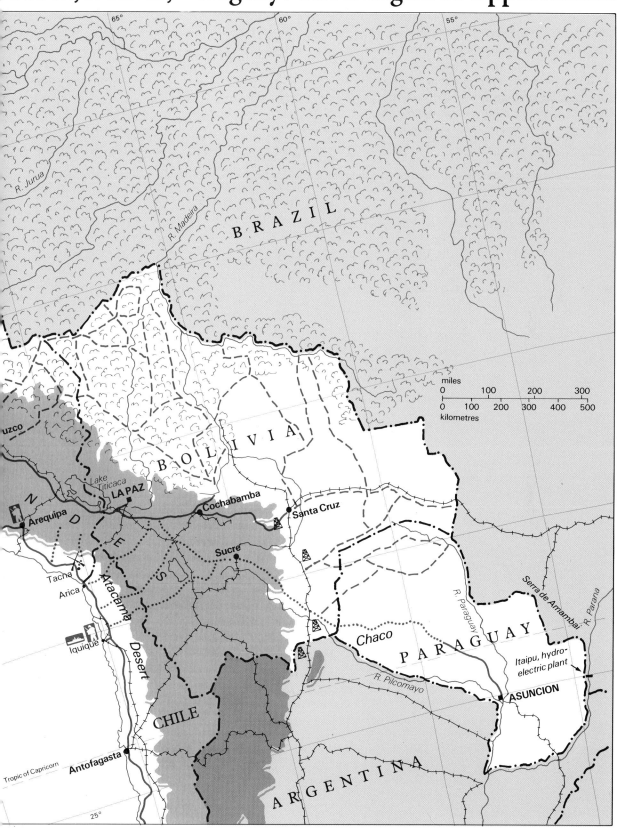

BRAZIL

R. Jurua

R. Madeira

BOLIVIA

uzco

Lake Titicaca

LA PAZ

Arequipa

Cochabamba

Santa Cruz

Sucre

Tacna

Arica

Atacama

Iquique

Desert

Chaco

PARAGUAY

R. Paraguay

Serra de Amambaí

R. Parana

R. Pilcomayo

Itaipu, hydro-electric plant

ASUNCION

CHILE

Tropic of Capricorn

Antofagasta

ARGENTINA

miles
0   100   200   300
0   100   200   300   400   500
kilometres

growing insurgent threat in Ayacucho province in the Andes. Ecuador suffers less from problems of social disruption. Great efforts have been made to improve land communications both towards the western frontier and into Amazonia. On the other hand, Ecuador's oil resources and her centres of population are desperately vulnerable to Peruvian attack. Any adventurism to improve the vague boundaries of the Rio Protocol could invite a repetition of the catastrophe of 1941. So, although the western frontier has been the site of most of the border incidents, a constant and largely invisible war is being waged in Amazonia with much slighter risks of precipitating a full-scale war.

The danger of war, however, remains very real. Peru has the possibility of transforming Ecuador's oil industry into Peru's oil industry by a dash across the frontier. Moreover, as the internal structure of the country is disturbed by the guerrillas, an external and profitable war might serve to distract popular anger. This is the *Argentine gambit*, played so disastrously in the Falklands in 1982. Peru, a faithful friend of Argentina in her hour of need, will not make the same mistake. The initiative lies with Ecuador, a minnow in the South American pond.

Paraguay – Bolivia

Paraguay, sandwiched between the two great nations of South America, Brazil and Argentina, has spent the whole period of her existence repelling her more powerful neighbours. There is little to Paraguay, except a dominating position on the rivers which flow down into the River Plate, a great navigable artery into the heart of the continent. Paraguay has fought two ferocious wars to protect her position on this river system. Between 1865 and 1870, Paraguay took on a combination of Brazil, Argentina and Uruguay in a war for the dominant position on the rivers Paraguay and Parana. The war is rightly blamed on the insane imperialism of the Paraguayan leader, Francisco Solano Lopez. By 1864, Paraguay possessed the most powerful army in South America and Lopez aspired to dominate the whole of the River Plate basin. The war demonstrated only the stubbornness and ferocity of the Paraguayan peasant soldiers. They fought until most of the male population was killed: the country ended the war in 1870 with only 28,000 surviving men. Paraguay survived because the community of interests between Argentina and Brazil could only be temporary. The occupying armies withdrew in 1876, having done much to restore the size of the population, but nothing else for Paraguay's society and economy. The true function of the reborn state was to keep the Paraguay and Parana river system out of the sole control of either of the great powers of the continent.

Paraguay falls naturally into two parts. The eastern and southern boundaries run along river and mountain lines – the Paraguay, Parana, and Pilcomayo rivers mark the border with Argentina, the Cordillera de Amambai and the Upper Paraguay river separate it from Brazil. But in the lands across the Paraguay river in the western half of the country, the boundary with Bolivia has always been indeterminate. This huge area, known as the Chaco, is land of poor quality except in a narrow strip close to the river: it had little real value to Paraguay. But to Bolivia, cut off from access to the Pacific coast by the Chilean victory in the war of 1879–83, the Chaco was the road to the River Paraguay and free access to the Atlantic coast. In 1929, the treaty settlement finally ended any Bolivian hope of recovering the lost ports of Arica and Antofagasta, and the probing actions into the Chaco in 1927–8 became a full-scale war in 1932.

As in 1865, Paraguay took the offensive against a notionally larger and more powerful enemy; and the advantage of the ground lay with Paraguay rather than Bolivia. What produced victory for Paraguay, at enormous cost in life and material, was the tenacity of the Paraguayan soldiers, the same quality which had sustained Paraguay in the earlier war of 1865–70. The Chaco was consolidated, and the Paraguayan armies advanced as far as the foothills of the Andes. But neither side could draw the war to an effective conclusion. Paraguay could not attack the Andean heartland of Bolivia, and the long lines of communication across the Chaco made the advancing Bolivian armies extraordinarily vulnerable. The Bolivians lost 57,000 dead, and the Paraguayans, with a much smaller population, over 36,000. Both countries were in a state of economic collapse. What they had fought for was largely symbolic. Paraguay, which gained full control over the Chaco, has never been able to find a use for it. Even the rumour of oil finds has done relatively little to stimulate development. Bolivia had effective access to the coast via Antofagasta, and the promise of access to the Paraguay river as part of the treaty settlement. But the promised treaty port on the river has never been built and Bolivia has never been much handicapped by its absence.

Symbolism continues to play an important part in the political structure of Paraguay. The Itaipu complex of hydroelectric plants being built along the Parana river provides vastly more power than Paraguay could ever require, and its rationale depends on the sale of electric power to Brazil and Uruguay, who are co-operating in the project. But the scheme still lacks a distribution network to absorb the power, and the area now has a surplus of energy available. The impetus for the project was political nationalism rather than economic calculation: Paraguay displays the same qualities of dogged perseverence in pursuit of irrational ends which have involved her in the two bloodiest wars of the continent.

26 Amazonia: The New Frontier

The river basin of the Amazon is almost the size of the continental United States; over 1,100 tributaries deliver their waters to make up its steady flow down to the coast. The development and exploitation of this vast area is altering the strategic geography of South America. Road access is being opened over areas of former jungle, even though the roads are rough and not yet suitable for heavy volumes of traffic. The flow of the Amazon and, more particularly, its tributaries is being used to create huge hydroelectric resources. The pattern of land clearance and the creation of small settlements, which exist mostly on mining and stock rearing, is Brazil's great 'march to the west', a development which is seen as a threat by all the Andean states which also claim a share of the headwaters of the Amazon.

The western frontier is the amplification of more than a century of Brazilian expansionism. The war with Paraguay in the 1860s settled the dominance of the Mato Grosso and the southern basin of the Amazon in Brazil's favour. Since then the forward pressure has been steady if not spectacular, until the creation of the new capital of Brasilia in 1960. The construction of a new capital hundreds of miles inland from the rapidly expanding coastal belt was in one sense an act of reckless

Human advance is destroying the delicate ecological balance of Amazonia: as the trees are cut down, the rainfall cycle disappears, and the earth turns to dust. But Amazonia will serve as a place of refuge for those unable to find room in Atlantic Brazil; teeming millions will surge westwards into the complex of frontier towns. Once there, there will be only a failing agriculture and no industry to support them. The great Amazonian adventure is ripe with political and human catastrophe.

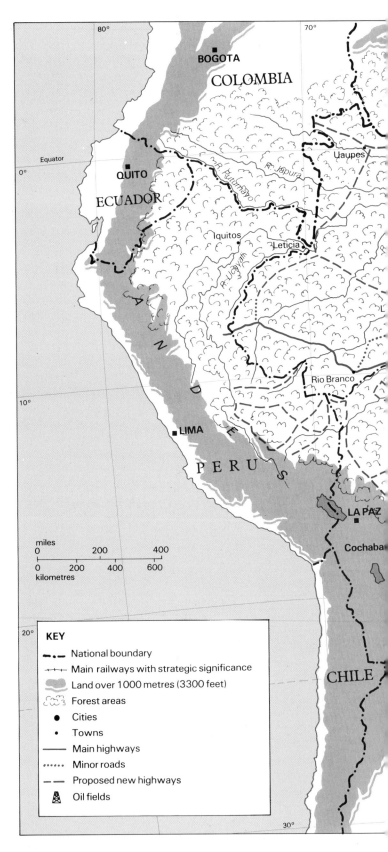

KEY
- **-**·**-** National boundary
- ***+++*** Main railways with strategic significance
- Land over 1000 metres (3300 feet)
- Forest areas
- ● Cities
- · Towns
- —— Main highways
- ······ Minor roads
- – – Proposed new highways
- ⛏ Oil fields

Amazonia: The New Frontier

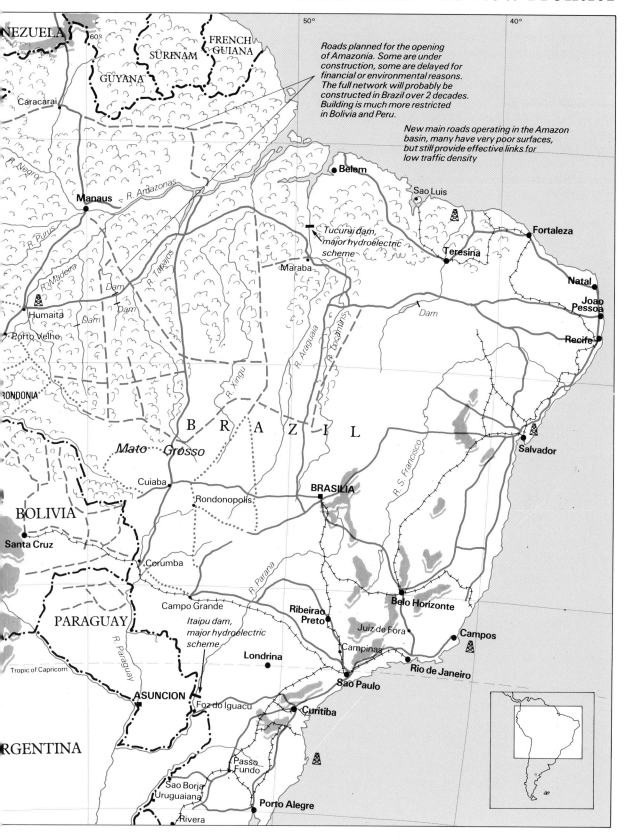

Roads planned for the opening
of Amazonia. Some are under
construction, some are delayed for
financial or environmental reasons.
The full network will probably be
constructed in Brazil over 2 decades.
Building is much more restricted
in Bolivia and Peru.

New main roads operating in the Amazon
basin, many have very poor surfaces,
but still provide effective links for
low traffic density

Tucurui dam,
major hydroelectric
scheme

Itaipu dam,
major hydroelectric
scheme

50°

40°

60°

VENEZUELA

SURINAM

FRENCH
GUIANA

GUYANA

Caracarai

R. Negro

Manaus

R. Amazonas

R. Purus

R. Madeira

R. Tapajos

Belem

Sao Luis

Fortaleza

Teresina

Maraba

Natal

Joao
Pessoa

Recife

R. Araguaia

R. Tocantins

R. Xingu

Dam

Dam

Dam

Dam

Humaita

Porto Velho

RONDONIA

B   R   A   Z   I   L

Mato   Grosso

Cuiaba

Rondonopolis

BOLIVIA

Santa Cruz

Corumba

BRASILIA

R. S. Francisco

Salvador

PARAGUAY

Campo Grande

Ribeirao
Preto

Belo Horizonte

Juiz de Fora

Campos

Campinas

R. Parana

Londrina

Rio de Janeiro

Tropic of Capricorn

R. Paraguay

ASUNCION

Foz do Iguacu

Sao Paulo

Curitiba

ARGENTINA

Passo
Fundo

Sao Borja
Uruguaiana

Porto Alegre

Rivera

grandiloquence, but it also symbolised the intention of Brazil to look to its interior. The programme of resettlement from the exhausted lands of the Sertão in the north-east into the new towns of the frontier, particularly in Rondonia in the far south-west, stems from the same political impetus. The cost of the advance in the west has been enormous, especially in the creation of the energy resources: Brazil is now the principal debtor country of the world. But what is being laid is the infrastructure, communications and power for the creation of massive industrial development in Amazonia. Much of the work has been carried out by the Brazilian army, and this military presence on the frontier causes alarm to Brazil's competitors. The road system means that the notionally Peruvian areas around Iquitos now have real access to the exterior either down the Amazon (the traditional route) or along the new roads. These begin as earth tracks, but are concreted over as use builds up. Thus the road linking Porto Velho with Manaus is now a properly metalled highway, opened in 1975.

The opening of the west has induced new strains and tensions into the strategic position of Brazil. The huge arc of empti-ness once protected the economic heart-land of the country, the coastal strip between 16° and 30° latitude, from any possible enemy, except perhaps Argentina. The creation of the new economic zone in the Amazon basin has altered the strategic geography. The borders are now more contentious and, because of their very length, almost impossible to police and defend. The concentration of energy resources in nuclear power and hydroelectric production has created new points of vulnerability to internal subversion or external threat. All these are potential rather than actual dangers. Brazil is the most powerful state in the continent, and aspires to great power status. But the huge cost of the various economic programmes has bought potential future advantage at the cost of present financial instability. Similarly, the programme to power most of the nation's vehicles with alcohol distilled from sugar production (Brazil has very small reserves of fossil fuels) has produced great social tensions: sugar for fuel has replaced subsistence farming. The road to greatness is strewn with many dangers; whether the political structure is resilient enough to avoid them is open to question.

27 Antarctica and the Falklands: The Southern Approach

The Antarctic continent is one of the largest islands in the world, its land mass covering 5,350,000 square miles; its ice-cap, which has an average thickness of 6,500 feet, and the surrounding ice barriers and glacier tongues contain about three-quarters of the world's fresh water. Effectively uninhabitable though the continent is, it has now been extensively explored and three of the exploring nations, Britain, Norway and France, together with four adjacent or nearby states, Argentina, Chile, New Zealand and Australia, lay claims to its territory; the claims of three of these, Argentina, Chile and Britain, overlap; one sector of the continent, Byrd Land, the most inhospitable, remains unclaimed. Numbers of islands within what is known as the Antarctic Convergence are also sovereign territory, though sovereignty is in several cases disputed. The South Sandwich and South Orkney Islands, South Georgia and Shag Rocks are disputed between Britain and Argentina, the South Shetlands between them and Chile also. The South Shetlands and South Orkneys form, with the British sector of the continent, British Antarctic Territory, proclaimed in 1962.

By the international Antarctic Treaty, signed in 1959 (effective 1961) between the seven claimants and five other states, most of which had established research stations on the continent – Belgium, Japan, South Africa, the USSR and the USA – it was agreed that claims should be held in abeyance until 1991, when they might, but need not, be revived. At the time of signing, the USSR and USA declared that they did not necessarily recognise the claims of others and reserved the right to make claims of their own. Like many of the other signatories, both the USA and the USSR maintain scientific bases in and around the continent, some of them large and elaborate.

Strategic interest in the Antarctic derives from two causes. The first is economic. The seas around the Antarctic are rich in fish and marine mammals and have long been exploited, in part from fishing whaling stations established on the adjacent islands. But the continent and its shelf is believed by many scientists to be mineral- and oil-bearing, in quantities that would repay the very costly effort needed to extract such deposits. Those who hold this view state that giant (half billion barrel) or supergiant (5 billion barrel) fields are likely to be discovered, and that these would be commercially exploitable. A contrary view, held by an equivalent body of opinion, is that the continent will not yield resources of any commercial worth. The evidence they cite is the failure to discover so far any large deposit of minerals; though coal and lead have been found, the quanti-

ties are very small. The balanced judgment of the Norwegian polar research institute is that 'Very little information on the potential accumulation of petroleum exists. Deposits have been located off the southern coast of Australia and in Argentine waters. If sedimentary sections of adequate thickness and extent exist in the Antarctic shelf, accumulations of hydrocarbons could be present.' The extraction of other minerals – traces of gold, silver, cobalt, chromium, copper, iron, manganese, platinum, titanium, tin, uranium and zinc have apparently been detected at various exposed points – might then become feasible.

The second cause of sovereignty disputes in Antarctica is strategic. Australia, New Zealand, Argentina and Chile have a precautionary interest in denying ownership of such nearby land to powers external to the region (South Africa, for the same reason, lays claim to certain sub-Antarctic islands, while Ecuador, because of its ownership of the Galapagos Islands, has a subsidiary dispute with Chile). The issue of free passage round Cape Horn is, however, of wider than regional importance. It provides the shortest oceanic route between the Atlantic and the Pacific and, in the event of the interruption of passage through the Panama Canal, would become the only route open in western hemispheric waters. Strategic concern, particularly that of the United States and Britain, focuses on maintaining free navigation of the Drake Passage, the stretch of stormy water separating South America from the Antarctic continent. Both countries, as well as the major states of the southern latitudes, have the strongest interest in maintaining the demilitarised status of Antarctica and the benevolent attitude of Chile and Argentina.

Argentinian sensitivities were of particular concern to the United States during its efforts to mediate in the Falklands

The importance of the Antarctic region only becomes clear from reversing the normal geographical perspective. The Falklands and the other British possessions occupy a strategically dominant position across the Drake Passage, which controls access from the Pacific to the Atlantic – a vital link. So even if the commercial value of Antarctica proves illusory, no power interested in the control of the line of access can afford to allow dominance to slip into unfriendly hands. This is the hidden key to Fortress Falklands.

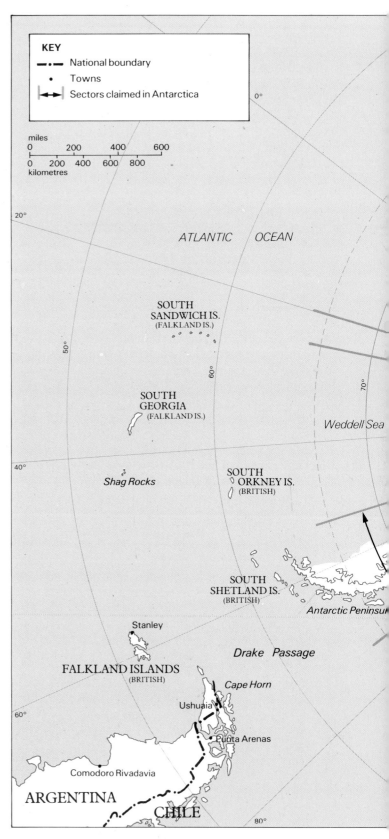

KEY

— · — National boundary

· Towns

Sectors claimed in Antarctica

miles
0   200   400   600

0   200   400   600   800
kilometres

0°

20°

ATLANTIC   OCEAN

SOUTH
SANDWICH IS.
(FALKLAND IS.)

50°

60°

70°

SOUTH
GEORGIA
(FALKLAND IS.)

Weddell Sea

40°

Shag Rocks

SOUTH
ORKNEY IS.
(BRITISH)

SOUTH
SHETLAND IS.
(BRITISH)

Antarctic Peninsul

Stanley

Drake   Passage

FALKLAND ISLANDS
(BRITISH)

Cape Horn

Ushuaia

60°

Punta Arenas

Comodoro Rivadavia

ARGENTINA

CHILE

80°

Antarctica and the Falklands: The Southern Approach

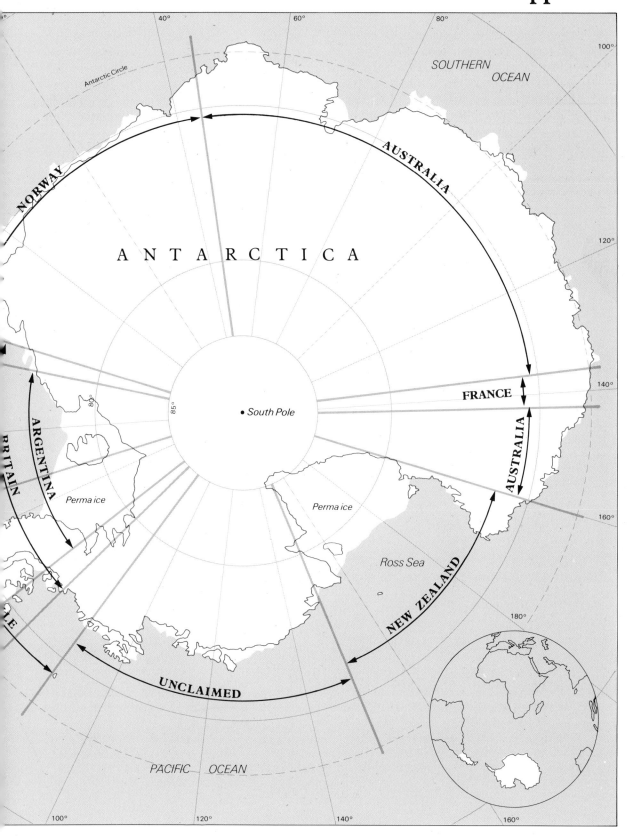

(Malvinas) crisis between that country and Great Britain in 1982. The Falklands, which belong geographically to the South American and not the Antarctic continent but are so located as to dominate the eastern approaches to the Drake Passage, have been under British government and settlement since 1833. Argentina claims the islands as hers, however, by nature of their inheritance from the Spanish Empire, to which they had been sold by France, the original claimant, in 1767. Britain, resting its title on 'prescription' (effective occupation), has always rejected the Argentinian claim but had done little or nothing to prepare to defend it before 1982, despite growing Argentinian pressure to settle the dispute. The Argentinian invasion of 2 April 1982 therefore both took the British government by surprise and overwhelmed the token force it had stationed on the island. Argentina simultaneously seized South Georgia, a dependency of the Falklands to which it had laid claim in 1927; it already had a base in South Thule, among the South Sandwich Islands, a group it had claimed in 1948.

The Falkland Islands seemed to many strategic observers to be irrecoverable, so great is the distance intervening between Britain's home base and the islands, some 8,000 miles; the distance to the Argentinian coast is only 300 miles. By making use of the intermediate base of Ascension Island, and by equipping a task force to reprovision at sea, the British nevertheless succeeded in landing two brigades of troops on the islands on 21 May; the Argentinian garrison surrendered, after costly fighting, on 14 June.

Britain is now, however, left with the task of defending the islands against a revanchist second attempt at capture; it has been forced to build an airport of international standard, at a cost of £500 million, to maintain a link with the large garrison now based there. It must also at some stage face the need to re-establish friendly relations with Argentina, since the long-term strategic interests of these two allies of the United States coincide in the region. They are that free movement through the Drake Passage shall be assured, that the Antarctic remain demilitarised and that no hostile military presence be established in the area, either land- or sea-based.

28 War in Space

Man's first entry into space, defined as the transmission of an object beyond the earth's atmosphere, took place in October 1957, when the Soviet Union launched its Sputnik satellite into orbit. The United States followed suit in January 1958. A Soviet man-carrying satellite orbited the earth in April 1961, an achievement soon repeated by the United States; shortly afterwards satellites carrying several crew had been successfully deployed. In 1970 the Americans sent a manned spacecraft to the moon and recovered it, while the Russians successfully landed an unmanned craft on a distant planet, Venus. The latest development in space technology is the launching and return to earth of a reusable spacecraft, the American Space Shuttle, demonstrated in 1981.

The very rapid development of space technology early provoked speculation that science-fictional stories of space warfare might soon be realised in practice. The launching of satellites with a military function began in 1959, when an American photographic spacecraft was put into orbit; an American early warning satellite was launched in 1960, an American communications satellite in the same year, an American electronic reconnaissance satellite in 1962 and a nuclear explosion detection satellite, also American, in 1963; the Soviets have now duplicated the deployment of all these types. Since 1957 some 2,100 military satellites of all types have been launched from earth, and those in use supply both the United States and the Soviet Union with the most important elements of their strategic surveillance and communications systems.

Nevertheless, until 1983, it remained the official view that space would not become a battlefield, largely because the spirit of the Anti-Ballistic Missile Treaty of 1972 and the terms of the Outer Space Treaty of 1967 seemed to outlaw such activity. In March 1983, however, President Reagan outlined a new programme of defence research and development to be known as the Strategic Defence Initiative (SDI), soon popularly nicknamed 'Star Wars', which overturned conventional thinking. The 1972 treaty had only exempted 'national technical means of verification' from interference, while the 1967 treaty demilitarised the planets and banned the stationing of nuclear weapons in orbit. Both omitted to legislate against the direct attack on missiles and warheads while in ballistic trajectory. Recent developments in technology appear to bring the achievement of such attacks within reach, and President Reagan's speech was an announcement that the United States intended to embark on research and investment that would make such an attack feasible. The justification for the Initiative, which has powerful electoral appeal, is that it would allow the United States to transfer its defensive strategy from a basis of Mutual Assured Destruction (MAD), by which a nuclear missile attack is deemed to attract an equal and opposite response, to one of assured interception, thereby relieving the populations of the United States,

and their allies, of the burden of a deterrence posture founded on the threat of retaliation.

The theory of the Strategic Defence Initiative derives from the dissection of the separate stages through which modern nuclear missiles travel in their journey from launch to impact. The total flight time of the current Multiple Independently Targeted Re-entry Missile (MIRV) lasts approximately thirty-five minutes, and falls into four periods. In the first (boost) phase, of five minutes, the missile leaves its silo and reaches the edge of space. In the second (post-boost) phase, also lasting five minutes, the nose-cone of the missile, known as the 'bus', follows a predetermined course through space towards its target area. In the third (mid-course) phase, the 'passengers' – some ten warheads and perhaps 100 decoys – leave the 'bus' and follow independent trajectories. Finally in the terminal phase, lasting again about five minutes, the warheads re-enter the atmosphere and home in on their targets.

Because of its short duration, the terminal phase is the least promising period in which warheads might be attacked. The mid-course phase is also unpromising, because of the large and confusing number of targets to be identified and sorted for destruction. The best prospect for successful interception is during the early post-boost and, yet more desirably, the boost phases, when each missile presents only a single target.

Successful identification and interception will depend upon the closely co-ordinated operation of three layers of defence. In the first, timed to destroy missiles during the boost phase, an early warning satellite in stationary orbit will detect the rocket launch and direct against its warhead one of three types of weapon, each designed to disrupt the missile rather than explode its warheads: a) a missile

War in space is a potential development rather than the fact that many analysts pretend it to be. To destroy a static, predictable, undefended satellite demonstrates the ability to run a celestial shooting gallery or a three-dimensional Space Invaders game. The resolution of the vast technical problems, making this a practical field for warfare, has yet to be achieved. What the Strategic Defence Initiative does provide is a huge state-directed investment in technology which could only be justified on military grounds.

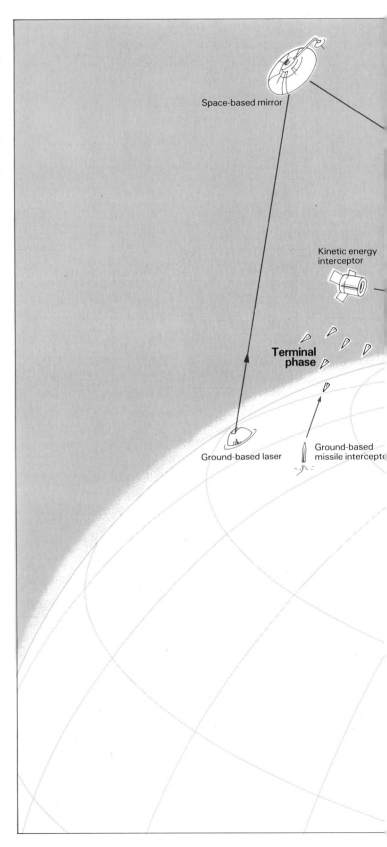

Space-based mirror

Kinetic energy interceptor

Terminal phase

Ground-based laser

Ground-based missile interceptor

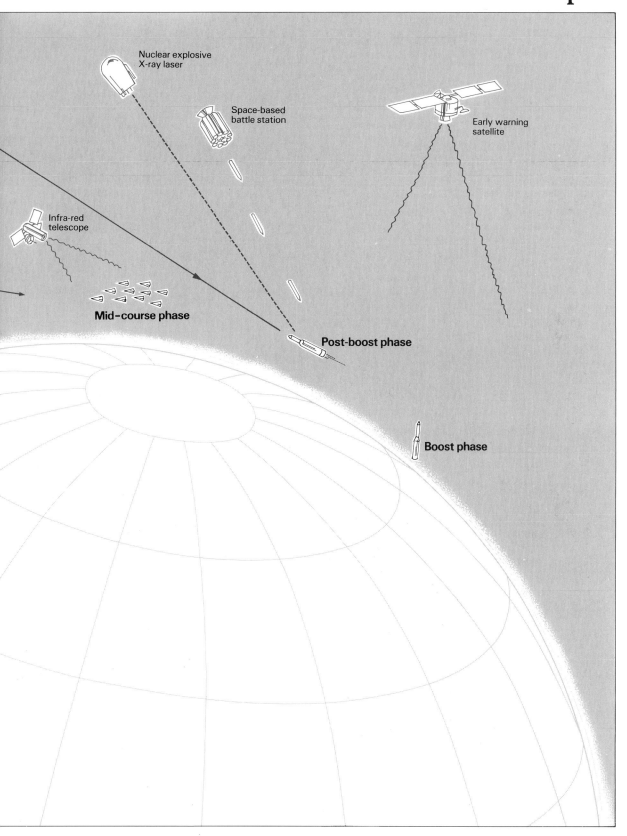

Nuclear explosive
X-ray laser

Space-based
battle station

Early warning
satellite

Infra-red
telescope

Mid–course phase

Post-boost phase

Boost phase

launched from a space-based battle station, b) a ground-based laser beam reflecting off a space-based mirror or c) perhaps a space-based nuclear explosive X-ray laser. Lasers are of particular worth in space because of the speed at which their beams travel, equal to that of light, and the precise focus they can be given; their disadvantage is that their required energy demands generating sources too heavy to be sent into orbit, so that it must either be produced by a nuclear explosion, which is unlawful under the Outer Space Treaty, or transmitted from a ground base and indirectly reflected.

Should some of the warheads 'leak' through the first layer of defence, a second, controlled by infra-red telescope, would fire non-nuclear kinetic energy missiles into their trajectory above the atmosphere. Finally, to mop up remaining 'leaks', ground-based radars would fire nuclear-tipped missiles into the atmosphere to consume the surviving warheads at close range.

Other ingredients of the SDI programme under development or discussion are particle beam weapons, which direct a disruptive stream of hydrogen atoms at the target, and the so-called 'smart rock', a space-based self-guiding projectile propelled either by rocket or by an electromagnetic 'rail gun'.

All systems, and more importantly their co-ordination, would depend upon the construction and programming of a very large computer, capable of tracking, identifying and sorting tens of thousands of objects in space, ordering weapons to take the hostile targets under attack and supervising the defending weapons' flight to the moment of destruction. Such a computer, it has been calculated, would require programming with 100 million lines of computer code, a program 100 times bigger than any currently existing.

Despite the scale and complexity of the research and development work required for SDI, to say nothing of its cost ($26 billion, 1985–90; perhaps as much as $1 trillion to deploy the system), the United States government is resolved to press ahead with it. President Reagan, in his speech of March 1983, spoke of rendering nuclear ballistic missiles 'impotent and obsolete', an outcome which the informed voters of a democracy could not fail to demand, or any democratic government find reasons to deny them. The government of the Soviet Union, already spending proportionately three times as much of its income on defence as the USA, and not needing to justify itself to or inform its electorate, is understandably hostile to the prospect of SDI becoming reality, since it must meet the USA's challenge in 'Star Wars' or fall irretrievably behind it as a world power.

THE LIGAMENTS OF
STRATEGY

The vast weight of armaments in the hands of the Soviet Union and the United States is symetrically disposed. Both nations are vulnerable to attack from the sea, on their lines of communication and from the threat of submarine missiles. The role of the submarine defiles is crucial, while both sides deploy sophisticated undersea surveillance systems to monitor the submarine threat. While both make use of 'advisers' and military assistance on an increasing scale, both sides are more chary of direct and overt military involvement. The Afghanistan involvement in the Soviet Union's 'back yard' should caution those who advocate direct US intervention in the United States' 'back yard' – Central America. European vulnerability lies more in the possible threat to oil supplies than in the tightly controlled European war zone; a long-term solution lies in overland supplies which avoid the perilous sea route.

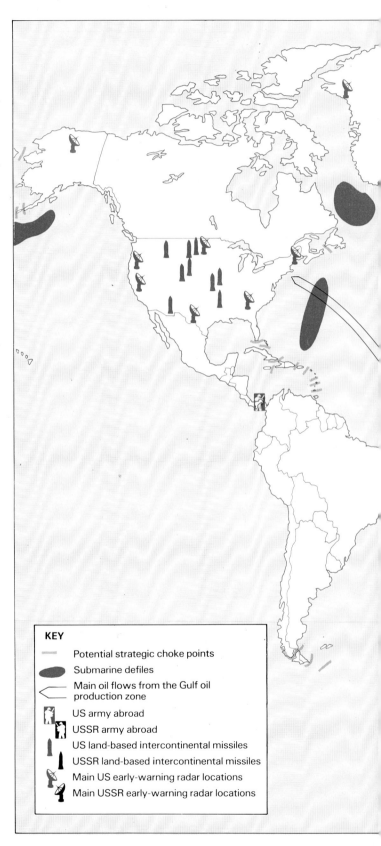

KEY

〰〰〰 Potential strategic choke points

⬮ Submarine defiles

◁— Main oil flows from the Gulf oil production zone

US army abroad

USSR army abroad

US land-based intercontinental missiles

USSR land-based intercontinental missiles

Main US early-warning radar locations

Main USSR early-warning radar locations

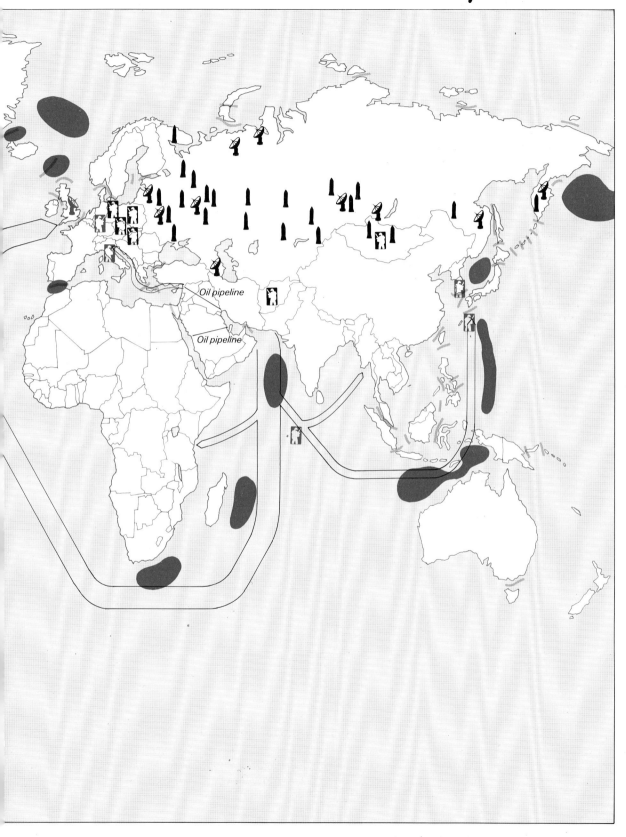

Oil pipeline

Oil pipeline

There are vast untapped rare metal resources in the offshore zones, and the possibility of even greater reserves in the deep sea zones and Antarctica. But the technology to exploit them is some way off; by comparison, the offshore oil technology had to resolve only minor difficulties in tapping the undersea fields. Some experts equate the difficulties, especially in the deep sea sites, with those faced by the space programme. So the land-based reserves remain, for the moment, the key strategic zones. Many are concentrated in areas of political instability, the real prizes of military adventurism. But many also lie in those areas where geography and climate have always made war difficult – deep jungle or forest, desert or semi-desert, high and cold mountain zones, the frozen north and the Antarctic waste.

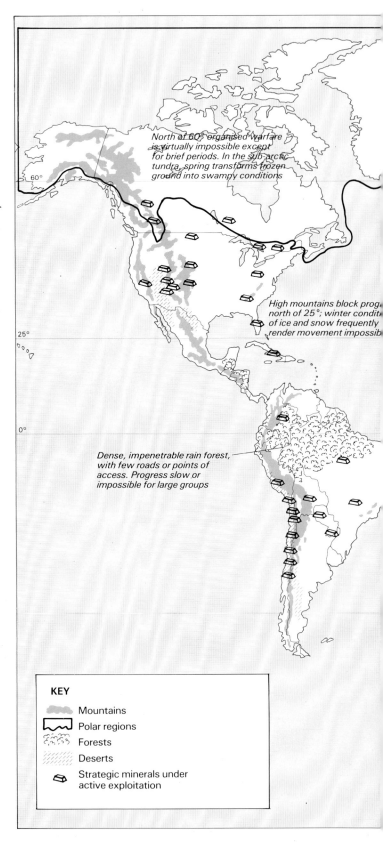

North of 60° organised warfare is virtually impossible except for brief periods. In the sub-arctic tundra, spring transforms frozen ground into swampy conditions

High mountains block prog. north of 25°; winter condit of ice and snow frequently render movement impossib

Dense, impenetrable rain forest, with few roads or points of access. Progress slow or impossible for large groups

KEY

Mountains
Polar regions
Forests
Deserts
Strategic minerals under active exploitation

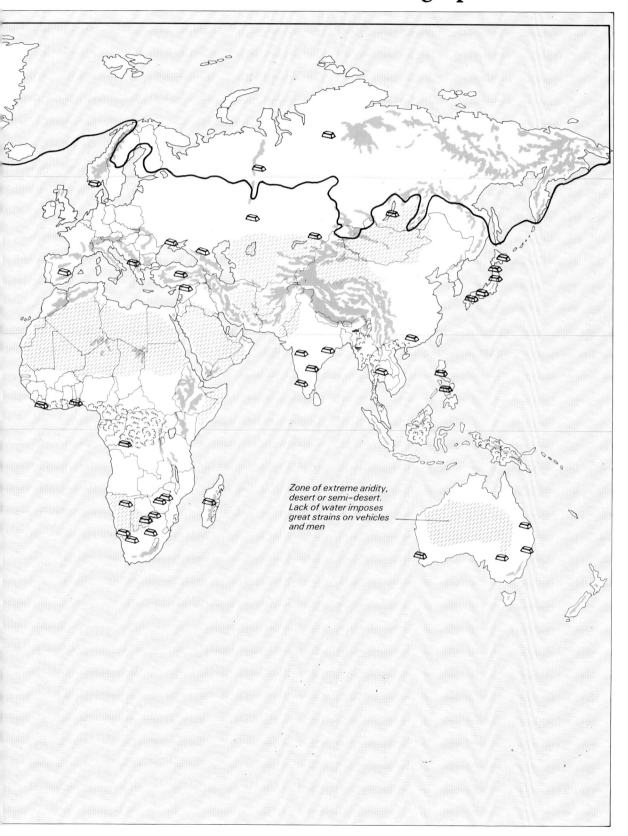

Zone of extreme aridity,
desert or semi–desert.
Lack of water imposes
great strains on vehicles
and men